Strategic Management in
High Technology Firms

MONOGRAPHS IN ORGANIZATIONAL BEHAVIOR
AND INDUSTRIAL RELATIONS, VOLUME 12

Editor: Samuel B. Bacharach, Department of Organizational Behavior, New York
State School of Industrial and Labor Relations, Cornell University

MONOGRAPHS IN ORGANIZATIONAL BEHAVIOR AND INDUSTRIAL RELATIONS

Edited by
Samuel B. Bacharach
Department of Organizational Behavior
New York State School of Industrial and Labor Relations
Cornell University

Strategic Management in High Technology Firms

Edited by **MICHAEL W. LAWLESS**
University of Colorado at Boulder

LUIS R. GOMEZ-MEJIA
Arizona State University

 **JAI PRESS INC.**

Greenwich, Connecticut   *London, England*

Library of Congress Cataloging-in-Publication Data

Strategic management in high technology firms / edited by Michael W.
  Lawless, Luis R. Gomez-Mejia.
      p.   cm. -- (Monographs in organizational behavior and
  industrial relations ; v. 12)
    Includes bibliographical references.
    ISBN 1-55938-105-1
    1. High technology industries--Management.   I.   Lawless, Michael
  W.   II.   Gomez-Mejia, Luis R.   III.   Series.
  HD62.37.S77   1990
  620′.0068′4--dc20   90-33863

Copyright © 1990 JAI PRESS INC.
55 Old Post Road, No. 2
Greenwich, CT 06830

JAI PRESS, LTD.
118 Pentonville Road
London N1 9JN
England

ISBN: 1-55938-105-1

Library of Congress Catalogue Number: 90-33863

Manufactured in the United States of America

CONTENTS

INTRODUCTION

The mutual effects of technology and competitive strategy in firms have attracted the attention of corporate managers, government officials and strategy analysts. The interaction is generally important to the success and even survival of firms in many industries, and a growing body of research has developed to investigate the various effects of technology in competitive markets. Because technology-driven industries assume a large role in national economies, and because technology affects competitiveness of firms and even countries in international trade, the attention appears warranted.

However, even in light of the accumulating knowledge on technology-strategy integration, the field of inquiry is still in the early stages. New conceptual and empirical research has the potential to influence the direction of future thought significantly. This volume, therefore, brings together the current work of 22 authors on technology-related strategy issues. Their 14 articles present a broad range of viewpoints on some important topics. The papers cover such diverse areas as the relative advantages of small and large firms in developing and commercializing new technology, the risks taken on by early market entrants, less developed countries as markets for high technology products, and the role of regional culture in technology management, among others.

The papers are presented here with the objective of stimulating further advances in management practice and in interdisciplinary research. A companion volume, edited by Luis R. Gomez-Mejia and Michael W. Lawless, deals with issues of organizational management in high technology industries. These papers should foster reexamination of some questions in the strategic management of high technology, and lead to new viewpoints on others. The volume is organized into three parts.

The first section is titled "Innovative Strategies," and covers issues related to firm conduct in technology-driven competitive markets. Barney and Baysinger compare large and small firms in regard to stages of the innovative process, using Schumpeter's model of technological change as a framework. They conclude that both types of firms have a weakness in some of the diverse skills needed to innovate, and then to successfully market the innovation. Their initial arguments complement and extend Teece's definitions of technology and complementary assets. Small firms are better equipped for innovation, and large ones for production and marketing. They conclude that, between the drawbacks of vertical integration, and contracting in high uncertainty, no organizational arrangement is superior a priori. However, their three alternatives do provide the seed of a solution for choosing the best possible structure for an innovating organization. Harianto and Pennings frame innovation as an outcome of organizational process and learning. They adopt the view that innovation at the firm level is influenced by an organizational inertia based on distinctive skills. Their analysis looks to the technology, firm, industry and "community" as they organize the received literature on innovation. They derive some hypotheses about organizations' behavior as both user and originator of innovations. They also describe preliminary observations on the hypotheses from case study data. Their multilevel approach to interfirm innovation suggests some new directions for research. Risks and rewards of early entrants in new markets are evaluated in the paper by Day and Freeman. They list several kinds of first mover advantages, which combined with their classification of product markets, lead to some new insights on risks of early market entry. Uncertainty is traced to customer acceptance, technological feasibility, availability of financial resources, and the responses of rivals. Their discussion has particular implications for market entry and implementation of product market strategies. Haynes and Hendrick's paper is novel for its focus on technological innovation in a service industry. They propose that fit between firms offering a new technology and the market's expectations can explain some technology market outcomes. They use ATMs (automated teller machines) in a case study of technology diffusion in retail banking. They group problems in ATM diffusion into five types, studying each in a way that draws out opportunities as well as threats. They close with prescriptions for preintroductory evaluation of a new technology to increase the odds of successful diffusion. Weiss and Delbecq add to the discussion of the context within which innovation and technology management take place. They compare "regional cultures," which they argue influence the nature of enterprise in particular geographical areas. Their exploratory study involves firms in Massachusetts and California. They speculate that there is a great deal of heterogeneity among regional cultures, resulting in differences across high technology firms that develop in each location. Regional behavior norms appear to produce contrasts in organizational structure, decision making types, risk propensity, and even creativity.

High technology and international competition seem to go hand-in-hand. It is fitting that Part II is dedicated to papers that treat these issues: national differences in institutional relationships and business practices, offshore sourcing and markets, and a broad range of others. Balakrishnan and Koza take a long view of globalization in high technology industries that generalizes quite well to businesses of all types. Their review of forces that push firms toward global scope puts protectionism, exchange rate volatility, worldwide diffusion of technology and other issues into perspective. They describe implications for survival and success, including ways to greater efficiencies and more effective integration. Their discussion of organizational forms leads up to the emergence of multinational enterprise, a potentially important development.

Ungson argues that theorists have not adequately specified the advantages that arise from institutional settings when firms compete internationally. He first distinguishes high technology in international markets, with emphasis on institutional arrangements in the host country. Ungson raises new issues like the timing of Japanese entry in U.S. technology markets in relation to competitive conditions and life cycle stage. He then evaluates responses of U.S. competitors. Ungson questions whether appropriate institutional arrangements can be developed in the United States to compete with those of other countries and regions. Daniels presents some new propositions which cast less developed countries (LDCs) as attractive markets for high techonology products. The new perspective is based on differences in opportunities, threats and adjustments between LDCs and industrial countries for technology driven enterprises. For example, market opportunities for high technology products in LDCs are complicated by a lack of installed base of technology, higher learning costs in starting up and the role of governments as buyers, among others. Daniels expects shorter lead times for adoption of new technology and offers suggestions for specific management measures to enhance participation in these markets. Brown and Daneke set strategy and technology in Japan in an historical, social and cultural context that gives new insights into Japan's success. Japanese business strategy is a good example of Quinn's "ethos," strongly-held values that include a vision of a firm's future. Innovation occurs in this context where a long-term direction is understood, but the immediate means are not overly prescribed. Brown and Daneke argue that the Japanese slowness to innovate is exaggerated and poorly understood in the West. Their detailed analysis of MITI, JIT and other production management methods, and multilearning by employees, brings out the complexity of the Japanese cultural and business environment. It is a clear summary of causes and outcomes of Japanese technology management. Janavaras' study brings out key issues in firms' participation in international technology transfer. He then surveys managers with international business responsibility on the issues. The empirical portion of the study involves 15 firms in technology industries where in-depth descriptive data were collected. Janavaras compares problems of exporting to various international markets—from LDCs to industrialized countries. He concludes with a listing of emerging trends in international technology transfer.

In the third section, the readings describe competitive strategies and management approaches that apply principally at the product-market level. Strategy-technology integration, a success factor that is still poorly understood, is approached from four different perspectives. In their paper on competitive strategy's relation with technology, Snow and Ottensmeyer develop a conceptual and analytical framework for the execution of strategy in high technology markets. They note that the link remains nebulous, despite its importance to firm success. Their starting point is the strategic management of technology, a perspective based on the Miles and Snow strategic archetypes. They extend their presentation into organizational forms to enhance strategy-technology integration, including network organizations in particular, addressing the need for alliances in high technology environments.

Kamm's study, based on two in-depth, longitudinal case analyses, describes effects on interpersonal management and relationships in entrepreneurial software firms. She is able to state propositions not previously explored concerning key issues like influence on communication and trust of equity sourcing, eventually influencing performance. Kamm's rich narrative gives a view from the "trenches" of small technology companies searching for ways to cope with rapid change in complementary goods markets, consumer behavior, global competition, and more. She concludes that some concrete measures can improve the position of small firms in an inherently uncertain condition. McGowan begins his discussion with the premise that effective innovation management incorporates multiple product-market life cycles and the organizational life cycle. His focus is ultimately on organizational barriers to change and innovation. His discussion of technology life cycle is based on the "S" curve phenomenon, and he ties it in with opportunities for management to exploit possible competitive advantage from the technology. The channels to competitive advantage are classified in a typology of technology-based strategy. McGowan describes uses of a model where technology, product and organizational life cycles are integrated. Hottenstein concentrates on a significant functional interface in high technology firms—that between R&D and production. The two are important, and at least potentially in conflict, due to competitive pressures to reduce costs while keeping quality up. He lists specific measures that managers can take, based on his survey findings. These lessons, particularly for increased communication and integration, are experience-based, and can serve either as the base for large-sample research or as heuristics for management.

Michael W. Lawless
Luis R. Gomez-Mejia
Editors

PART I

INNOVATIVE STRATEGIES

THE ORGANIZATION OF SCHUMPETERIAN INNOVATIONS

Jay B. Barney and Barry Baysinger

This paper argues that there is no such thing as a "single best way" to organize the invention, development and commercialization of major technological innovations. It does so by examining the strengths and weaknesses of three particular approaches to organizing the innovation process: (1) where all stages of the innovative process are accomplished in a small, entrepreneurial firm, (2) where all stages of the innovative process are accomplished in a large, well established firm, and (3) where a small firm specializes in the invention and development phases of innovation, while a large, more established firm specializes in the commercialization phases of innovation (Souder, 1987).[1]

Even casual observation suggests that all three of these innovation processes are used by real firms. The first commercial personal computers, for example, were invented, developed and marketed by what at the time was a relatively small and entrepreneurial firm, Apple Computer. On the other hand, the first 256K and 640K semiconductor devices were invented, developed and put into commercial use by IBM, and IBM is far from being a small and entrepreneurial organization. Finally, there are numerous examples of technologies being invented and developed in a smaller, more entrepreneurial organization, later to be brought to market and commercialized by larger, more established firms (Souder, 1987).

Given that all three of these innovative processes *can* be used by firms to manage innovation, an important question becomes when *should* they be used. The traditional approach to this question has been to examine, in detail, the attributes of the technological innovation in question, under the assumption that these attributes would determine what the appropriate innovation process would be (Perrow, 1972). However, this technology-attributes approach has proven to be inadequate. Consider, for example, the 256K semiconductor device discussed earlier. IBM decided to invent, develop and commercialize this innovation within the boundaries of IBM. However, a set of Japanese electronics companies decided to develop this same technological innovation through a joint research and development project (Ouchi, 1984). That the same technology can be developed successfully in two different ways suggests that the attributes of that technology do not totally determine how innovation should be organized.

This paper examines the organization of innovation processes for one particularly important class of innovations: Schumpeterian innovations (Barney, 1986; Schumpeter, 1950). Schumpeterian innovations differ from other forms of innovation in that they replace, rather than modify or augment, previous technologies. In this sense, Schumpeterian innovations render older technologies obsolete. Any list of Schumpeterian innovations is likely to include transistors (which made vacuum tubes obsolete), semiconductors (which made transistors obsolete), the basic oxygen process for steel smelting (which made the open hearth furnace obsolete), and so forth. Schumpeterian innovations are particularly important because they are closely linked with major technological progress in an economy. Also, firms that are able to bring Schumpeterian innovations to market have the potential of earning substantial economic rents.

The paper is organized into four sections. In the first section, the strengths and weaknesses of organizing Schumpeterian innovation processes entirely within a single firm are discussed. Innovation entirely within both small firms and larger firms is examined. Then, the strengths and weaknesses of organizing these kinds of innovations such that small firms specialize in invention and development, while large firms specialize in commercialization, are evaluated. In section three, the ability (and inability) of firms to overcome the limitations of each of these innovative processes is discussed. In a final section, how firms should decide which innovative process to use is analyzed.

SCHUMPETERIAN INNOVATION WITHIN A SINGLE FIRM

There is substantial evidence that suggests that small firms are more efficient in the invention and development of Schumpeterian innovations than larger firms. The evidence also suggests that small firms are typically not as well equipped as large firms to commercialize these innovations by bringing them to market (Kamien & Schwartz, 1982).

Inventive Efficiency in Small Firms

The reasons for the relative efficiency of small firms in invention and development, compared to larger firms, are not difficult to find. First, small firms typically do not have the enormous bureaucratic overhead that is common in many larger organizations (Williamson, 1975). Innovation, especially Schumpeterian innovation, tends to be "untidy," not well suited for more formalized and routinized bureaucracies (Schumpeter, 1950). When those bureaucratic constraints do not exist, inventive activity is more likely.

Second, small firms are much better able to structure employment contracts to attract and hold highly innovative personnel (Zenger, 1987). In large bureaucratic firms, there tends to be a close correspondence between an individual's position in the firm's hierarchy, and his or her compensation. Such incentives, according to Williamson (1975, p. 201), "are poorly suited to satisfy the entrepreneurial appetites of individuals who are prepared to risk their personal savings and careers in pursuit of big stakes." Risk-taking innovative individuals are not likely to be attracted to larger organizations with these kinds of compensation schemes.

Moreover, since innovation is often a team production process, it is difficult to distribute rewards in anything but what must seem to the innovator as a highly arbitrary and, hence, counterproductive manner. In anticipation of these difficulties, innovative individuals in large organizations that do invent an important new technology are likely to break out on their own, start their own firm, and thereby obtain a greater percentage of the economic rents associated with an innovation. Thus, even if large firms are able to induce some innovative risk-taking individuals to join, it will be difficult for these firms to retain these individuals once innovations have actually occurred.

These attributes of large organizations have led several authors to conclude that small firms will be more efficient at invention than large firms. Indeed, Williamson (1975, p. 201) has suggested that a "large, mature bureaucracy is (not) constitutionally well-suited to handle" inventive activities that can lead to Schumpeterian innovations.

Commercialization Advantages in Large Firms

While small firms possess an advantage over large firms in the invention and development stages of Schumpeterian innovations, there is significant evidence that suggests that large firms are more likely to possess the skills and capabilities needed to commercialize a new technology by bringing it to market. These advantages of large firms in commercialization reflect substantial economies of scale in production, advertising, and distribution (Scherer, 1980). Moreover, production, advertising and distribution are precisely the functions required in order to successfully commercialize an innovation (Souder, 1987). Thus, in general, large firms have an advantage in commercialization compared to small firms.

Vertical Integration in Innovation

The analysis to this point suggests that firms that attempt to engage in all phases of the innovation process can expect certain predictable problems. Small firms that are vertically integrated into innovation have a comparative advantage in the invention and development stages of innovation, but have a comparative disadvantage in commercialization. Large firms that are vertically integrated into innovation have a comparative advantage in commercialization, but may be weak in the areas of invention and development. Given this analysis, a vertically disintegrated approach to innovation, where small firms specialize in invention and development, and large firms specialize in commercialization, seems a reasonable alternative.

SCHUMPETERIAN INNOVATIONS ACROSS FIRMS

A vertically disintegrated approach to innovation has several advantages. First, vertical disintegration lets each type of firm specialize in that phase of innovation they do best. Stigler (1956) has emphasized that different parts of the innovation process may require very different skills, and that there is no a priori reason to believe that the same firm or individuals will have the necessary expertise across all stages of innovation. Specialization, through vertical disintegration, overcomes this problem.

Second, vertical disintegration, because it imagines essentially a market relationship between inventing small firms and commercializing larger firms, builds greater flexibility into the innovation process than would be the case if innovation occurred entirely within a small or large firm. For example, once a small firm invents and develops an innovation, it can choose from many large firms the one that possesses the skills needed to commercialize the innovation. Also, large firms can shop around among small inventive firms for that innovation that they will most effectively be able to commercialize. In vertically integrated innovation, innovations pass from invention and development to commercialization, even if the division given the assignment of commercialization does not possess exactly the right set of skills and capabilities.

These apparent advantages of vertically disintegrated innovation can only be realized if an efficient transfer mechanism can be created between the inventing firm and the commercializing firm. Without this transfer mechanism—be it a contract, a joint venture, or some other institutional arrangement—innovations will never move from the invention and development stage to commercialization.

Transactions cost economics (Williamson, 1975) is a powerful theoretical framework that can be used to describe the attributes that this transfer mechanism must have in order to efficiently transfer an innovation from invention to commercialization. Among the several transaction characteristics cited by Williamson as important in determining the nature of an efficient transfer mechanism are the level of complexity/uncertainty and the level of transaction specific investment (Williamson, 1975). The logic here is well known, and will only be briefly reviewed.

Because economic actors are boundedly rational and opportunistic, transactions that are highly uncertain or complex and transactions that are characterized by high levels of specific investments (i.e., investments that have considerably more value in the current transaction than in any alternatives) are difficult to govern through even the most complex contractual relations. Market contracts do not work well in this setting for several reasons. First, because of uncertainty and complexity, contracts cannot anticipate all future states of the relationship. In some of those future states, one or another party to this exchange may suffer a significant economic loss. However, because this loss could not have been anticipated, appropriate remedies could not have been created and built into the contract. Second, because of specific investments, parties to an exchange have an incentive to appropriate the difference between the value of that investment in the current transaction and its value in its next best use. This postcontractual opportunism puts parties to this exchange at risk. For these reasons, Williamson (1975) argues that economic transactions characterized by high uncertainty/complexity and high transaction specific investment will typically not be governed through market relations, including market contracts, but will be more efficiently governed through vertically integrated hierarchical relations.

The transaction cost model can be applied to analyzing exchanges between inventive small firms and commercializing larger firms. First, it seems clear that these exchanges will be characterized by uncertainty and complexity. This is especially the case for Schumpeterian innovations, which by their very nature are typically complex, and their future economic value very uncertain. Second, the transfer of innovations, especially Schumpeterian innovations, almost always requires enormous transaction specific investments. In order to commercialize an innovation, a large firm must understand, in a complete and subtle way, the nature of that innovation. Obtaining that understanding requires significant transaction-specific investments on the part of the large firm. It also requires significant transaction-specific investment on the part of the small firm, for the small firm is sharing its technology with a particular partner. Once the partner understands the technology, it could appropriate all the economic rents coming from that technology, effectively shutting out the inventing firm.

Uncertainty, complexity and specific investments create a variety of exchange problems in the transfer of technological innovations between firms. Several of these have been cited in the literature. For example, if the commercialization of an innovation requires large specific investments by the commercializing firms, relatively few of these firms will be willing to enter the market to acquire the rights to a new invention (Williamson, 1975, p. 205). Small firms, selling into these concentrated markets, may find that bids from firms specializing in commercialization will opportunistically fail to reflect full valuations of the invention (Williamson, 1975, p. 204). Thus, specific investments can lead to a larger than normal economic burden being borne by small firms.

Large firms can also find themselves at risk in these settings. Suppose a small and large firm agree to a cost-plus contract specifying that the small firm will provide major technological innovations to the large firm, which will subsequently commercialize them. Such a contract recognizes the difficulty, a priori, of specifying the costs of inventing and developing a Schumpeterian innovation. However, once such a contract is in place, the small firm has few incentives to keep their costs under control. In this way, the small firm could take opportunistic advantage of the large firm, and such contractual relations would be difficult to form.

Each of these contractual difficulties is exacerbated in the transfer of Schumpeterian innovations, where the levels of uncertainty, complexity, and specific investment are very high. In the end, a transactions cost analysis of transferring technology from an inventive small firm to a commercializing large firm suggests that this transfer cannot be efficiently accomplished in a simple market setting, and must be done in a hierarchy, through vertical integration.

MANAGING THE PARADOX OF INNOVATION

The above analyses suggest a paradox that is at the heart of managing innovation. On the one hand, managing innovation in a vertically integrated manner does not allow different kinds of firms to specialize in that innovative activity they do best. Vertical integration requires inventive small firms to commercialize innovations, even though they are not able to exploit the economies of scale associated with commercialization. Vertical integration requires commercializing large firms to engage in inventive activity, even though the structure and control systems in large firms tend to discourage Schumpeterian invention. On the other hand, managing innovation in a vertically disintegrated fashion creates severe contracting problems. These contracting problems are due to uncertainty, complexity and transaction specific investments, and may prevent the efficient transfer of an innovation from inventive small firms to commercializing large firms. Moreover, uncertainty, complexity and transaction specific investments are all likely to be very high when Schumpeterian innovations are transferred, making the vertical disintegrated approach to this type of innovation all the more problematic.

We are left with a somewhat uncomfortable solution to the organization of innovation problem: there apparently is no single optimal solution. Vertical integration, whether it be in small or large firms, creates problems. Vertical disintegration creates its own problems. Given this situation, what can managers do to organize Schumpeterian innovation as efficiently as possible?

Managing Vertically Integrated Innovation in the Small Firm

Three alternatives present themselves. First, managers in small firms may opt for vertical integration in the small firm, and attempt to develop the skills and capabilities needed to commercialize an innovation. Several small firms have apparently opted for this, including Apple Computer. This option is possible when the skills required for commercializing a product are not characterized by substantial economies of scale, and thus are within reach of smaller entrepreneurial firms (Bain, 1956).

Small firms seeking to improve their commercialization skills so that they approximate the skills of larger firms run at least two risks. First, these firms face the real possibility of becoming "second rate" commercializers—obtaining enough skills to bring an innovation to market, but not enough skills to fully exploit an innovation's potential. Second, if these small firms are successful in exploiting the full economies of scale in commercializing an innovation, they run the risk of becoming so large, and so bureaucratic, that they are unable to continue as inventive small organizations. There are numerous recent examples of small firms that became large through their commercialization efforts, only to discover that they lost their ability to invent Schumpeterian innovations. These newly large firms have many of the same problems as other large firms, including the apparent inability to retain their most inventive and entrepreneurial managers (e.g., Apple Computer's recent loss of its original entrepreneurs).

Managing Vertically Integrated Innovation in the Large Firm

A second managerial response to the paradox proposed above is for managers in large firms to vertically integrate the innovation process, but then attempt to debureaucratize the inventive activities in their firm. This debureaucratization can take one of two forms. First, managers in large firms can attempt to directly modify the management systems in their organization. This is the approach recommended by Quinn (1985), Souder (1987), Peters and Waterman (1983), and others. Whether these "direct" debureaucratization efforts work has yet to be fully evaluated. Some researchers are not optimistic. Williamson (1975, p. 206), for example, has observed,

> Conceivably, the perceptive large firm can attempt to debureaucratize itself and overcome certain of its worst tendencies. Replicating the characteristics of the small firm is not, however, apt to be easy ... intensive efforts at debureaucratization are apt to be relatively expensive. If, naturally, organizations experience certain (mainly irreversible) life cycle changes, it may be more economical to simply acknowledge these ... rather than force innovation through the internal development route.

Even if direct debureaucratization does work, large firms run the risk of losing their comparative advantage in commercializing a new innovation. When commercializing an innovation involves exploiting significant economies of scale, bureaucracy may be the most efficient way of coordinating efforts to exploit these economies (Perrow, 1972). A fully "debureaucratized" large firm may be very inventive, but may not be able to fully commercialize the inventions it develops.

As an alternative to direct debureaucratization, managers in large firms may opt for an indirect approach. Here, rather than attempting to debureaucratize the entire organization, relatively small, quasi-independent innovation organizations might be developed. This quasi-independent entity in many ways duplicates the small firm, but does so in the context of the large firm's commercialization resources.

Unfortunately, the creation of this independent entity does not solve all the problems associated with inventiveness in large organizations. First, if this independent entity is successfully created, all the technology transfer problems discussed above for transferring Schumpeterian innovations from a small company to a large firm reappear. Those charged with inventing a technology may feel that they will not get their fair share of the rents generated by transferring that technology. Second, and perhaps more importantly, the compensation schemes in large firms, even when they are successful in creating quasi-independent invention units, will not typically attract or retain the most inventive, entrepreneurial and risk taking managers. These managers can still be best served (and rewarded) in independent small organizations. Thus, in the area of Schumpeterian innovations, these quasi-independent invention teams seem likely to only generate "second rate" innovations, and thus to be at a comparative disadvantage vis-à-vis small inventive firms.

Managing Vertically Disintegrated Innovation

A final broad alternative presents itself. Managers may opt for a vertically disintegrated innovation process, despite the transactions cost difficulties outlined above, and then learn to manage the transfer of technology efficiently. This might be done by developing what Williamson (1975) calls a "relational contract" between a small inventive firm and a large commercializing firm. Such relational contracts entail a whole range of social norms and common values that parties to an exchange use to mediate their relationship. Such contracts can manage higher levels of uncertainty, complexity and specific investment more efficiently than pure market contracts.

The existence of relational contracts has been widely documented (Williamson, 1975; Macaulay, 1963; Ouchi, 1984). Unfortunately, how these relationships are developed has not received as much attention. It does seem clear that trusting an exchange partner before that exchange partner has demonstrated trustworthiness puts a firm at significant risk. This is especially the case where Schumpeterian innovations are concerned, because a large firm that is actually not trustworthy has a very strong incentive to appropriate the substantial economic rents associated with this type of an innovation.

Nevertheless, previous research seems to indicate that small firms that are able to develop trusting, long lasting relationships with larger firms will be able to more efficiently transfer Schumpeterian innovations to those large firms for commercialization than small firms without these kinds of relations.

CHOOSING AN INNOVATION ORGANIZATION

Once again, this analysis leaves managers in a difficult situation. Vertically integrated innovation and vertically disintegrated innovation both have significant liabilities. Managerial attempts to reduce these liabilities are uncertain, at best, and possibly counter-productive. How then should innovation be organized?

This analysis suggests that there is no such thing as an *optimal* innovation organization; that is, there is no "one best way" of managing Schumpeterian innovations. Rather than attempting to duplicate one of the three alternatives examined here (as is recommended by Peters & Waterman [1983], Quinn [1985], Souder [1987], and many others), the most reasonable alternative facing management seems likely to be to choose that innovation organization they already are most skilled in doing, and then be aware of, and manage, the problems associated with that alternative. In this sense, the choice of an innovation organization reduces to managers choosing those sets of problems they would prefer to manage.

Thus, for example, small firms that already have some commercialization skills might best opt for completing the entire innovation process, from invention to commercialization, themselves—always recognizing the risks to future inventiveness that these actions entail. As was suggested earlier, Apple Computer has apparently followed this road to innovation, for not only was the original Apple computer invented and developed within Apple, Apple also took the lead in creating a distribution network, advertising and other aspects of commercialization. It is interesting to note, however, that Apple's approach to commercialization did not require significant economies of scale. For example, Apple used a network of independent dealers and electronics distributors to distribute its products, rather than attempting to duplicate Tandy Inc.'s retail sales outlets. It is also interesting to note that, as Apple has become larger (and perhaps more bureaucratic), it has had some difficulty retaining its most creative and innovative staff. These difficulties are consistent with the analysis presented here (Swanger, 1984).

A small firm without any commercialization skills should probably attempt to exploit some preexisting relationship it maintains with a larger firm. If no preexisting relationship exists, then the small firm may need to develop one, although it should always be aware of the risks the development of such relationships entails. The key for managers in these small firms is to remember that simply because Apple was successful in commercializing its product does not mean that they would be, nor does it mean that some alternative approach to commercializing a product will not be successful (Love, 1986).

Large firms have many of the same options. If a large firm is relatively nonbureaucratic in its management systems, perhaps it should opt for vertical integration. The Hewlett-Packard Corporation is widely known for its nonbureaucratic management system (Peters & Waterman, 1983). For HP, the most optimal innovation structure may be to vertically integrate, to conduct invention, development and commercialization. And indeed, HP tends to develop most of its own technological innovations (Peters & Waterman, 1983).

A more bureaucratic large firm, or a large firm that has a compensation scheme that does not reward risk taking among its managers, may need to opt for obtaining major technological innovations from smaller inventive companies. This is the approach to innovation that is followed by firms like Westinghouse and GE (Ouchi, 1984; Peters & Waterman, 1983). While these firms do some R&D in-house, in general, major Schumpeterian innovations are developed elsewhere and commercialized using these firms' impressive commercialization skills. If, in fact, firms like Westinghouse and GE have a competitive advantage in commercializing major innovations developed elsewhere, it does not appear to be good business practice for these firms to abandon this competence in favor of some "ideal" nonbureaucratic, vertically integrated innovation process, especially when that process may be very difficult and expensive to obtain, and when it may reduce the commercialization efficiency of the firm (Quinn, 1985).

Other large firms may have unusual skills in developing close trusting relationships with small inventive firms. McDonald's is apparently one of these firms (Love, 1986). When McDonald's determines that it needs some new food processing equipment, it approaches a set of small inventive firms with whom it has established relations. These small firms invent and develop the new technology, it is transferred to McDonald's, which then commercializes it. McDonald's manages the technology transfer problem by developing an atmosphere of trust and cooperation with its small innovative suppliers (Love, 1986). In this sense, their reputation for trustworthiness and nonopportunistic behavior is the source of McDonald's distinctive innovative competence. Given their distinctive competence in managing innovation in this manner, it appears, again, to be poor business practice for a firm like McDonald's to attempt to be innovative in the same way that Apple, HP, GE, or Westinghouse is innovative.

That there are multiple "good" ways to manage the innovation process, but no single "optimal" way explains why one observes the same technological innovations being managed in very different ways in different firms. As long as firms are heterogeneous along the dimensions described above, the innovation process that is best for one firm may not be the best for other firms, and all innovation processes have some limitations. In this sense, attempts to mold firms, whether they are large or small, all into a single innovation process seems to be a misguided policy.

NOTE

1. Two other innovation processes are not examined here. The first of these is for invention and development to occur in a large firm, with commercialization occurring in a small firm. This alternative is not examined because it is empirically very rare (Souder, 1987). The second is invention and development occurring in a small firm, and a larger firm purchasing this smaller firm for subsequent commercialization. However, this second alternative is really a special case of the vertically disintegrated process (option three) discussed here.

REFERENCES

Bain, J. (1956). *Barriers to new competition*. Cambridge, MA: Harvard University Press.

Barney, J.B. (1986). Types of competition and the theory of strategy: toward an integrative framework. *Academy of Management Review, 11*, 791-800.

Kamien, A., & Schwartz, N. (1982). *Market structure and innovation*. Cambridge, MA: Harvard University Press.

Love, J. (1986). *McDonald's: Behind the arches*. New York: Harper & Row.

Macaulay, S. (1963). Non-contractual relations in business: A preliminary study. *American Sociological Review, 28*, 55-66.

Ouchi, W.G. (1984). *The M-form society*. Reading, MA: Addison-Wesley.

Perrow, C. (1972). *Complex organizations: A critical essay*. Glenview, IL: Scott, Foresman.

Peters, T., & Waterman, R. (1983). *In search of excellence*. New York: Harper & Row.

Quinn, J.B. (1985). Managing innovation: Controlling chaos. *Harvard Business Review, 63*(3), 132-138.

Scherer, F.M. (1980). *Industrial market structure and economic performance*. Skokie, IL: Rand McNally.

Schumpeter, J.A. (1950). *Capitalism, socialism, and democracy* (3rd ed.). New York: Harper & Row.

Souder, W.E. (1987). *Managing new product innovations*. Lexington, MA: D.C. Heath.

Stigler, G. (1956). Industrial organization and economic progress. In L.D. White (Ed.), *The state of the social sciences* (pp. 256-281). Chicago: University of Chicago Press.

Swanger, C. (1984). *Apple Computer, Inc.—Macintosh (A)*. Unpublished manuscript, Stanford University.

Williamson, O.E. (1975). *Markets and hierarchies*. New York: Free Press.

Zenger, T. (1987). *Agent sorting, agency solutions, and diseconomies of scale: An empirical investigation of employment contracts in high technology R&D*. Unpublished manuscript, University of California, Los Angeles.

TECHNOLOGICAL INNOVATION THROUGH INTERFIRM LINKAGES

Farid Harianto and Johannes M. Pennings

This paper presents a theory and empirical account of the organizational location of technological innovations. The questions to be answered are, under what conditions will firms be likely to embark on an innovation, and under what conditions will firms collaborate with other firms in developing new ideas, products or processes. Why do they relinquish control to outsiders, rather than preserving ownership of innovative results by keeping the research and development activities in-house? A related question pertains to the emergence of wholly new industries such as the videotex market. Such new industries appear to primarily consist of joint ventures and other forms of diversification into neighboring technologies.

A major issue in the field of innovation research involves the level of analysis. Whether one seeks to explain invention, innovation, or diffusion of innovation, at least four levels are discernible, and somehow they all seem to be pertinent to one another. Innovation has been treated at the *organizational* level, the *industry* or market level, the *interindustry* or "community" level and at the macroeconomic or *technology* level.

Typically, treatments of organizational innovations have implicitly assumed that organizations are innovation bearing milieux; that for the origination and diffusion of innovation we have to understand the organizational attributes or conditions in their environment. For example, adoption of innovation studies have examined whether aspects such as size, bureaucratization or the presence of significant gate keepers affect the innovative conduciveness of organizations (e.g., Rogers, 1983).

Other studies have adopted an industrial organization perspective. The theories or assumptions about innovation revolve around concepts of competition, shifts in market demands, size distribution of firms and the like. At this level people seek to answer questions such as whether innovation is the result of market pull, or market push (compare, for example, Rosenberg, 1982). Individual firms constitute part of the impetus that triggers the diffusion of innovation in their industry, but other innovation producing forces can only be accessed at the level of the industry.

Other economists move to a still higher level of analysis and have studied the interplay between various industries. Scherer (1982), for example, has generated an input-output matrix involving multiple industries, based on the production and consumption of innovation. It shows that the financial sector is a major consumer of information technology innovation, but that this sector is neither an innovator for itself, nor for other industries. The implication is that for us to understand innovation of the firm or industry, we ought to move to the interfirm or community level of analysis. This is implicit, for example, in the framework of Porter (1980), when he includes the threat of "substitutes" in his competitive analysis framework. This framework is essentially a conventional industrial organization framework. The reference to substitutes pertains to events in other, unrelated industries.

Finally, there is a group of authors that has adopted a macrosocioeconomic perspective. They have treated innovation as a somewhat autonomous process, in which firms or industries participate. The evolution of certain technologies may solidify or disrupt existing industries and create turmoil for individual firms. Mensch (1979) and Sahal (1981) are exponents of this level of discourse.

Confounding the issue of level is the enormous diversity of theories, perspectives or research traditions. Innovation diffusion theories embody learning, inertia and adoption theories from sociology and social psychology and focus primarily on the organizational level of analysis (e.g. Mohr, 1982; Norman, 1971; Rogers, 1983). Research and theory on the origination of innovation have been the realm of industrial and institutional economists (e.g., Mensch, 1979; Nelson & Winter, 1982; Rosenberg, 1982; Sahal, 1981; Teece, 1986), or historians (e.g., Gilfillan, 1935). Yet, as we will see, these approaches share equivalent conceptual foundations and permit meaningful integration. In essence, they personify a learning and inertia view. The core view adopted here holds that organizational inertia due to the acquisition of distinctive skills provides the stage for innovation beyond the confines of firms and their traditional industry boundaries.

We seek to understand innovation at the firm level, recognizing that a comprehensive explanation requires us to incorporate elements of higher levels of analysis. The empirical examination focuses on the financial services sector and the introduction of new forms of information technology in the form of videotex into that industry. First, we will briefly review relevant literatures, then integrate them into a multi-level model of organizational innovation. Finally, several hypotheses are presented and illustrated with case material from video banking developments.

RESEARCH ON INNOVATION

As a starting point, we review pertinent innovation literature according to the level of analysis used. As mentioned earlier, four levels are identified to organize the previous research: technology, firm, industry and multiple industries (i.e., community).

Technology as the Unit of Analysis

The dominant view about technological evolution is represented by the *incrementalist perspective*. In this view, major innovations are viewed as emerging from the cumulative synthesis of simple innovations, each one of which requires "an act of insight" (Rutan, 1959, p. 601). The cumulative process itself may produce a synthesis, where a new relationship among various individual experiences becomes fully understood and effectively cultivated into their entire context (Usher, 1954). A proposition advanced is the *learning by using hypothesis*: it is through the accumulation of relevant experience in a given technology (e.g., through the identification and elimination of weak spots or bottlenecks in the system) that its optimal performance can be realized. For a single technological domain, the increased production and application of the technology would pave the way for refinements of its attributes and performance.

The incremental technological improvements can occur through a variety of avenues, some of which are perceived as more attractive than others. The prevailing path is the technology's *natural trajectory* (Nelson & Winter, 1982). In a given technological regime, research engineers are guided by a paradigm about what is technically feasible in potential technological improvements.

While some historians[1] focus on the origin of a technology, others emphasize the discontinuity and consequence of technological evolution. Mensch (1979), for example, surmises that technological progress follows an S-curve. Once a basic innovation emerges, it is followed by a series of *improvements* with accelerating rate and culminates in decays when the potential for additional improvements is exhausted. Further improvements are not only difficult but also costly. At this junction, the technology faces a *stalemate* that can be offset only by the development of other basic innovations. Astley (1985) and Tushman and Anderson (1986) have further modified Mensch's model by depicting a pattern of evolutionary technological progress punctuated by revolutionary change. These technological discontinuities are attributed as significantly altering competitive environments (Tushman & Anderson, 1986) or opening up new strands of activities which concomitantly creates new branches of industry (Astley, 1985).

One of the difficulties in the distinction between radical and evolutionary innovations concerns the actual definition of "radical." Some may judge the "radicalness" by the intrinsic attributes of the technology itself, its social consequences or the characteristics of the adopting organizations. The distinction is helpful whenever we track a technological history, but less so in explaining the origination of an innovation when "frame breaking" is hard to judge. Furthermore, it can be difficult to distinguish accumulated incremental changes of a technology from the radical ones since the first can lead to a very different product for a different market (i.e., "radical"). Rosenberg (1982) has shown that major technological changes grow out of and build directly upon the accumulation of experience with the technology.[2]

From the innovating firm's viewpoint, similarly, there is a difficulty in distinguishing between radical and incremental changes. Clearly, attempts by firms to employ techniques that depart significantly from their existing ones are very costly and uncertain. One of the problems is that firms do not obviously know, ex ante, what is the best technique to be searched for. This leads us to the second area of innovation research, namely, the innovation by the firm.

Innovation Within the Firm

The bulk of innovation research at the firm-level of analysis revolves around the *adoption perspective,* in which organizations are viewed as recipients of innovation developed elsewhere (Normann, 1971; Rogers, 1983). This perspective has primarily addressed the conditions that enhance or impede the decision to innovate, to experiment with or to acquire a new process or product or to consider a change in organizational practices in general. The basic ingredients of adoption research involve the identification of organizational attributes such as size (Rogers, 1983), types of organization structure and the role of organizational elites (Normann, 1971), which are viewed as critical factors in fostering innovation. The innovation adoption research has also dwelt on the role of leaders and boundary spanning individuals. This perspective, therefore, has often addressed issues at the level of groups and individuals within organizations, and the role they might play in bringing organizations into contact with new developments (e.g., Pettigrew, 1974). Such individuals are deemed crucial in converting organizational constituencies and in forging the stage for adoption and implementation. Other research attempts to identify various innovation attributes (Rogers, 1983) and the "fit" between organizations and the nature of the innovation (Normann, 1971; Pennings, 1987).

The setback of the adoption perspective lies in its reliance on internal structures and processes as explanatory factors of innovativeness. Another criticism is that adoption research has been static, of the *variance* rather than the *process* type (Mohr, 1982). From an organization-level of analysis, we can and need to distinguish the role of organization either as producer, adopter, both user and adopter or as the innovation itself (Kimberly, 1986). In this respect, our interests rest on the category of organization as both producer and user of innovation, a category that is less researched.

Another stream of research starts with the presumption, unlike the adoption perspective, that firms are not merely a recipient of technology developed elsewhere. Rather, it emphasizes practical experiences as innovation antecedents. This stream complements the research at the macroscopic, technology-level above, by stressing the role of the individual firm in shaping technological evolution. Part of the work of Nelson and Winter (1982) is typical. Firms are depicted as actively engaging in a continuous search for better techniques. In their search, firms seek incremental improvements to current techniques and exploring preexisting, albeit to be found, technological possibilities. The search is modeled as not extending very far beyond the alien domains that might also be contested by others. In the Simonesque tradition (Simon, 1947), they affirm that for a given technology, progress occurs as the firms gradually explore and locate new possibilities.

The depicted search behavior by the firm implies that the firms gradually learn about technology through modification and trial and error. This organizational learning takes place within specific practical experiences: it is mostly context (e.g., product and plant) specific. The view that the firm may modify an innovation (produced by others) is also shared by the adoption perspective (Rogers' [1983] *reinvention*). Different organizations may develop different system configurations of the very same technology, and can at times reinvent the technology for other use functions. These ideas imply that there are built-in difficulties in transferring the technology, as innovations largely are built upon knowledge accumulated from within and not so much on imported knowledge from outside. As learning through experience implies cost, there is no free technical know-how at the disposal of every firm in the market.

When commercial application or adoptions fail, we tended likewise to examine the industrial factors that can account for the failure. These draw our attention toward the structural characteristics of the market that foster or inhibit innovation.

Industrial Analysis of Innovation

The heart of the traditional industrial organization perspective is to explicate the structural determinants of innovation with an aim to provide a sound ground for public policy. In his comprehensive review, Scherer (1970) relates R&D efforts and outcomes to market structure parameters such as concentration, entry barriers, firm size and pattern of firm conducts. While innovation research at the technology-level or at the firm-level deals with a specific technology or innovation (particular new product or process), the industrial organization analysis takes the *innovative activities* in general (measured as the number of patents, R&D personnel, R&D expenditure) as its unit of analysis.

The relationship between market structure and innovative activities is complex. Although market structure (e.g., concentration) may influence the pace of innovative activities (e.g., Mansfield, 1968), the market structure itself is subject to the influence of technological advances. R&D outputs may influence the optimal scale of production and the erection of entry barrier (Hamberg, 1967). As discussed earlier, major innovation may bring new firms to the forefront and displace the old ones, defining a new set of structural conditions (Mensch, 1979; Tushman & Anderson, 1986). Also, it has generally been accepted that the *demand pull* and *technology push* arguments are not necessarily mutually exclusive; these two views can be regarded as a complementary rather than competing explanation.

Interestingly, as we have indicated earlier, in his industry analysis framework Porter (1980) implicitly includes the notion of interindustry linkages. Buyer-supplier relationships and the notion of "substitute" loosen the boundary of the analysis to include other, even seemingly unrelated industries. As we will see, such linkages may have a profound effect on the development of new technological possibilities and hence the direction of innovation that firms undertake.

Innovation Within the Web of Interindustry Linkages

As was indicated before, the bulk of the innovation research has adopted an organizational or macroeconomic (e.g., technology) level of analysis. Research at the level of the firm and its industry, however, is too restricted as increasing technological interdependencies are discernible. This requires us to move to a higher level of analysis, meaning, interindustry level of analysis. This observation is related to the earlier mentioned technological trajectory that draws firms and their industries together and apart, and that requires firms to search beyond conventional industry boundaries.

Only scattered publications have emerged covering the subject of innovation in an interorganizational context. There is, for example, the research by Astley and Fombrun (1983) on the competition and fusion of populations of organizations, as witnessed in the changing relationship between the semiconductor and telecommunication industries. Firms witness dissolution of their industry boundaries as their respective technologies evolve increasingly toward each other. Astley and Fombrun suggest that we have to move to the level of "community" (populations of industries) if we want to understand how interpopulation dynamics are played out at the level of individual firms. Their revision and expansion of the population ecology paradigm nicely complement the work that is done concurrently by industrial economists.

Several economists have carried out research on the flows of technological innovation and technological relatedness among industries. Rosenberg (1979) claims that the applicability of an invention is very much conditioned by the availability of complementary technologies that reside in different industries. Examples are telecommunications and computers, pharmaceutical and biotechnology. Complementary technologies were not always available at the time of invention, but had to await the realization of other inventions. Perhaps this may explain the long to very long time lag between inventions and their actual conversion to practical use (Mensch, 1979).

It is this notion of technological relatedness that can be linked to interindustry flows of innovation: the diffusion of innovations from one industry toward other ones. The overwhelming majority of innovations found their applications in industries different from where they originated (Scherer, 1982; Pavitt, 1984). The implication is that innovating firms do not initiate their own breakthroughs. Diversification, where innovation flows to different industries but stays within the bounds of a corporation, is extremely limited and accounts for only 18 percent of interindustry flows. Naturally, there are variations among industries. Pavitt classified them into three categories: science-based, supplier dominated and production-intensive. The first are among the highest exporting industries, while the latter are rather mixed with some approaching autarchy to high external dependency (compare also von Hippel, 1976).

An interesting observation made by Pavitt (1984) is that general knowledge and specific technology have to be supported and combined with firm-endogenous skills if innovations are to be effectively adopted—a notion that is quite akin to the adoption and incremental perspective. In some cases, the development of in-house expertise also makes significant contributions, or even dominates, upstream innovations such as in the instrumentation industry. In such cases, informal ties between producer and user firms are significant. Another insight pertains to the direction of technological innovation across industry categories. In the science based industries, innovations take place largely to improve product quality and productivity. In production intensive industries they enhance efficiency through improved scale economies. In supplier-based industries most innovations are process innovations. In different industries, technological trajectories are, therefore, the result of a unique symbiosis.

Despite their diversities, the literature with four different levels of analysis above, as we will see, share equivalent conceptual foundations and permit a meaningful synthesis. In essence they embody a learning and inertia view. We will show that the organizational inertia due to the acquisition of distinctive skills creates interesting consequences for the firms and their industries and provides the stage for innovation beyond the confines of focal firms.

Firms have, as already implied, idiosyncratic technologies with distinctive skills or competence and unique assets. It is because of such idiosyncrasies that the issue of interorganizational relationships acquires strategic significance. The fundamental question is, how interindustry flows mirror interfirm linkages whose creation is a crucial factor for preserving or enhancing the firms' competitive position. As has been stipulated numerous times (e.g., Pennings, 1981), cooperative arrangements between firms engender external control, thereby making firms less vulnerable to uncertain, meaning, unanticipated events.

Interfirm arrangements include cartels, trade associations, interlocking directorates, licensing agreements and joint ventures. The last two, licensing agreements and joint ventures, represent an interesting class of phenomena. They are germane to the question of how a firm seeks to commercialize its innovations or merge its distinctive skills with those of others. The firm becomes confronted with transaction difficulties when it seeks to address the choice of expanding its proprietary technology or to contract it in the market. As Teece (1986) has indicated, such a choice is conditioned by the degree of specificity of its complementary asset, the efficacy of its "appropriability regime" (i.e., factors that determine an innovator's ability to reap the innovation's benefits) and the relative position of the competitors and their potential for contributing distinctive skills into a joint venture. Von Hippel (1988) puts it more simply: firms (whether a producer or a user of innovation) will carry out the necessary innovation only if they believe that they can expect an attractive economic rent from the innovation.

Relationships between firms in general and evolving linkages between the industries they belong to represent the embeddedness of the diffusion of innovation. It provides a mapping for supraorganizational inducements for search and adoption.

TOWARD A CONCEPTUAL FRAMEWORK

Firms and their Skills

As producers or users of innovation, firms are defined here as a set of integrated resources that are more or less unique. The foremost important set are those related to the skills or know-how as these reside in its human and nonhuman assets. The skills may be specific to the organization if they cannot be exported or alienated. The dominant assumption is that firms consist of members whose behavior is governed, enacted and modified by layers of routines. The routines are the scripts that embody the skills of the firm and its members; they facilitate and inhibit the production and adoption of innovation.

Skills are defined as the accumulated practical expertise and know-how that allows the beholders to function smoothly and efficiently.[3] For a firm, they are the ingredients that make up the firm's distinctive competence. As knowledge-based resources, skills possess some significant characteristics. Knowledge can be viewed as a public good as well as a fixed cost in its production. A chunk of knowledge, once developed, can be used over and over at any scale of operation without reducing the amount of information possessed by the first person who produced it. As with any fixed cost, by definition, knowledge is a source of scales economies in production. These characteristics, as we will see, contribute to the direction of innovations that a firm will undertake.

Because many skills are anchored in the interdependence of tasks and embedded in complex social relationships that are unique to the firm, they cannot be separated from the firm that possesses them, a view that is highly similar to Nelson and Winter's (1982, p. 124) well-known notion: "routines are the core skills of an organization." The information required for the functioning of the enterprise is stored in routines, in which much of the underlying knowledge is tacit, not consciously known or articulable. Tacit skills are unprogrammed, hard to teach or package, as they are embedded in the web of social and technical interrelationships in the organization. Individual skills may be highly articulable, but within a complex division of labor they may become unarticulable. Next to tacitness, skills can also be classified by their degree of specificity to their beholders. Skills, interestingly, may be highly tacit but not idiosyncratic to the firm. Examples of such skills are those that remain unique to a class of applications or those that are an integral part of an occupation's body of knowledge. We will examine the implication of these skill attributes for the innovation behavior of the firm.

The Quest for Expansion and the Direction of Innovation

In the quest for expansion, diversification or enhancement of a firm's skills, its own baggage of skills forms a key constraint upon the scale and direction of innovative activities. Whenever there is a perceived imbalance, that is, a hiatus in its skill repertoire, there is a motivation to search. There are, however, also environmental search triggers such as market conditions. Under pressure of competition, firms are induced to imitate their most efficient competitors or to use alternative techniques with comparable results.

Firms located at a junction of interindustry linkages, likewise, face a technological trajectory that makes their own technology overlapping with that of other firms in traditionally different industries. These flows draw the attention of the firm's leaders to other industries and technologies. Remote and unrelated technologies and skills now become related and potentially highly interdependent. They become proximate to a firm's distinctive skills, yet may remain alien or ill-understood, and not within the purview of its *problemistic search*, at least initially. It becomes, therefore, a crucial question how or under what scenarios those disparate yet interdependent technologies and skills arrive at an innovative synthesis.[4]

The technological or competitive conditions alone cannot be assumed to trigger such a search, if only for the inertial reasons as specified by the Carnegie school (e.g., Cyert & March, 1963). Figure 1 provides a simple diagram for presenting these interindustry inducements for innovation and the way these should be consolidated with the focusing effects of a firm's skills, or escalated commitments such as prior investments. It is proposed that the external and firm-specific inducements jointly explain a great many manifestations of innovations in an interorganizational context. They may also explain why some firms refrain from externalizing their R&D efforts, or why they prefer to acquire the new technology by contractual means. In this sense, the model combines both the "demand pull" and the "technology push" arguments. The significant differences are that our model takes the firm-level of analysis, and that we need to look at the coupling of various technologies in question.

Inducing Effects from the Environment

Firms operating in a web of interindustry linkages are exposed to a realm of technological prospects. Some of these technologies are symbiotic in that their combination in an integrative fashion can greatly simplify the overall

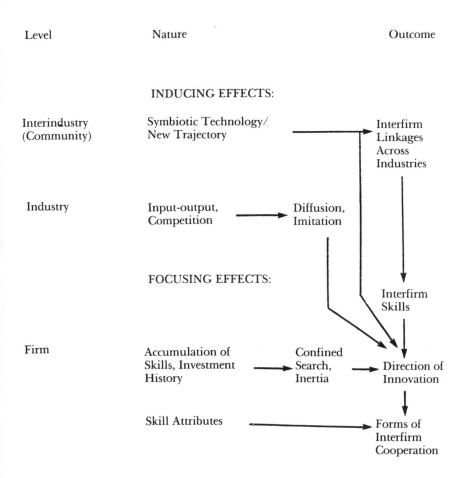

Figure 1. Factors Shaping the Innovation Activities of the Firm

system and advance their evolution. The interindustry linkages, reflected by interindustry flows of ideas and innovations, induce firms to look upon production activities of different firms as a source of new markets or technological prospects. As such, this inducement may preempt internal imbalances as an object of managerial action.

Hypothesis 1. Innovating firms at the junction of convergent technological evolution will acquire both relevant technological skills from the neighboring industries, and commensurate interorganizational skills.

Focusing Effects of Internal Conditions

As argued, interindustry linkages and the pressure of competition expose and induce firms to search for new opportunities. Whether firms will innovate (join the bandwagon of technological trajectories) also depends on their internal resources configuration, including technical, organizational, financial and human. We discussed earlier that innovation takes place incrementally. At any given time, a firm can only skillfully master a limited set of capabilities. The skill configuration of a firm is very much the product of where it has been, including its position in interindustry linkages, and what it has accomplished during its entire history.

The existing skill configuration of the firm imposes some constraints upon the scale and direction of its activities. Prevailing skills may focus the efforts of the managers upon the improvement of existing deficiencies. The innovation implemented to resolve the deficiency or imbalance of existing skills, however, does not typically create a permanent new balance. The change, elimination or addition of an existing set of skills is likely to result in another, different imbalance. As Normann (1971) noted, modifications of existing product or production dimensions will diffuse to other subsystems: any adjustment in one activity therefore will require adjustment in other activities as well. At the same time, the changes may also open up new opportunities not encountered before. All things considered, it is proposed that firms accumulate their skills gradually.

The *problemistic search* invoked here implies that managers can only deal with a limited set of opportunities. Such cognitive limitations shape the scope of firms' innovative activities. The accumulated skills of the firm can be viewed as a fixed production cost: their use in any scale does not proportionally increase the cost to produce them. In essence, this attribute of the skills can reinforce the firm's search to the limited area with which it is already familiar.

Because innovation ensues very much from built-up knowledge inside the firm, it is expected that the latter will facilitate, and confine, the initiation of innovation in adjacent areas. In other words, the ability of a firm to carry out an innovation is very much conditioned by the accumulated innovation-relevant skills, reflected in its investment histories.

Hypothesis 2.   The more a firm has amassed relevant skills for a given technological innovation, the greater is its likelihood for adopting the innovation.

Locating and Organizing Forms of Innovation

Another pertinent issue is the identification of conditions under which firms collaborate with others in their quest for new ideas, products or processes. Many arguments and theoretical perspectives have addressed this question. We do not claim that our arguments are complete; still, we believe that our core concept about accumulation of skills and the attributes of skills contribute to the explanation of observed variances in the the interfirm organizing forms chosen to carry out the innovation.

Assume that an innovation requires the combination of skills A and B. Assume further that a focal firm (with skills A) wants to innovate, hence needs the complementary skills B, traditionally belonging to industry B firms. For analytical clarity, we can depict the innovating firm as having a sequential problem-solving task. Figure 2 summarizes this chain of possibilities. When embarking on an innovation, a firm needs to resolve whether to have full control over expected rents or share them with other firms. Some factors that condition a firm's ability to monopolize the full benefit of the innovation include its relative strategic position in the market (e.g., Teece, 1986) and the saliency of the innovation to the focal firm, such as the expected displacement of existing business due to the innovation (von Hippel, 1988). If the focal firm has a strong strategic position (high market share in a given niche, oligopolist/monopolist) or if the innovating firm believed that the innovation will replace its existing business (e.g., the earlier, controversial belief of Knight Ridder management that videotex services would replace printed news), it is expected that the firm will control the development and commercialization of the innovation.

Given that the focal firm wants to monopolize the benefit of the innovation, it can decide either to develop the complementary skills B in-house, or to acquire the ownership rights of such skills from outsiders. The latter implies that the complementary skill B is "packageable" and can easily be transferred. We expect that if: (1) the complementary skills B are packageable (i.e., low tacitness); (2) there are many potential suppliers for skills B (i.e., low specificity); and (3) the focal firm has only a limited exposure and accumulation of skills B; it is likely that the focal firm will purchase outright such skills from potential suppliers from industry B. Otherwise, we expect that the focal firm will develop it internally.

If the focal firm is willing to, or has to, share the expected rent from the innovation, the firm does so by licensing the complementary skills B from other firms, or by creating a joint venture with firm(s) having the capability of providing the complementary skills B. We assume here that the licensing arrangements involve continuous technical support for the use of the technology and with the licensing fee at least partially proportional to the output of the service. We also limit ourselves here to the licensing and joint venturing arrangements that are intended to share diverse technologies and skills for creating a new process, product or service.[5]

A joint venture is an independent legal entity, founded by two or more partners, each one of which contributes assets and collects rents. The joint

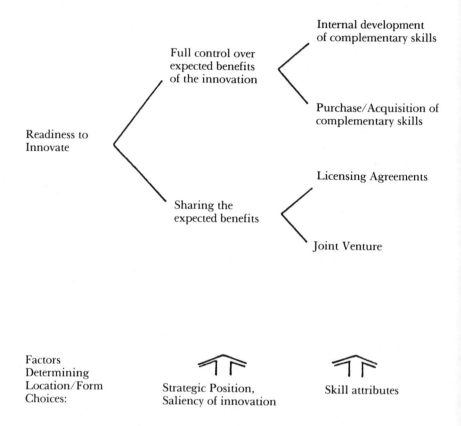

Figure 2.   Locating and Organizing Forms of Innovation

venture is potentially a producer of innovation, whose outcome might be used by the parent. More importantly, the joint venture might be less encumbered by its parents' organizational practices and can, therefore, be seen as a vehicle for radical innovations, charting strange territories and following certain technological trajectories. At the onset of this chapter, we pointed out that the organizational entity may be an innovation itself.

In licensing, again it is implied that the complementary skills are relatively *packageable* and can easily be transferred. The licensing is more attractive, as compared to outright purchasing, if the focal firm has not had an extensive exposure and accumulation of related skills B. Furthermore, from the viewpoint of the potential provider of skills B, licensing makes sense if such an arrangement is enforceable and especially if there are relatively many potential users of skills B.

Compared to the licensing arrangement, joint venturing involves a higher stake for each party involved. The equity ownership in the joint venture functions as a bond for each party to ease the problem of moral hazard and to ensure the success of the venture. The bonding is especially crucial if there is a high degree of difficulty in transferring and combining the two traditionally distinct technologies and skills. Interestingly, the focal firm is in a position to see this potential difficulty, especially if it has relatively extensive experience with the complementary skills that the potential partner is about to provide.

By its nature, the dual governance structure of a joint venture is laden with potential conflict of interests, disagreement about the means to achieve an end and interpersonal differences. Because such an on-going governance structure requires a high degree of interorganizational skills, we expect that a firm with extensive experiences to link with other firms that are potentially capable of providing the complementary skills is more likely to engage in joint venturing than licensing. In short, joint venturing is more likely than licensing if: (1) both skills are difficult to transfer (hard to package) or specific to both partners; (2) the focal firm has extensive experience with the complementary skills; and (3) the firm has extensive interorganizational skills, especially with firms from the complementary industry.

The scenario presented above is obviously a static one. While some skill attributes are relatively "fixed," the expected economic benefit of the innovation as well as the strategic position of the innovating firm may change over a period of time, rendering the previously chosen form of interfirm arrangements obsolete. It is conceivable, therefore, that the interfirm linkages evolve from one form to another.

A CASE STUDY: THE FINANCIAL SERVICES INDUSTRY AND ONE OF ITS KEY PLAYERS, CITICORP

In the previous pages, general propositions on innovation in an interorganizational context have been presented. They will now be illustrated and clarified with the case of converging technologies in the financial services sector. This sector is very significant as its output constitutes almost 66% of the total revenue of the information industry. This percentage is relatively constant over the period of 1970-1980 (Compaine, 1984). Indeed, the sector witnesses a microelectronic "sweep" and is by far the most important recipient of the U.S. information technology.

In examining our framework as presented in Figure 1, there is a methodological issue of levels of analysis. For example, we can take the industry as our unit of analysis, then identify the nature of interindustry linkages and examine the variation in interfirm linkages across industries.

Another strategy confines the study to a single industry, permitting an examination of both the diffusion of innovation and the concomitant interfirm activities. As it happens, a major technological trajectory is discernible at the interface of financial services, telecommunications and computers. Additionally, an examination of the first as a focal industry "controls" for industry differences.

We will first look at the interindustry linkages surrounding the financial services context, then examine the extent of interfirm linkages in these convergent technologies and services. Finally we will examine one firm, Citicorp, with special emphasis on its move into the videotex/video financial services.

Interindustry Linkages Around the Financial Services

Traditionally, the financial services sector is fully dependent on innovations developed elsewhere, notably from the computer and telecommunications sectors. In 1974, this sector generated virtually no R&D outlays. In contrast, it consumed approximately $410 million of R&D inflows, 42.8% of which came from computers and another 5.1% from telecommunications industries (Scherer, 1982). Contrast this with the computer industry, which produced $1,153 million in R&D outlays, $110.5 million of which was used internally (accounting for 83.8% of total R&D input). Major users were the financial sector (15.5% of the output), trade (8.5%) and defense (6.5%). The telecommunications sector, produced $1,227.7 million in R&D outlays, and consumed $728.4 million of input, almost 72% of which came from within. The major recipients included defense (18.0%), transportation (7.1%), trade (2.6%) and finance (1.7%). Clearly, the financial sector and these two parts of the information technology sector were extraordinary in their mutual dependence.

The figures presented above, based on Scherer's (1982) study, pertain to the year 1974. Interindustry input-output patterns may have changed during the last decade. For example, it has been reported that the financial services have been increasingly active in developmental activities (*Computer World*, 1988). Our point, however, is that under such conditions, financial services firms find themselves at an intersection of interindustry R&D flows that may forebode certain technological trajectories. A central question revolves around their core skills and the way these get complemented with those of others.

The Converging Technology and Services

By the sheer number of financial transactions (37 billion checks, 3.5 billion credit card drafts and over 30 billion shares/securities traded annually) it has become imperative for financial firms to venture into information technology. The initial introduction of information technology (e.g., the use of magnetic ink character recognition, MICR, to encode checks; on-line work stations for tellers and platform personnel) facilitated automation of back office operations. Beyond automation, current applications such as automated teller machine networks, remote banking through home computers and work stations in corporate offices represent only a further departure from the manual storing and transmission of information. Such an innovation delegates the rendering of financial services to actors external to the firms. The merger of microelectronics and telecommunications is nowhere more evident than in the financial services sector.

Telecommunications are critical for financial services delivery. Delivery systems such as automated teller machine networks, both regional and national, and wholesale automatic clearing houses depend very much on the availability of efficient telecommunications networks. Securities trading firms have long used private video cable networks. Merrill Lynch sponsors the planned teleport installation for New York, while Aetna Insurance jointly owns Satellite Business Systems. Citicorp is one of several firms that operate or lease their own satellite.

With these technological developments, there is indeed a real possibility of altering the structure of the financial services: the way the services are produced, priced, delivered and used (Office of Technology Assessment, 1984; Revell, 1983). At the retailing level, the proliferation of automated teller machines and point-of-sale networks in major gas stations and retailer/supermarket chains has changed the function of payment networks. The electronic information services have also changed, and at some extent diminished, the role of brokerage services (for insurance, mortgages and securities). A highly integrated global capital market, for example, has emerged when financial institutions began moving capital at a national and even international scale. Local brokerage agents can now provide an *added value* service, combining their access to the integrated capital market information system with their in-house database and expertise. From these developments, The Office of Technology Assessment, in its 1984 study on the effect of information technology on financial services, concluded, among other things, that the major players (e.g., Citicorp, Merrill Lynch, Sears) have accumulated expertise and capabilities in distribution processing and/ or communications systems. By virtue of competition, it is expected that all financial firms must acquire similar know-how in the computer applications as well as telecommunications.

Interfirm Linkages

We also hypothesize that under a condition of interdependence among financial services, computer and telecommunications sectors, financial firms

Table 1. Number of Significant Innovations in Banking Industry And Interfirm Linkages, 1977-1987[a]

	1977	78	79	80	81	82	83	84	85	86	87	Total
Technological Innovations[b]	11	8	2	9	25	41	37	60	67	49	56	365 (34%)
Technology-Related New Services[c]	2	3	1	1	0	7	5	7	4	9	6	45 (4%)
Other New Services[d]	7	5	8	11	9	12	26	32	30	28	31	199 (19%)
Administrative Innovations[e]	13	8	13	33	18	38	26	40	58	90	127	464 (43%)
Total	33	24	24	54	52	98	94	139	159	176	220	1073 (100%)
Technology-Related:												
Int. Development	7	8	2	6	10	15	14	28	25	27	27	169 (41%)
Licensing, J.V.	2	0	0	1	5	26	26	27	34	27	24	172 (42%)
Other New Services/ Admin. Innov.												
Int. Development	20	13	20	43	26	46	43	64	78	113	153	619 (93%)
Licensing, J.V.	0	0	0	0	1	2	6	6	9	4	5	33 (5%)

Notes: [a] There are 148 banks in the sample. The numbers are innovation activities as reported in the Predicast Corporate Index.
[b] Included in this category are: ATM, POS, computerization, Telecommunications, smart card, home banking and corporate electronic banking.
[c] This category includes: information/data base services, transaction-related services (e.g., shopping by phone charged through customer's account), informational value added services.
[d] This includes the introduction of new types of accounts such as NOW, interest-bearing traveller cheque, and other type of financial products offered by banks.
[e] This category includes general administration (e.g., restructuring of bank organizations), marketing (new incentive programs aimed at people over 55) and personnel (the introduction of personnel database, new incentive packages).

would forge various interfirm connections with firms belonging to those industries. Astley and Fombrun (1983) have documented the interfirm, interindustry linkages, especially in the telecommunications, computer and entertainment (as information providers) sectors. The documentation on interfirm linkages in the financial sector, however, is sparse, if it exists at all.

To address this deficiency, we collected data about innovation activities from approximately 150 of the largest banks in the United States. We collected secondary data from public sources, as they are readily available. The criteria for selecting the data base for this purpose were: (1) it had to contain multiple years of observation; and (2) it had to contain information from sources relevant for banks (e.g., American Bankers, *Wall Street Journal*), computers and telecommunications (e.g., *Computer World*). The only data base that fulfilled these criteria was the Predicast Index on U.S. Corporations.[6] Results are presented in Table 1.

Table 1, covering the period 1977-1987, shows several interesting results. While administrative innovations show a constant increase, technological innovations reveal a sudden increase in 1981, followed by a downturn after 1985. Second, during the decade, technological innovations are more likely to be carried out with computer and/or telecommunications firms (e.g., 47%) compared to nontechnological innovations where only less than 10% involved reliance on other firms. Third, prior to 1981, interfirm structures for technological innovations projects were relatively rare (e.g., 12.9%), whereas in subsequent years such structures became exceedingly prominent (e.g., 47.9% in 1985).

Videotex Innovation in the Financial Service Industry

A technological convergence is discernible in the financial sector from the rise of videotex/videobanking services in the financial sector. Videotex refers to computer-based interactive systems that electronically deliver screen text, numbers and graphics, or execute transactions. It brings together firms from information delivery, financial and merchandizing sectors on the one side (as information and service provider) and semiconductor and telecommunications firms on the other side.   Particularly during the early videotex development in the 1980s, one could witness a surge in interfirm cooperation (see Table 1). Interestingly, they represent mostly multiple interfirm linkages. AT&T, for example, was involved with Knight Ridder (*Viewtron*) as well as with CBS (*Venture One*) and later formed a joint venture (*Covidea*) with Time Inc., Chemical Bank and Bank of America in 1985. Chemical Bank had already developed its own electronic banking and information service (*Pronto*) for residential and business users and licensed the Pronto system to other banks (e.g., Crocker National, American

Security). L.M. Berry, a national advertising company for yellow pages directories, offered an on-line shopping service through the CompuServe of H&R Block (a tax consulting firm). Buick Motor, apart from its links with Viewtron and Gateway, was also participating in Electronic Mail.

Cooperation among financial firms has also emerged. The Automated Data Processing (ADP) has developed *Home Banking Interchange*, and licensed the system to around 15 banks nationwide (as of 1985), including Bank of Montreal, Barnett Banks of Florida, Continental Illinois National Bank, First Wisconsin and Marine Midland. Seven major banks, besides their individual videobanking efforts, have jointly formed *Video Financial Services* (VFS). Among these banks are Bank One, Security Pacific, Chase Manhattan and First Chicago. The VFS is a national videotex gateway operator that organizes and packages on-line financial services.

The form of interfirm cooperation varies widely, with some firms seeking high levels of control over the expected benefit of innovation (e.g., internal ventures), while others are willing to share (e.g., joint ventures). Over time, the firms' cooperative forms either evolve into closer ties or the opposite. It appears that many follow two sets of learning curves: technological and interorganizational. Different interfirm arrangements may cover different types of innovation; for example, satellite leasing versus software development.

Attributes of Skills Involved in the Videotex and Videobanking Services

Videobanking can be viewed as a subset of the general videotex services. Videobanking involves only financial transactions such as transfers between accounts, bill payments or securities trading. General videotex, on the other hand, offers a full array of services ranging from data retrieval, electronic billboard, teleshopping and electronic banking in general. While videobanking requires relatively simple representation on the customer's terminal (mostly in digital form), others require sophisticated images. Teleshopping and games, for example, require graphics and even analog animation.

From a bank's viewpoint, the skills required for videobanking involve full automation of its back office. With the proliferation of automated teller machine (ATM) and point-of-sales (POS) networks, one can expect that the expansion into videobanking technology is unavoidable. There are hundreds of software vendors of electronic fund transfer processes, 83 of which specialized in financial services (Directory of Electronic Fund Transfers, 1985/1986). Videobanking software is highly codified (as is most software) and can be transferred relatively easily, subject to the compatibility of the host computer system.[7] Complementary skills require that software and hardware are *packageable* and not specific to any potential suppliers.

Of course, some potential suppliers have developed proprietary software (e.g., Chemical's *Pronto*), but the availability of hundreds of other potential suppliers render it difficult for a single supplier to monopolize the products.

A full-fledged videotex service, on the other hand, requires not only more sophisticated software, but also an extensive array of nonfinancial services. Teleshopping, for example, needs a full understanding about comprehensive retailing operations: clear target customers, logistics and promotional capabilities. It is doubtful that banks, if legally permitted, would be willing to develop such skills. Entry barriers for banks (as well as for retailers and other potential entrants into the videotex industry in the form of inadequate relevant skills) necessitate cooperative arrangements. Such cooperative agreements render videotex service delivery more feasible. As a result, there are two options available for a bank to participate in the videotex services: to act as a financial service provider for a videotex system operator (together with other information and transaction services providers) or to assume the role as system operator with financial services as one of the core components. As we have argued earlier, the latter option is more likely to be carried out through joint venturing. *Covidea* and NCR Partners are examples of the second option, where banks (i.e., Chemical for Covidea and Citibank for NCR Partners) jointly provide comprehensive videotex services.

Citicorp

We proposed that a firm that has amassed innovation-relevant skills is more likely to carry out the innovation. For banks, the skills required to provide videotex are computer and telecommunications capabilities, and information or service provision. As the merging of disparate technologies unfolds at the interindustry level, it can be surmised that interorganizational experiences with computer, telecommunications or merchandizing firms are also conducive to videotex innovation. Citicorp is prototypical for banks having such capabilities.

Figure 3 provides a condensed historical map of Citicorp involvement in information technology in general and videotex in particular. Automation in Citicorp originated in the early 1960s. Under the current CEO, John Reed, Citicorp was reorganizing its operating departments, as a part of its strategy to be a leader in information technology. It pioneered back office automation. A new internal venture, the Transaction Technology Inc., was in charge of developing Citicorp's transactional technology, either through internal developments or through licensing from other software houses (e.g., with Scantlin Electronic in 1971). The company also pioneered automated teller machines (ATM); its massive network in the New York area was first installed in 1977. The company has also developed an *enhanced telephone* technology, using a small portable device

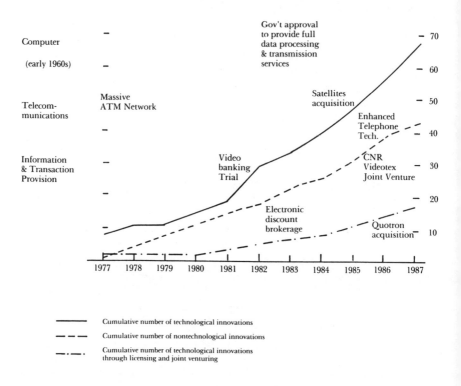

Figure 3.   Chronological Events of Citicorp Involvement
In Information Technology

to enable a telephone receiver to function as a mini terminal. To handle
its millions of credit card holders, Citicorp obviously required sophisticated
information technology capabilities.

In telecommunications—a complementary technology—the firm has also
been very active. In 1977 it signed a five-year agreement with Graphic
Scanning Corp. to develop automated data and messaging systems for the
firm. In 1984, the company bought the *Spacenet 1* satellite from GTE
Spacenet and then leased it back to the seller. Soon afterward satellite
transponders were purchased from American Satellite, followed by a lease-
back. Its ATM expansion in 1981 into regional as well as national networks
certainly contributed to the buildup of telecommunications proficiency.
Citicorp has also signed agreements with various institutions to link their
product and services, including their computer network (e.g., with Good
Year in 1983 and American Airlines in 1987, and with Daichi Kangyo Bank,

Japan also in 1987). In 1985, Citicorp joined Cirrus, a national automated teller machine network, and practically became the first national consumer bank.

Citicorp started providing information and transaction services as early as 1969, when it offered computerized individual tax returns. This diversification was triggered by the collaboration with Tax Corp. of America. In the same year, it became the first participant in the Big Board's automated stock clearing operation. In 1977, consumer information libraries were created, this being another seed in its branching out into information delivery. In 1985, Citicorp created a joint venture with McGraw-Hill to form "Global Electronic Marketing Co.," providing commodity traders buy and sell opportunities through computer terminals, although this joint venture was eventually discontinued.

In 1982, Citicorp started a joint marketing program with the brokerage houses of Lehman Brothers, Kuhn Loeb Inc. and Quick & Reilly. In 1983, discount brokerage services were made available in its 225 New York branches, where Quick & Reilly would handle the accounts. In 1985, it also planned a joint venture with NMW Computers P.L.C. to become a clearing member of the London Stock Exchange. The expansion into securities brokerage became more apparent when it bought Quotron System Inc. in 1986. A year later, Citicorp signed an agreement with Sun Microsystems Inc. to supply intelligent work stations to be sold in tandem with Quotron's computerized stock information and transaction services.

With these additional encroachments into different but related technologies necessary for videotex services, it is consistent with our hypothesis that Citicorp is highly likely to be a premier player in this new industry. It undertook its first videobanking experiment in 1981, and then after entering into a joint venture with RCA and Nynex, further entrenched itself into these alternative delivery systems. While the death of the joint venture can be viewed as a setback, it certainly has not eliminated the firm's interest in building competitive strength in electronics and telecommunications. Uncertainties due to regulation, consumer acceptance and capital resources surface as key issues in the survey of banking executives.

CONCLUSION AND DISCUSSION

A multilevel approach to the study of interfirm innovation has been suggested. Technological innovations at the firm level may necessitate a consideration of events, conditions or developments which occur at higher levels of analysis. Technological developments among firms or among industries comprise important inducements for individual firms to commit significant resources. Yet, it is also apparent that conditions internal to the firm are crucial in understanding their quest for technological innovations. Crucial are the skills and know-how relevant to a certain technology that induce a firm to search for and to commit resources. Finally, we have argued that whenever technological evolutions span multiple industries, such as semiconductor, telecommunications and financial services, firms which seek to diversify into those directions enjoy a significant advantage if they have accumulated interorganizational experiences. The merging of disparate skills often unfolds in interfirm structures that combine the industry-idiosyncratic resources that different firms contribute.

The survey of the videotex industry in general and the historical description of Citicorp in particular highlight the propositions that are embedded in these considerations. As an exponent of the financial services sector, Citicorp has repeatedly branched out toward telecommunications and computer firms, thus mirroring the trend toward greater entanglement of these industries. However, compared with its competitors, it enjoys a considerable advantage in that it was a first mover in various related technological innovations such as the automated teller machine. It has been a participant in several joint ventures and licensing agreements, and has been an aggressive acquisitive diversifier, thus endowing it with an extensive repertoire of interfirm skills. The firm's behavior neatly illustrates the need to consider both its history as well as technological trends in the banking industry alone, and those in conjunction with encroaching electronic and telecommunications industries.

Previously, it was argued that the forms of interfirm linkages are determined by the accretion of relevant skills, subject to the focal firm's ability to reap monopoly rents from the innovation's expected benefit as well as the innovation's saliency from the strategic standpoint of the firm. Little was said about the expected benefit itself, which appears crucial in the case of videotex.

Of course, we have seen many instances of innovations with a great deal of potential (recent examples include cochlear implants, teleconferencing and windmill energy) that have failed to find commercial acceptance. Will videotex join that class of innovations? Despite the rosy picture about the future of the videotex services in the early 1980s, its appears unable to expand; rather it encounters relatively cold acceptance by consumers (see Aumente [1987] for an appraisal). In trying to emulate the success of the French Minitel, where some six million outlets are connected with tens of thousands of information sources through a single gateway, a Federal Judge in Washington, D.C. in July 1987 made a ruling that assigns the Regional Bell Operating Companies the role of gateway, but prohibits them from diversifying into the content of such gateways. For example, to preempt a surge in their market power, they are prevented from providing electronic directory assistance. The idea is to promote standardization leading to growth in demand for services. Another possibility is to transform videotex services into simpler forms, such as data retrieval services which are currently blossoming. We believe that when the survival of the new services are perceived to be questionable, participating firms will change their original strategic priorities. Rather than monopolizing the expected benefit of the innovation any longer, they may seek to promote and enhance the market first. It is this uncertainty and common fate that results in the multiple linkages cooperation among rivals as well with firms from other industries. New research might shed light on such conjectures.

This chapter has adopted the strategy of examining a single innovation to understand how a complex set of factors at multiple levels of analysis can account for the adoption and diffusion of innovation. Such studies should not only clarify technological evolutions or innovation adoption decisions, but also enhance our theoretical understanding of an evasive and elusive phenomenon in organization theory and strategic management.

ACKNOWLEDGMENT

We gratefully acknowledge the support from the National Science Foundation under the grant number SES-8709674. We thank Leng Kean Meng for his research assistance.

NOTES

1. The much quoted works in this area are the studies by Gilfillan (1935) and Hunter (1949) on the history of ship technology.

2. Pavitt (1987), in his review on Tushman and Anderson's (1986) paper, provides an elaboration of the difficulty in distinguishing the two types of innovations.

3. This definition is adapted from von Hippel's definition of know-how (1988, p. 76).

4. While Nelson and Winter (1982) are relatively silent about the origin of a technological regime, we assume that a new regime can simply emerge as a result of a synthesis of various developments (including those in other regimes) that have taken place.

5. Indeed there are other instances where firms are involved in a joint venture not for sharing their technologies, but for some other reason, such as exploiting economies of scale (e.g., when several firms in the same industry, or in the same stage of a value-added chain, join together to venture into another stage of the value-added chain).

6. We found the *Predicast Index* to be biased toward big firms. The correlation between company size (asset log adjusted) and the number of news entries reported in the index is 0.74. See Hladik (1985) for a review on the benefits and disadvantages of using the *Predicast Index*.

7. Our survey results covering about 30 bank executives responsible for bank automation confirm this assessment.

REFERENCES

Astley, G.W. (1985). The two ecologies: Population and community perspectives on organizational evolution. *Administrative Science Quarterly, 30*, 224-241.

Astley, G.W., & Fombrun, C.J. (1983). Technological innovation and industrial structure: The case of telecommunications. In R. Lamb (Ed.), *Advances in strategic management* (Vol. 1 pp. 205-229). Greenwich, CT: JAI Press.

Aumente, J. (1987). *New electronic pathways*. Beverly Hills, CA: Sage.

Compaine, B.M. (1984). *Understanding new media*. Cambridge, MA: Ballinger.

Computer World [Special edition on the Premier 100]. (1988, September 21).

Cyert, R.M., & March, J.G. (1963). *A behavioral theory of the firm*. Englewood Cliffs, NJ: Prentice-Hall.

Directory of Electronic Fund Transfers (1985/1986). *Directory*. Washington, DC: DEFT.

Gilfillan, S. (1935). *Inventing the ship*. Chicago, IL: Follett.

Hamberg, D. (1967). Size of enterprise and technical change. *Antitrust Law and Economics Review, 1*, pp. 43-51.

von Hippel, E. 1976. The dominant role of users in the scientific instrument innovation process. *Research Policy, 5*, 212-239.

_____ (1988). *The sources of innovation*. New York: Oxford University Press.

Hladik, K.J. (1985). *International joint venture: An economic analysis of U.S.-foreign business partnerships*. Lexington, MA: Lexington Books.

Hunter, L. (1949). *Steamboats on the western river*. Cambridge, MA: Harvard University Press

Kimberly, J.R. (1986). The organizational context of technological innovation. In D.D. Davis (Ed.), *Managing technological innovation* (pp. 23-43). San Francisco, CA: Jossey Bass.

Mansfield, E. (1968). *Economics of technological change*. New York: W.W. Norton.

March, J.G., & Simon, H.A. (1958). Organizations. New York: Wiley.

Mensch, G. (1979). *Stalemate in technology*. Cambridge, MA: Ballinger.

Mohr, L.B. (1982). *Explaining organizational behavior*. San Francisco, CA: Jossey-Bass.

Nelson, R.R., & Winter, S.G. (1982). *An evolutionary theory of economic change*. Cambridge, MA: Belknap Press.

Normann, R. (1971). Organizational innovativeness: Product variation and reorientation. *Administrative Science Quarterly, 16*, 203-215.

Office of Technology Assessment, Congress of the United States. (1984). *Effects of information technology on financial service systems*. Washington, DC: U.S. Government Printing Office.

Pavitt, K. (1984). Sectoral patterns of technical change: Toward a taxonomy and a theory. *Research Policy, 13*, 343-373.

_____ (1987). Commentary on technological discontinuities and organization environments. In A.M. Pettigrew (Ed.), *The management of strategic change* (pp. 123-127) Oxford: Basil Blackwell.

Pennings, J.M. (1981). Strategically interdependent organizations. In P.C. Nystrom & W.H. Starbuck (Eds.), *Handbook of organization design* (pp. 433-455). New York: Oxford University Press.

_____ (1987). Technological innovation in manufacturing. In J.M. Pennings & A. Buitendam (Eds.), *New technology as organizational innovation* (pp. 197-216). Cambridge, MA: Ballinger.

Pettigrew, A. (1974). *The politics of organizational decision making*. London: Tavistock.

Porter, M.E. (1980). *Competitive strategy: Techniques for analyzing industries and competitors*. New York: Free Press.

Revell, J.R.S. (1983). *Banking and electronic fund transfers*. Paris: Organization for Economic Cooperation and Development.

Rogers, E.M. (1983). *Diffusion of innovations* (3rd ed.). New York: Free Press.

Rosenberg, N. (1979). The direction of technological change: Inducing mechanisms and focusing devices. *Economic Development and Cultural Change, 18*, 1-24.

_____ (1982). *Inside the black box: Technology and economics*. Cambridge: Cambridge University Press.

Rutan, V. (1959). Usher and Schumpeter on invention, innovation, and technological change. *Quarterly Journal of Economics, 73*, pp. 596-606.

Sahal, D. (1981). *Patterns of technological innovation*. Reading, MA: Addison-Wesley.

Scherer, F.M. (1970). *Industrial market structure and economic performance*. Chicago, IL: Rand McNally.

_____ (1982). Inter-industry technology flows in the United States. *Research Policy, 11*, 227-245.

Simon, H.A. (1947). *Administrative behavior*. New York: Macmillan.

Teece, D. (1986). Profiting from technological innovation: Implications for integration, collaboration, licensing and public policy. *Research Policy, 15*, 285-305.

Tushman, M.L., & Anderson, P. (1986). Technological discontinuities and organization environments. *Administrative Science Quarterly, 31*, 439-465.

Usher, A. (1954). *A history of mechanical inventions* (2nd ed). Cambridge, MA: Harvard University Press.

BURNOUT OR FADEOUT:

THE RISKS OF EARLY ENTRY INTO HIGH TECHNOLOGY MARKETS

George S. Day and Jonathan S. Freeman

Pioneers that survive often outperform later entrants. One study of a broad cross section of mature industrial businesses found that the average market share at maturity for pioneers was 30 percent, for followers 21 percent and for late entrants market shares were 15 percent (Robinson, 1988). The pioneers in the fluorescent lamp and plain paper copier markets have been leaders for years. This finding is comforting for managers of pioneering firms that have survived, for it confirms the wisdom of their strategy. It also accounts for some of the allure of new markets to those preparing to take the plunge.

The pursuit of these prospective rewards exposes aspiring pioneers to formidable and sometimes fatal risks. One class of fatalities is afflicted with the "winners' curse." These firms act on overly optimistic estimates of market acceptance and their technical prowess to prematurely enter embryonic markets. Meanwhile, more conservative aspirants take a pessimistic posture and defer entering until the market is viable. By this time the pioneer that moved too soon has exhausted both credibility and resources and vanished from the scene.

The second class of fatalities manages to avoid premature entry, hits the profit-making window (see Figure 1) and establishes a leadership position as the market begins to take off. Yet they are soon overtaken because they fail to adapt to changing requirements for success. This was the plight of

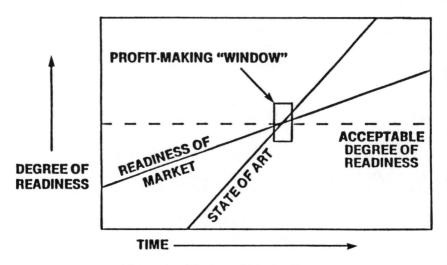

Figure 1. Timing of Market Entry

Bowmar Instruments (hand-held electronic calculators) and Osborne (portable computers) (Hartley, 1986).

To manage these risks, an aspiring entrant must first assess the prospective gains from early entry. The key question is whether these benefits are likely to be lost either by premature entry or later inability to maintain a lead. This paper offers a framework for understanding these risks and provides some general propositions on appropriate strategies for surviving a shakeout.

THE BENEFITS OF PIONEERING

Most of the benefits of early entry come from the opportunity a pioneer has to define the rules of competition to their advantage (Day, 1986).

Preemption of Competition

A pioneer can develop and position products for the largest and most lucrative market segments, while leaving less desirable segments to later entrants. The capacity needed to serve the most attractive segments signals a commitment to maintaining output, with the implied threat of price cuts to make later entrants unprofitable.

Early entrants with a viable product usually have the pick of the best brokers, distributors and retailers. The followers have the thankless task of persuading the pioneer's distributors to shift and divide their commitment. Failing this the followers have to find a new channel or settle for less desirable channel members. This creates acute problems for followers in the personal computer market where the scarcest resource is the shelf space controlled by the large chains of computer retailers such as Computerland.

Leadership Reputation

The first company in a market naturally has a unique position, which also confers a potential leadership image that is not available to followers. Whether this advantageous reputation has more than temporary value depends on the credibility of the firm, its capacity to invest in marketing and whether a firm with a strong reputation in an adjacent category follows the pioneer into the new market (e.g., IBM's credibility in the mainframe market secured its position even though it was a follower in the PC market, as customers were sure that it would be in business in the long term. IBM's PC thus instantly achieved a degree of acceptance that had been vainly sought by earlier, smaller firms). Small firms have often introduced innovations to the industrial battery market, but have not been able to capitalize on them. For instance, their failure to develop an extensive distribution system denied them credibility as suppliers of batteries for consumer goods (Wilson & Atkin, 1976).

Customer Loyalty

A customer may be forced to be loyal to the first supplier in the market because switching costs are high. These are one-time costs the buyer absorbs when switching suppliers, associated with employee training, new ancillary equipment, the need for technical assistance and product redesign and the time required to test and qualify a new source. For example, hospital management contracts are costly to change, because of the disruption caused by a new administrator, a new computer system and budgeting and operating procedures.

Loyalty may also occur as a natural result of satisfactory performance of the pioneer. When consumers consider a pioneer their reference points are those existing products that presently satisfy their requirements. However the follower will be compared to both the old alternatives, and the new product offered by the pioneer that has proven its value as a substitute. The follower, however, is an unproven entity. Unless the follower is able to provide significant additional benefits over and above what the pioneer can offer, inducing trial will be more difficult for the follower than the pioneer (Schmalensee, 1982). This advantage is likely to be more significant for pioneers whose initial offering is based on a technological development that is followed by incremental rather than radical improvements. In either case, however, it is likely to depend on the pioneer's ability to be able to overcome the initial unreliability of new products and achieve satisfactory performance.

Proprietary Experience Effects

A pioneer gains an initial cost advantage when learning gained through cumulative experience becomes an important contributor to cost reductions. Such experience effects are more likely to be significant in markets that are large (Teece, 1988), as they often result from sizeable levels of cumulative production. Whether a cost advantage is sustainable depends on how difficult the learning is to imitate, and whether it will be nullified by a competing technology. Protection against imitation can sometimes be afforded by a strong patent position, but even this advantage must be vigorously policed and can often be "invented around." Firms utilizing new process technologies can often obtain better protection simply through trade secrets, in which case the availability of the product often does not afford an opportunity for competitors to determine the new process (Teece, 1988). For instance, in the chemicals industry the availability to competitors of a new product created by a new process technology is often of little help to them in understanding the process by which the product is created.

Sustainable Lead on Technology

Such a lead will result if competitors are unable to duplicate the technology, or the firm innovates at a faster rate than the competition so followers are never able to catch up. For example the first firms to introduce the dominant designs in ten international semiconductor markets tended to have an advantage in improving the design throughout the product lifecycle (Flaherty, 1983).

In summary, specific advantages can accrue to the pioneering firm. However, none is inevitable. In the main the accrual of these advantages depends on four basic factors:

1. In order to preempt competitors the pioneer must have *significant resources* at its disposal if it is to serve large segments with significant marketing support. In addition, it must often also have significant resources to invest in marketing to establish a leadership reputation and to invest in R&D to maintain a technological lead.
2. Cost advantages may only be available to pioneers able to rapidly exploit large markets.

3. Competitors, especially large established competitors in associated industries or markets, can often determine the ability of a pioneer to retain its advantages.
4. A technological advantage is generally maintainable only if the technology cannot be imitated or superseded.

DEGREES OF PIONEERING

Abell (1980) devised a multidimensional business definition which has been adapted to the definition of product-markets (Day, 1984). The four dimensions in this definition are technology, customer function, stage of value-added and customer segments. Thus a product-market can be regarded as the use of a certain technology at one or more stages of the value added chain to provide specific functions to identifiable customer groups. A firm may pioneer on any one of these dimensions alone or in combination. Although in this chapter we are taking the use of a new technology as a given, it is important to recognize that a pioneer has further choices to make on the other dimensions. The degree to which each of these is also radically new will increase the amount of uncertainty facing the firm, and, potentially, will affect its likelihood of success. Furthermore, the pioneer also has a choice about the speed (or aggressiveness) with which it will carry out its strategy.

Technology

Olleros (1986, p. 5) suggests that there are two types of technological change: incremental and radical. The former "tends to refine and extend the established technologies, thereby favouring the incumbent firms and reinforcing the status quo." The latter "tends to undermine and displace the established set of competences, whether in R&D, production, or marketing."

Function

New technologies need not necessarily imply the provision of new functions for customers. A pioneer may develop and market a new product that provides the same functions for customers as existing products but do so more reliably, or at lower cost. On the other hand a firm can also be a pioneer in providing a product with a new function and this may or may not use a new technology. However, the provision of new functions not derived from new technologies is likely to be associated with product line extensions in existing markets than with the pioneering of new markets;

the payback required for new technologies is likely to be significant and new markets are likely to offer the greatest potential rewards.

Customer Group

Firms can be pioneers in recognizing new markets, or segments in existing markets, and these can often be linked to the functions existing products provide. Thus the pioneers of diet soft drinks recognized a significant segment when they realized that their product, a low calorie soft drink targeted to diabetics, was being bought by nondiabetics concerned about their weight.

Stage in the Value-added Process

Pioneering firms can enter the value-added process at any stage from supplier to retailer. While we are concentrating here on pioneering manufacturers it is important to recognize that innovation in one stage of the system often implies innovation in others. This point is made forcefully by Sahlman and Stevenson (1985, p. 24) in describing the development of the Winchester disk drive industry. The new drive manufacturers were uncertain both about the development of other systems components that their customers (computer manufacturers) required in order to be able to make use of the Winchester drives, and about the development of their own suppliers' products (e.g. heads, platters, motors and controls), many of which "were also new and untested and their specifications were elements of their own ambitious business plans." Thus the uncertainties and risks expounded in this chapter are magnified when a pioneer enters the value-added system at a point at which both up and down stream industries are also populated by pioneers.

Overall, the availability of a new technology need not prescribe a pioneer's choices on the other three dimensions. However, uncertainties are compounded when a technological pioneer is also a pioneer in all four dimensions, and even more so when the pioneering firm is new.

THE RISKS OF EARLY ENTRY

Failures of pioneers stem from either premature entry that results in "burnout" in the face of the struggle to overcome market resistance or an inability to hold a lead once the market is established. The likelihood of "burnout" is greater than "fadeout" if the technological innovation is radical rather than incremental.

Premature Entry and "Burnout"

The early history of most major technologies (typewriters, televisions, semi-conductors and genetic engineering, to name a few) reveals major industries emerging "over the dead bodies" of the pioneers (Olleros, 1986). The true pioneer, opening an uncharted territory, must incur many costs and absorb considerable market and technological uncertainty before revenue starts to flow. The lengthy payback often exhausts the meager resources, leaving the pioneer no choice but to be absorbed by bigger later entrants or go out of business.

Sahlman and Stevenson (1985, p. 23) describe the problem facing pioneers as "the classic growth industry dilemma":

> If they did not staff, build and finance for growth, they could never achieve it. If they prepared for growth and it did not arrive on schedule they were faced with the painful and often permanently damaging need to scale back people and plant and give great disappointment to the financial backers.

This in essence is the basic "burnout" problem facing pioneers.

Technological uncertainty.

Here some of the key questions are:

1. Will the technology function as expected when placed into volume production? For example, Thomson-CSF in France has been pursuing low-cost flat screen displays as an alternative to the usual cathode ray tube for low-cost data processing terminals. There are growing doubts that acceptable cost levels can be achieved.

2. Which technology will be dominant? This is a particular problem with radical technological changes, such as local area networks. These are data communication networks that enable word processing, data processing, and communications equipment to interact, or "talk to," each other in a limited physical environment such as an office building. This would be a major step forward in achieving office automation. Unfortunately, major differences exist among vendors as to whether the best technology has a digital, single-channel, or analog, multichannel capability. Each has performance advantages, so it is highly uncertain which technology will eventually prevail.

Radically new technologies need the support of a sizable, high-performance oriented specialty market segment that is willing to nurse the pioneering firm through the teething period (Erikson & Maitland, 1982; Romanelli, 1987). They are willing to pay price premiums to gain the performance advantages and be able to accommodate the early deficiencies in reliability and service.

Uncertain Costs

Despite the beneficial effects of experience on costs, doubts are always present as to whether high initial costs can be offset by sharp drops in the costs of critical components. Without these cost declines, the relative attractiveness of the new product will be seriously diminished. However, strong demand may create its own problems if shortages of essential components such as microprocessors result in high prices.

Competitive Uncertainty

During the introductory stage, the structure of competition is in flux. Both present and prospective entrants face major questions:

- What protective actions will be taken by the producers of products that are being supplanted?
- What are the commitment and resources of other entrants?
- Who are the potential direct competitors, and what entry strategies might they employ?
- What about other emerging technologies that can provide similar functions? Both pay TV and video tape recorders have had a big impact on the acceptance of videodiscs in major applications.

Uncertain Customer Acceptance

The rate of customer acceptance will be slowed by lack of product standardization, perceived likelihood of technological obsolescence and the unpredictable quality of the products first into the market. If these problems are significant, most prospective buyers are likely to adopt a "wait and see" attitude. This tendency in turn reinforces the inertia that comes from satisfaction with existing alternatives and reluctance to change established behavior patterns. These problems have created a significant barrier to the large-scale acceptance of assembly line robots, which often require a complete redesign of manufacturing processes before they can be effectively utilized.

Indeed, the robotics industry is an excellent example of an industry for which, after almost thirty years, the light is still at the end of the tunnel. In 1960, General Electric was believed to have concluded that though the market potential of industrial robots was "adequate" it would not be profitable because of marketing costs. At that time there were only a few manufacturers in the United States (Buzzell, Cox, & Brown, 1969). In the mid 1970s it was predicted that the robotics market would reach $1 billion by 1983. It actually reached $169 million ("shakeout," 1984). In 1984, the prediction was that the $1 billion mark "will be delayed at least until 1989," but that in the meantime "sales will turn soft for the next year or two," and that the market is "heading for a shakeout" ("GM throws a wrench," 1986, p. 36).

Financial Uncertainty

Burnout is often precipitated by the failure of firms to obtain sufficient resources to carry them through the unprofitable early stages of development of a market. In some cases these resources may involve skills or knowledge but quite often they are financial. Problems can stem both from exceedingly liberal initial funding for an industry with glowing prospects, and from the withdrawal of those funds at a critical time.

Sahlman and Stevenson (1985) studied the role of venture capital markets in financing the explosion in the numbers of firms in the Winchester hard drive industry. The predicted success of most firms was contingent on the joint occurrence of many factors, the likelihood of each of which was fairly low. Though in an excellent position to anticipate the problems the industry was likely to face, these investors failed to do so and most companies were grossly overvalued as a result. For example, many of the investors who specialized in the industry supplied capital to more than one firm and therefore were provided with a number of detailed business plans. In addition, industry experts repeatedly revised their forecasts upwards encouraging further new entrants. However, after the risks began to materialize, there was a commensurate withdrawal of financial support, which further fueled the demise of many firms that required funds to remain competitive.

Financial difficulties of this type are influenced by expectations of both incumbents, entrants and investors, yet their ability to make such forecasts is often limited. For instance, experts in the computer industry have often been quite inaccurate in their forecasts, which has been attributed to inadequate market research ("It's getting harder," 1985).

Inability to Maintain a Lead and "Fadeout"

There are some benefits to being a later entrant that may reduce or negate the advantages of the pioneer. If the pioneer can't adapt to the changes in circumstances that encourage the later entrant, the price may be failure through "fadeout." These exits due to an inability to adapt are anticipated to occur after the emergence of a dominant design in the industry, as it is after this point that customer uncertainty is reduced and strong market growth often occurs. Tushman and Romanelli (1985) indicate that the emergence of a dominant design delineates a switch in technological development from major product changes to process changes. This switch results in the declining costs and greater standardization that a dominant design enables, as well as improved quality. These in turn open up new markets.

Competitor copying or leap-frogging

There are a number of ways a competitor can "free ride" on the pioneer's investments in R&D, buyer education, gaining regulatory approvals, developing an infrastructure and encouraging ancillary or complementary products such as software.

1.   The follower can learn from the pioneer's mistakes by hiring key personnel, by teardown analysis of the competitor's product and by conducting marketing research to learn the problems and unfulfilled expectation of customers and distributors.

2.   A later entrant may "leap-frog" the pioneer by using the latest technology or building a plant with a larger current scale of operations (Yip, 1982). Thus, Caterpillar became a major factor in the diesel engine market with a new production facility using high-technology machining systems and automatic transfer lines to reduce unit costs and guarantee better quality.

3.   All competitors should benefit from cost reductions achieved by outside suppliers of components or production equipment. In the spinning and weaving industry most of the advances in technology come from textile machinery manufacturers who share these improvements with all their customers.

4.   A follower may have cost advantages for reasons independent of experience, such as facility location, government subsidy or different cost structures.

Technological obsolescence

The pioneer is usually better protected if the first generation technology is followed by a series of incremental improvements. Sometimes, if the following generations of technology are significant departures that offer superior performance and are also incompatible with the first generation, an early commitment to a technology may later turn out to be a disadvantage. Once a commitment is made to one technology it is frequently difficult to assess and adapt to a new technology. Managers are naturally reluctant to withdraw too quickly from mature technologies that are highly profitable (Yip, 1982). Thus Metronic's leadership position in the cardiac pacemaker market was eroded when it waited too long to switch to a new lithium-based technology. An outside firm, without the constraint of the established technology, was able to exploit this delay and successfully enter the market.

Changes in Customer Requirements

These present significant opportunities to followers. Until recently, Japanese manufacturers of chip-making machinery could not keep up with the rate of technology change in the successive generations of aligners, etchers and other processing gear. This confined them to their home market, where they served captive customers with superior reliability and short setup times. Trends underlying the evolution of products in this market are now working in their favor. Advances in wafer processing technology seem nearing the point of diminishing returns. Instead, chip makers are emphasizing automation to improve yields. While U.S. suppliers excel in the software needed to link processing machinery into an automated system, the Japanese have an edge in electromechanical technology for precision handling of chips at high speed.

Inability to Adapt

As markets evolve the key success factors are likely to change. If the pioneer is unable to gain access to the new skills and resources, or can't adapt to the new reality, the game is likely to be lost.

The demise of the three pioneers in the Personal Computer industry (see Table 1) has been attributed to an inability to adapt to the shift in demand from the original specialty markets of computer buffs to the less sophisticated mass end-user markets that were hard to reach and very price sensitive (Olleros, 1986). These pioneers were engineer-run, technology driven, with few of the skills needed to analyze and reach fast-changing markets.

As a market grows the key success factors may change. For example, during the early growth stage of the CT scanner market the key success factor was technology, and the industry could support many firms. As this market matured a service capability became necessary that was difficult for some smaller firms to obtain. As the medical imaging industry matures, a further key success factor will be to have synergies with components, computer technologies, software technologies and instrumentation. The firms that ultimately survive will likely be the large diversified electronics firms like GE, Hitachi, Phillips and Siemens.

Sometimes late movers are in the best position to compete when a new set of key success factors emerges. Thus, IBM in personal computers and Matsushita in VCRs (Schnaars, 1986), were able to exploit existing capabilities in marketing, distribution and customer reputation.

Table 1.   Pioneers and Poachers in
The U.S. Personal Computer Market
(in percent)

	1976	1978	1980	1982	1984	1986
MITS	25	—	—	—	—	—
IMSAI	17	—	—	—	—	—
Processor Technology	8	—	—	—	—	—
Commodore	—	12	20	12	6	3
Radio Shack	—	50	21	10	7	6
Apple	—	10	27	26	16	9
IBM	—	—	—	17	31	26
H-P	—	—	9	7	4	4
Others	50	28	23	28	36	52
Total	100	100	100	100	100	100

Overcrowding and Shakeout[1]

Even if pioneers overcome the perils of burnout and avoid a fadeout they may still be fatally wounded if there is a competitive shakeout triggered by overcrowding.

- In 1982 the $200 million facsimile transmission market in Japan had 13 competitors, attracted by a 35 percent annual growth rate. It was unlikely anyone had sufficient earnings to support investments in new digital technologies and extensive sales and service networks.
- By 1987 there were 12 companies scrambling for a piece of the $300 million transdermal drug release market. The technology used skin patches to slowly release drugs into the bloodstream through the skin. As the market is unlikely to top $1.5 billion there are certain to be a number of fatalities.
- At the end of 1982 there were more than 150 manufacturers of microcomputers, plus another 300 or so firms dealing with add-on products, software, service, sales and support. Most did not survive as independents.

This pattern of overcrowding of competitors beyond the foreseeable capacity of an emerging market sets the stage for a wrenching adjustment, and realignment, triggered by a slow-down in market growth below expectation, or aggressive share-building moves by attackers or defenders. However, it is not always easy to foresee the timing of a shakeout nor does it happen in all industries. An examination of the data provided by Knight,

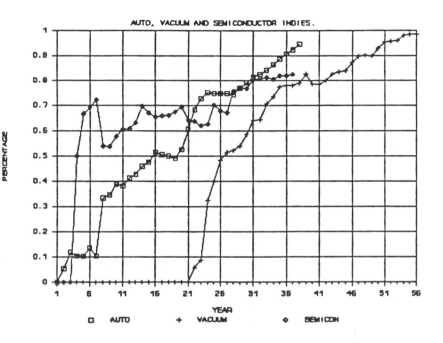

Figure 2. Percentage CUM Entrants To Have Exited

Dowling, and Brown (1988) in this volume sheds some light on this question.[2]

Identifying Shakeouts

Conventional wisdom would suggest that essentially one major shakeout occurs during the life of an industry. However, our analysis of data gathered by Knight, Dowling and Brown (1988) suggests that this need not be the case, and therefore, knowing when one is in or has been through a shakeout may not be easy. We have summarized the number of entrances and exits in three industries in one diagram. Figure 2 shows the cumulative percentage of firms to have left the U.S. automobile,[3] vacuum tube[4] and semiconductor[5] industries each year. For example, 70% of all firms that had entered the semiconductor industry by year six had also exited by that point.

The number of firms involved and the pattern of exits and entrances differed considerably among the three industries. Note that the vacuum tube industry, unlike the others, appears to have had a long lead-in period of growth with no exits[6] and that the degree of variation in annual exits differed considerably between the three. Note also that for the auto and vacuum tube industries almost every firm which had entered the industry had exited by the end of the period examined.

The steep rises in the curves at certain points indicate periods when disproportionately large numbers of firms left the industry. Interestingly, in all three industries, once exits began, there was a sharp rise in the early years, and it is tempting to speculate that these might have been early firms "burning-out." However, without further data about the circumstances of these firms one should be cautious in classifying them as such. Note also the declines in the curves, particularly for the semiconductor industry, which indicate exceptional rises in the relative number of entrants to exits.

The question then arises whether these data support the generally accepted view that shakeouts account for the departure of a large proportion of incumbents. The central part of the curve for the auto industry displays a classic shakeout pattern. Between years 19 and 24, 25% of cumulative entrants left the industry. However, such a pattern is not obvious for the other two industries. Based on the number of actual exits, one might argue that the shakeout period for the vacuum tube industry occurred between years 31 and 40, and that for the semiconductor industry it occurred between years 26 and 32. However Figure 2 shows that for these two industries such events accounted for the departure of only about 18% and 12% of cumulative entrants respectively.[7] Though not insignificant, these numbers suggest that the impact of shakeouts varies among industries. Note also that for two of the three industries, the industry remained attractive for many firms despite the occurrence of a shakeout.

It would be interesting to know which firms were "shaken out," whether it was recent entrants attracted by factors in the industry but unable to develop a sufficiently strong position within it, or whether it was the long standing firms unable to adapt to a changing environment that the newer entrants were better able to exploit. Unfortunately the industry level data displayed here does not enable us to answer such questions. However, risks that firms face at this stage in the development of an industry have been specified.

The Risks of a Shakeout

The risk of a significant shakeout depends on the following factors (Aaker & Day, 1986):

1. *The industry and its growth rate have high visibility*—as a result, strategists in related firms are encouraged to seriously consider the industry and, in fact, may fear the consequences of turning their backs upon an obvious growth direction.

2. *Very high forecast and actual growth in the early stages*—this is pointed to as evidence confirming high industry growth as a proven phenomenon.
3. *Threats to the growth rate are not considered or are discounted*—little exists to dampen the enthusiasm surrounding the industry. In fact the enthusiasm may be contagious when venture capitalists and stock analysts become advocates, (Sahlman and Stevenson, 1985).
4. *Few initial barriers to entry exist* to prevent firms from entering the market.
5. *Products employ an existing technology rather than a risky or protected technology.* Technology sometimes provides a more obvious and formidable barrier than for example, a finance or marketing barrier. The true significance of a marketing barrier to entry, such as limited retail space, may only be evident after the market is overcrowded.
6. *Some potential entrants have low visibility* and their intentions are unknown or uncertain—thus the quantity and commitment of competitors is very likely to be underestimated.

Beyond the Shakeout—The Appropriability of Profits

Survival, of course, is a minimal requirement for most firms. What is desired is survival and significant levels of performance. However, Teece (1988) suggests that though pioneers may survive, the degree of their success can be adversely affected by their need for specialized (e.g., shelf-space for PCs) or cospecialized (e.g., video programs for VCRs) assets if their barriers to imitation do not afford them a lengthy lead time. Thus a survivor's potential profits may be eroded by the powerful position of another firm in the value-added system. For instance, the example of the surviving firms in the PC market finding it increasingly difficult to obtain distributors' shelf space would suggest that such distributors may be able to appropriate a large proportion of the profitability of innovation.

STRATEGIES FOR SURVIVING

What do we know about the strategies and capabilities of pioneers that have weathered the early storms in a fast-growing high technology market, to prosper in the later stages of the life cycle? The short answer is not much; little or no empirical work properly addresses the question because it is so difficult to compare the actions of survivors versus failures when the failures drop out of sight so quickly. An exception is a study conducted by Willard and Cooper (1985) into the U.S. color television manufacturing industry that was based on retrospective reports of industry members of both successful and unsuccessful companies and experts. This study found that surviving firms provided high quality products at average prices, thus yielding consumers high value. Consumers in turn apparently recognized and rewarded this by providing those firms with their support. Yet Willard and Cooper state that there was no unique strategy common to all survivors and different from those who did not survive.

However, the foregoing suggests that sustaining a lead in technology is critically important. Understanding the factors affecting such sustainability is thus essential to developing strategies to maintain a lead. In the following we consider that and other ideas that flow from our examination of the risks facing pioneers.

Retaining a Technological Lead

A technological lead is likely to be sustainable under the following conditions (Porter, 1985):

1. The technology has been developed largely within the industry. If the source of technology is external, such as suppliers of machinery or components, or construction engineering firms that design production processes, the latest advances will be available to all present or potential competitors. Indeed the last entrant will be the greatest beneficiary by having access to the latest technology.
2. The rate of diffusion of the technology is slow, because the advances are difficult to copy. But when design improvements can be readily revealed by reverse engineering, the advances are communicated in scientific proceedings, or are carried outside by mobile personnel, then the cost or differentiation advantages will be transitory.
3. The firm has a relative cost advantage or greater effectiveness in continuous technology development. Two factors contribute to this area of advantage. One is economies of scale in R&D. The largest firm can have the largest budget, but still not incur a cost penalty because their R&D spending as a percent of sales will be lower than their direct competitors. Second, distinct learning effects have been observed in the development and launching of new products. Each new feature and improvement costs less than prior changes because of the accumulated stock of skills and experience. Of course, if there is a major shift in technology then this hard-earned base of knowledge may be more of an impediment than an advantage, especially if the personnel are strongly committed to the old technology.

Perhaps surprisingly, patents appear to give only minimal protection against imitation. In examining the question of retaining proprietary technological knowledge Von Hippel (1988) examined the effectiveness of both patents and trade secrets. Studies spanning thirty years all concluded that patents are not useful for either excluding imitators or capturing royalty income. However, Von Hippel shows that this varies by industry, for example, patents were ineffective in the semiconductor industry but effective in pharmaceuticals. One reason for this is that patents often provide competitors with information that enables them to invent a way around the restriction. In the case of pharmaceutical products however, the mechanisms by which the products achieve their effects are not well understood and examining a competitor's product does not give a potential imitator much useful insight. This also helps explain why trade secrets can sometimes be more effective than patents. Von Hippel found that trade secrets are effective in the case both of products which incorporate technological barriers to analysis (e.g., in the case of electronic products, "potting": encasing the innovation in a medium which destroys it if tampered with) or process innovations that can be hidden from public view.

Timing the Entry

Bennett and Cooper (1984) argue that the question of timing of entry is not simply answered by jumping in at the earliest opportunity. Instead, they look for clues in the adoption process of new technologies. Since new products, when first introduced, are often of inferior quality, the key is to find specific applications in niches where the new technology is highly valued despite its shortcomings. This requires careful monitoring of these limited niches, combined with forecasts of the development of the new technology. Careful attention to the needs of lead users is also important at this stage. These are users that face needs that will eventually be general in the market place (but face them months or years before the bulk of the market) and stand to benefit handsomely from any solution to these needs (Von Hippel, 1988).

Influencing the Dominant Design

When there are radical differences between competing technologies, the point at which one design becomes accepted as the industry standard can have a major impact on the industry's growth rate. Olleros (1986) argues that firms that share the same technology should be more concerned with intratechnological rivalry than intertechnological rivalry. In such a situation he recommends that a pioneer should encourage the spread of its technology and should welcome the entry of other firms using it in so far as the different technologies are perceived by consumers to provide distinctly different benefits or levels of benefits. Increasing the number of suppliers of products based on a specific technology may help establish its dominance as the increased number of firms sharing the same technology increases the overall resources that can be put towards overcoming the obstacle preventing dominance.

Reducing Financial Uncertainty

In order to avoid burnout, or create weaknesses that will lead to eventual fadeout, Olleros (1986) suggests several strategies for reducing the payback period and minimizing the investment base by (1) subcontracting manufacturing activities, subject to retaining control over proprietary aspects of technology; (2) undertaking joint ventures or marketing agreements with established companies having access to the target market; or (3) undertaking a widespread program of licensing of the technology that will encourage others to share the costs of developing the market. These moves will help maintain financial viability to ensure the firm can continue to invest in each generation of technology as they unfold.

The strategy followed by a food products company is illuminating here. This firm, set up by ex-employees of a large company in the same field, developed a technology enabling consumers to cook a well-established food more conveniently. Their strategy is to license this technology to a large company that would use extensive advertising in launching its brand and therefore the category. The original company also intends to launch its own brand, which is expected to hold the second position in market share. The licensed brand will have a larger market share because of the considerable advertising that will support it, but those resources will also have expanded the category to a size considerably in excess of what the original company could have achieved on its own. In addition, the original company will get a royalty income from sales of the licensed brand.

Adapting to Change

Specialization, by targeting a high-performance oriented specialty market segment willing to nurse the pioneer through the earliest periods of the industry, was advocated to avoid the burnout of firms introducing radically new technologies. Recent research sheds some light on and extends this advice.

Romanelli (1987) examines the question of how the early strategies of firms influence both early survival and later capacities for change. She develops a typology of organizational strategies based on the two dimensions of Market Penetration (Conservative versus Aggressive) and Market Breadth

(Generalist versus Specialist). The first, Market Penetration, is related to being able to rapidly and extensively exploit the opportunities presented by a sufficiently large market before others enter. Firms can also make strategic decisions on the second dimension, whether to concentrate on a narrow or broad range of the market. Often these choices are constrained by the level of managerial expertise and other available resources.

Early decisions on these two dimensions will shape the firm's future opportunities because they necessitate "investments in personnel, technology, reputation, distribution and so on that are not easily shed as conditions of environments change" (Romanelli, 1987, p. 163).

In other words, firms suffer from "structural inertia" (Hannan & Freeman, 1984) due to an investment in specialized assets that can make later adaptation difficult. Structural inertia refers to the speed of adaptation of an organization to changes in its environment. It is thus relative. A small firm may be able to adapt quickly but not as quickly as its environment is changing. Conversely, a large firm may only be able to adapt slowly but its environment may be changing even more slowly. Hannan and Freeman propose that the frequency of required change is often size dependent, with smaller firms facing more frequent critical changes than larger firms. For example, short-term variations in the availability of credit may be critical for the survival of small firms while only a minor nuisance for large ones.

As we have seen, many of the difficulties pioneers face can be traced to the degree of uncertainty about how the market will develop. By being conservative, a firm may be able to retain the resources and thus the flexibility necessary to adjust to rapid changes (e.g. of technology or market), thus avoiding fadeout. If such changes cannot be anticipated uncertainty is high and the conservative approach may be preferable.

However, this is counterbalanced by the possibility that the firm that adopts an aggressive strategy can, in doing so, influence the way the market develops. Thus those factors that may be uncontrolled environmental factors for a conservative firm may become controllable, (or at least influenceable) factors and therefore less uncertain, for an aggressive firm.

Many of the factors discussed in this chapter are illustrated in Romanelli's (1987) description and assessment of the strategies of three successful firms in the minicomputer industry, Digital Equipment Corporation, (DEC), Data General and Tandem, each of which entered the industry at different stages of its evolution. Of the three, DEC was the pioneer that opened up the industry and demonstrated the existence of a sizeable demand for mid-sized computers that combined on-site availability and the flexibility to carry out multiple functions. However, faced with great uncertainty at first about the market potential of such machines DEC targeted a specialized segment, scientists and engineers.

Though both DEC and DG were aggressive in their approach to gaining market share, they differed in their market breadth strategies. Whereas DEC was a specialist, DG was a generalist, providing a broad range of computers that were distributed through customizing OEMs to the minicomputer market in general. It is significant though, that this difference in strategies was likely influenced by the timing of the two firms' entry and the degree of uncertainty inherent in the market. DG, entering early, (founded in 1967), but somewhat later than DEC (founded in 1957), was able to take advantage of the explosion in the growth of sales that began in the late 1960s and in the preliminary work that DEC had undertaken in opening the market and identifying its potential. Romanelli indicates that DEC's decision to specialize in the scientific and engineering segments was influenced by the company founder's "computer scientist background," despite the fact that the market segments that DG later exploited were known to DEC at the time. DEC's decision to specialize in the segments about which its founder had associated knowledge seems reasonable given that such a segment should therefore be the least uncertain to him. The further afield from the pioneer's realm of experience are the segments it chooses to serve, the greater the uncertainty the pioneer would be likely to face. As Romanelli (1987, p. 170) later remarks: "The appropriateness of DEC's specialization, however, appears to have been driven by uncertainty. The viability of the minicomputer had to be proved and specialization provided the freedom to gain experience with the needs of one kind of user."

The initial provision of minicomputers had enabled customers to envision new applications. An aggressive market penetration strategy has obvious advantages here in helping the pioneers to keep in touch with their customers' evolving needs, especially those of lead users, and thereby to anticipate the development of new segments. It is thus noteworthy that the founders of DG were ex-DEC computer engineers, who, presumably, had an awareness of those new needs, and who felt the time was right to exploit a market opportunity which DEC did not.

In general, therefore, it would appear that when the market potential is large but unexplored and therefore uncertainty is high, as in the emergence phase of a new market, a pioneer would be best to adopt an aggressive, specialist strategy. As the market develops and uncertainty diminishes (i.e., in the growth phase), successful entrants will be those pursuing a generalist strategy. In some industries, mainly those characterized by mass markets (Teece, 1988), changes in key success factors occur at this time with the emergence of a dominant design and the shift to cost reductions and efficiency. We might presume that a generalist strategy is more suited to that phase when the key success factors shift to efficiency, decreased costs and price, as serving a broad market is likely to enable the generalist firm to obtain greater economies of scale and experience effects than the specialist.

However, a firm's ability to pursue a generalist strategy is constrained by the resources at its disposal. Specialization may be the only feasible alternative for many firms with limited resources.

In addition, Romanelli found that some pioneers survived even though they adopted a generalist strategy from the outset. Her explanation for this was that they were all aggressive generalists. However, given the uncertainties enumerated above, a pioneer that chooses to be both aggressive and a generalist must be able to call on considerable resources to avoid burnout.

It thus seems that the earliest pioneers will tend to be successful as specialists while their early followers, entering in the growth phase, will tend to be successful if generalists. The question then arises whether a specialist pioneer can make the transition to generalist as the market shifts from emergence to growth. There is some evidence to indicate that this is difficult, and that making the attempt increases the likelihood of failure.

Romanelli examined the relationship between long-term survival and changes in strategy. She found that those firms that survived tended not to change their strategies, on the strategic dimensions that she examined. Conversely, she found that those firms that eventually failed did change their strategies. However, there is an obvious question of causality here. Though it may be that strategic consistency helps ensure survival, it may also be that the firms that failed foresaw their demise and tried to change their strategies to avoid it. Their eventual failure may therefore have been due to an unsuccessful first strategy and a myopic assessment of their environment, which prevented them from taking timely action.

Research in this area is still in its infancy and it is too early to know whether firms that failed to adapt did so because of inadequate strategies and incompetence or, as Romanelli suggests, because of the difficulties involved in the attempt. It is hoped that this paper sets out a framework for analysis that will enable pioneering firms using radical technologies to avoid falling into either category.

NOTES

1. The term "shakeout" is increasingly being used in the business press to refer to any large exit of firms from an industry at any time in its evolution. We are holding to a narrower definition as explained in the text.

2. Note that this data is not ideally suited for our purposes as the earliest pioneers have often been excluded, and some "burnouts" may therefore be omitted. Additionally, it would be preferable to have corresponding data for sales growth and expectations to help identify the occurrence of the shakeout in each industry. We have simply inferred the pattern of exits from Knight, Dowling, and Brown's graphs and used these to infer the occurrence of shakeouts, a less than ideal method.

3. Commencing in 1903.

4. Commencing in 1926.
5. Commencing in 1945.
6. This may simply result from the fact that the data for the automobile and semiconductor industries does not cover a long enough period.
7. Note also that for both the auto and semiconductor industries, almost 20% of all firms that had entered the industry still remained after the shakeout had occurred.

REFERENCES

Aaker, D.A., & Day, G.S. (1986). The perils of high-growth markets. *Strategic Management Journal, 7*, p. 409-421.
Abell, D.F. (1980). *Defining the business: The starting point of strategic planning.* Engelwood Cliffs, NJ: Prentice Hall.
Bennett, R.C., & Cooper, R.G. (1984). The product life cycle trap. *Business Horizons, 27*(5), p. 7-16.
Buzzell, R.D., Cox, D.F., & Brown, R.V. (1969). *Marketing research and information systems: Text and cases.* New York: McGraw-Hill.
Day, G.S. (1984). *Strategic market planning: The pursuit of competitive advantage.* Minneapolis: West Publishing.
————— 1986. *Analysis for strategic market decisions.* Minneapolis, MN: West Publishing.
Erickson, W.E., & Maitland, I. (1982). Healthy industries and public policy. In M. E. Dewar (Ed.), *Industry vitalization* (pp. 144-170). New York: Pergamon.
Flaherty, M.T. (1983). Market share, technology leadership and competition in international semiconductor markets. In R.S. Rosenbloom (Ed.), *Research on technological innovation, management and policy* (pp. 69-102). Greenwich, CT: JAI Press.
GM throws a wrench into the robot market. (1986, August 25). *Business Week,* p. 36.
Hannan, M.T., & Freeman, J. 1984. Structural inertia and organizational change. *American Sociological Review, 49*, 149-164.
Hartley, R.F. (1986). *Marketing mistakes.* New York: Wiley.
It's getting harder for computer gurus to sound wise. (1985, May 27). *Business Week,* pp. 108-110.
Knight, K.E., Dowling, M., & Brown, J.B. (1988). *Venture survivability: An analysis of the automobile, semiconductor, vacuum tube and airline industries.* Working paper, University of Texas.
Olleros, F. (1986). Emerging industries and the burnout of pioneers. *Journal of Product Innovation Management, 1*, 5-18.
Porter, M.E. (1985). *Competitive advantage: Creating and sustaining superior performance.* New York: Free Press.
Robinson, W.T. (1988). Sources of market pioneer advantages: The case of industrial goods industries. *Journal of Marketing Research, 25*(1), 87-94.
Romanelli, E. (1987). New venture strategies in the minicomputer industry. *California Management Review, 30*(1), 160-175.
Sahlman, W.A., & Stevenson, H.H. (1985). Capital market myopia. *Journal of Business Venturing, 1*(1), 7-30.
Schmalensee, R. (1982, June). Product differentiation advantages of pioneering brands. *American Economic Review, 72*, 349-365.
Schnaars, S.P. (1986, March-April). When entering growth markets, are pioneers better than poachers? *Business Horizons,* pp. 27-36.
Shakeout (1984, July 16). *Forbes,* pp. 67-70.

Teece, D.J. (1988). Capturing value from technological innovation: Integration, strategic partnering, and licensing decisions. *Interfaces, 18*(3), 46-61.

Tushman, M.L., & Romanelli, E. (1985). Organizational evolution: A metamorphosis model of convergence and reorientation. In B.M. Staw & C.L. Cummings (Eds.), *Research in organizational behavior* (Vol.7, pp. 171-222). Greenwich, CT: JAI Press.

von Hippel, E. (1988) *The sources of innovation*. New York: Oxford University Press.

Willard, G.E., & Cooper, A.C. (1985). Survivors of industry shakeouts: The case of the U.S. color television set industry. *Strategic Management Journal, 6*, 299-318.

Wilson, A., & Atkin, B. (1976). Exorcising the ghosts in marketing. *Harvard Business Review, 5*(5), 117-126.

Yip, G. (1982). Gateways to entry. *Harvard Business Review, 60*(5), 85-92.

NEW PRODUCT INTRODUCTION:
STRATEGIC MATCHING PROBLEMS

Ray M. Haynes and Thomas E. Hendrick

Automated Teller Machines (ATMs) were introduced in the United States in 1970, yet it has taken nearly 15 years for this "new" product to be fully accepted to the level of installation saturation. The ATM can generate productivity increases of more than 400 percent when compared to traditional, teller-initiated banking transactions of specific types. Several writers have discussed the concept of matching operations capabilities to the market demand from a strategic perspective. The ATM purveyors suffered for many years due to a mismatch between their distinctive competencies and the market expectations. This paper will consider the historic perspective of ATM deployment in the United States and propose ideas that may preclude a similar mismatch in future high technology product introduction in other industries.

The opportunities available to a company that considers strategic matching are well documented for both the manufacturing (Buffa, 1984) and the services industries (Sasser, 1976). Strategic positioning of the operations function within the organization has been proposed by Wheelwright and Hayes (1985). The current thinking in operations management is that successful competitive advantage can only be achieved through a long-term planning perspective. While this does not directly preclude attention to tactical positioning, there is a definite need to maintain the strategic vision. The basic premise is to selectively match internal capabilities to external opportunities to secure long-term benefits. This is applicable to both existing and emerging industries. A careful analysis of the opportunity is particularly critical when considering a new product in a new market when there is little historical information available. It becomes even more important if the product involves new or leading-edge technology that may be relatively unproven. Finally, when the "product" is introduced in a service industry, it may have certain intangibles that defy accurate measurement relative to traditional evaluation mechanisms.

Service operations are somewhat more difficult to describe than manufacturing operations based on several factors identified below. An example of each characteristic is also presented.

1. The deliverable may be intangible; not a hard product. The user of legal advice may leave with only information.
2. There may be simultaneous production and consumption at a single site. Interacting with your tax accountant produces information which is instantly consumed.
3. The customer may be directly involved in the actual delivery process. A barber cuts your hair and requires your physical presence to deliver the service.
4. The deliverable may be time perishable with little potential for carrying inventory for future utilization. An empty airplane seat is forever lost for that particular flight.
5. The deliverable may be heterogeneous to a limited degree with some variation in the service. An instructor may give particular attention to students with special needs within the same classroom situation.
6. Services are traditionally labor intensive which creates even more variability. A live preacher in the church auditorium creates a distinctly different impression from a tape downlinked to a television in your home.
7. The delivery facility must generally be convenient to the user as well as pleasant to the senses. A nearby doctor's office may have soft seats, plenty of magazines and soothing music to help calm the patient.
8. Services often require a wait prior to obtaining the deliverable. Getting a driver's license generally requires waiting in several lines prior to getting the end product.
9. The quality of the service delivered is often in the eyes of the beholder and not necessarily linked to the actual deliverable. A workout in a popular health club facility may be more enjoyable than exercising by yourself in the living room, even if the same number of calories are burned.
10. Services typically have a soft, implicit component linked to the psychological aspect of taking delivery, which may be more overt than when a physical product is the deliverable. This generally

makes the deliverable unique to each consumer. A bank customer receiving an auto loan may be more satisfied than one merely cashing a check for spending money.

Berry, Zeithaml, and Parasuraman (1984) have discussed these elements with particular attention to the perceived quality of the service. This can be shown in the following sequence of motions during the delivery of a service:

A. *ENTRY EXPECTATIONS*—What do I expect to get from this service encounter?
B. *DELIVERY PERCEPTIONS*—What actually happened from my unique one-on-one perspective?
C. *QUALITY OF SERVICE*—Did the perception match the preconceived expectation? There are three general possibilities.

1. *Better*	=	high satisfaction	=	high quality
2. *Worse*	=	low satisfaction	=	low quality
3. *Match*	=	satisfied	=	some quality

There is an implicit assumption that the service actually was able to provide the basic deliverable required by the consumer. A potential customer of a laundry and dry cleaners requesting one day service and not able to get it may, in fact, go to another laundry to get his particular service needs met and never really see the delivery cycle to completion in the first encounter. One set of rules presented by Page-Jones (1980) in the context of software development seems to make sense on a universal basis, particularly with respect to other "high technology" systems implementation.

1. It must be effective—it must actually be capable of performing the function that it was designed to accomplish.
2. It must be usable—the intended user must be able to utilize the product in the manner expected with some reasonable amount of training.
3. It must be reliable—the product must function repeatedly without any significant degradation due to additional use.
4. It must be maintainable—the mechanism itself should be easily and economically repaired, serviced or enhanced as necessary.
5. Finally, when all of the above is in place, efficiency may be pursued as a reasonable goal in order to gain economic or operational advantage.

PRODUCT APPLICATION

Automated Teller Machines were a new product in the late 1960s that were designed and developed with "efficiency" (number 5, above) as the primary goal. This created a problem in the implementation experience that affected the suppliers, the financial institutions and the end-users. The ATM scenario will be explored in more detail to discover lessons that may be useful in other high technology product strategies.

Several issues that resulted from the ATM experience appear to be of interest. First, there was not a clearly defined demand for this service. Second, the effectiveness of the ATM, in the beginning stages, was questionable. Finally, the service provider was apparently looking for productivity increases by focusing on efficiency. When considering a basic productivity model, certain equivalencies can be proposed:

$$\text{Productivity} \quad = \frac{\text{Output}}{\text{input}} \rightarrow \left\{ \frac{\text{effectiveness}}{\text{efficiency}} \right\} \rightarrow \left\{ \frac{\text{deliverable}}{\text{resources}} \right\}$$

Total productivity concepts indicate that gains can be made by decreasing the denominator while holding numerator fixed, increasing the numerator while holding denominator fixed, simultaneously decreasing the denominator and increasing the numerator or increasing the numerator at a faster rate than the denominator. While Fitzsimmons and Sullivan (1982) and Chase (1981) suggest that service productivity is linked to both automation of the service (efficiency) and involving the customer directly (effectiveness) to a greater degree, there must be a rational approach to this implementation. The substitution of an ATM for a live teller was in direct competition to hundreds of years of traditional person-to-person banking experiences and it was discovered that the customer had no intention of getting involved; effectiveness was poor.

THE SETTING

The traditional business of banking is extremely low-technology and relatively simple. Banks take deposits and make investments. Along the way they act as facilitators for transferring funds on behalf of their customers. Profit is a result of the interest paid on the deposits, compared to the interest received on investments, less the operating expenses. At one time, certain types of institutions specialized in specific investments: savings and loans made mortgage loans while commercial banks made business and auto loans. Today, because of deregulation, the business of banking is highly homogenated and a typical financial institution will offer up to 150 distinct services to its customers. This creates a highly competitive environment where cost containment becomes both a tactical and a strategic concern. The reduction of the number of named institutions has been a result of merger/acquisition strategies and poor business practices that have driven the marginal providers from the market entirely. The importance of economies of scale (actual size) and economies of scope (market breadth) have become a primary planning focus. The changes in the business of banking in the United States over the past decade have been well documented by Mayer (1974,1984).

This is the environmental setting that was slowly emerging when the ATM was introduced by Docutel in the late 1960s. Docutel Corporation was a subsidiary of Recognition Equipment Incorporated of Dallas, Texas. The parent company was a major vendor of automated check processing equipment for commercial banks. The history of Docutel is chronicled in a case study by Abell and Hammond (1979). The first ATM was installed in late 1969. Technically, it was a cash dispenser with only a single function, but the technology was essentially available to build the full-function teller machine. Docutel was one of the first vendors, which grew to include IBM, NCR, TRW, Diebold and others. The ATM was the flagship product of an new area of banking-designated electronic banking or electronic funds transfer systems (EFTS). It included a variety of elements such as bank-to-bank wire transfer, corporate-to-bank automated payroll deposit, retail point-of-sale, credit/debit card authorization and ATMs. The strategy was to eliminate the proliferation of paper-based transactions in all areas of commercial banking in an effort to both streamline the entire operation and reduce, or at least contain costs (Lipis, Marschall, & Linker, 1985). The one product in this lineup that directly interfaced with the bank's customer was the ATM and this one-on-one linkage created operational "opportunities." An insight into the level of the potential significance of EFTS was evidenced by the formation of the President's Commission to study this new aspect of banking delivery systems in 1975 (Benton, 1977).

THE OPPORTUNITIES

Earlier works by Haynes (1987) and Murphy (1983) address the possibility of learning from the electronic banking experience and the necessity of looking at the factor interrelationships so that problems may be translated into opportunities. Analyzing the factors critical to success at the detail level is beyond the scope of this paper but will be summarized by major classifications relative to ATM implementation. The problems can be categorized into five types:

1. *Environmental*—Those having to do with the setting of the service being delivered.
2. *Technological*—Those dealing specifically with the ability of automated equipment to deliver the service "as advertised."
3. *Financial*—Those related to cost justification of the capital and ongoing expenditures required to deliver the service.
4. *Behavioral*—Those dealing with the substitution of a machine for the traditional one-on-one personal contact.
5. *Marketing*—Those dealing with the identification and selection of specific target customers.

The *Environmental* problems centered around the various banking regulatory bodies that governed the different banking entities. These ranged from local to federal regulations that could specifically limit the way an institution could do business. The ATM held money, which required that it be built within a "safe" enclosure with designated attack resistance and alarm systems. The designation of the money contained as "vault cash" could allow it to be considered part of the bank's reserves. However, if the ATM was not attached to the facility, it might require a branch permit and fall under an entirely different set of regulations. In addition, each of these might be interpreted uniquely on a state-by-state basis. The ATM's physical environment also required attention. The ATM is a collection of electro-mechanical components that are controlled by a self-contained computer. The physical site required a minimum of 50 square feet floor space supported by telephone, electrical, and air conditioning services. Very few banks were ready to address these problems in any detail in the beginning. However, the typical analysis for considering electronic banking has always been a relatively straightforward payback analysis based on the cost comparisons that show electronic transactions are typically one-half the cost of paper-based transactions (D.G. Long, 1982).

The *Technological* problems were better defined but often complex because of the integrative nature of the ATM delivery system. Each machine was customized to a certain extent for each financial institution, which made maintenance more costly. The cash dispensing mechanisms were very sensitive and often required new currency. Large quantities of currency were also needed as a given machine might be capable of holding up to 5000 bills. The card reader was also highly sensitive with transport and registration mechanisms frequently requiring close tolerance adjustments. Software was also an ongoing concern whether the machine was off-line or on-line and power fluctuations could easily destroy the system's memory. Keyboards and displays offered other opportunities for the ATM to malfunction. While the ATM was not necessarily leading-edge technology, it was a unique combination of existing technologies that functioned in

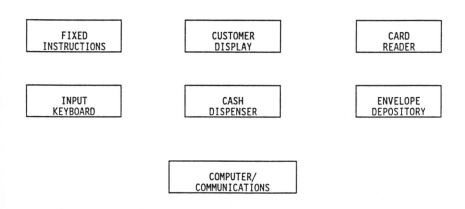

Figure 1. Functional Modules

a stand alone, unattended mode of operation. An early work that considers the scope of the technology shift was done by Long (1974). The physical functional components are shown in Figure 1. While the top six modules interface directly with the user, the local computer system integrates the functional modules into a homogeneous operational entity and provides necessary communications linkage to the bank's main computer system.

The *Financials* associated with ATM implementation offered the institution a wealth of opportunities to consider. The cost was approximately $60,000 per installation including site preparation and the actual ATM unit. Vendor maintenance averaged between $300-500 monthly for basic eight-hour coverage; however, many buyers opted for the premium 24-hour contracts. Return-on-investment figures were keyed to a relatively high transaction volume for a theoretical breakeven that was based on the projected cost savings between ATM and branch teller expense. The net result was an investment that had high fixed capitalization, high operating expenses and virtually unknown returns. Bank marketing people were generally excited about a new product but selling to the finance committee was difficult. One thorough study of the theoretical financial benefits associated with ATMs was done by Felgran (1984).

The *Behavioral* problems surfaced in two distinct populations. The primary in-bank customer contact for marketing the ATM was the branch teller. This was the same teller that the ATM was designed to replace. The enthusiasm was often less than necessary to change banking habits developed over years. The other contact point was the actual customer. The access card, in many cases, was the customer's credit card and ATM usage was the secondary application that was not easily compromisable in the event that the card was retained by the ATM for any reason. The actual ATM ergonomics were somewhat intimidating. The card was entered into a small slot and pulled inside a metal-faced machine. The next step required the successful entering of a 4- or 6-digit security code assigned by the bank or alternatively, chosen by the customer. Generally, only three tries were allowed and if not done correctly, the card was retained. The next function was to select the appropriate transaction and amount. If all of this was done in the appropriate manner and sequence, the card was returned with a customer receipt and actual cash (assuming a cash withdrawal transaction). The customer had to be thoroughly educated in the actual machine operation, had to possess the proper access card, and had some confidence that the machine would not malfunction. Finally, many of the ATM installations were in prominent, exposed locations that created some sense of insecurity to users, particularly at night. A recent study of ATM users versus nonusers was done by Stevens, Martin, Carter and Cogshell (1986) and includes some of the behavioral considerations that can be characterized by demographic profiles. The typical ATM user is younger (age 24-40), better educated (some college) and has higher income (average $32,500) than nonusers.

The target *Market* for this product were the 15,000 commercial banks that generally offered their customers a plastic card (credit, debit or check guarantee) that could function as the ATM access card. Unfortunately, in 1970, most of these banks did not have on-line processing capability and had three options: (1) they could run the machines off-line, which created security and control problems; (2) they could upgrade their existing mainframe system to support real-time processing, which was expensive and time consuming; (3) they could opt to install a front-end processor that would provide intercept processing of ATM transactions and feed the primary system a memo-post log daily. In addition, there was a distinct need for high-availability systems so that customers would not be faced with an inordinate amount of system down time. This was a key factor in the proliferation of fault-tolerant systems based on the computer equipment from Tandem and the IBM Series/1 multi-processor configurations. These front-end processors cost the installing institution a minimum of $250,000 to support a minimum of 50 ATMs, plus software development, plus maintenance and assorted support personnel. The costs escalated!

Meanwhile, there were 5000 savings and loan institutions, generally on-line with their teller terminals who did not have a card base necessary to access the equipment. One abortive attempt to replace the passbook associated with the savings account using a universal card (called Prestige) was made and marketed by a third party to the savings industry. Customers were extremely reticent to substitute the card for their passbook, in spite of financial incentives in the form of additional interest (typically .25%) to do so. This essentially precluded widespread implementation of ATMs in this type of financial institution for more than five years.

Finally, the ATM required a system-wide evaluation of a financial institution's data processing capabilities. Unfortunately, many of the banks did not have sufficient technical expertise to undertake this study and the hardware vendors were generally biased (Stamps, 1985). All things considered, the market niche was not accurately defined during the first decade of ATM deployment. Specifically, here was a high technology, high-priced product being sold to an intermediary (bank) with little, if any, end-user market demand. This created an unknown cost-benefit relationship.

MATURATION

The problems noted above were slowly and patiently solved over a period of approximately 10 years. ATMs became less physically intimidating and incorporated such features as CRT displays, voice/tone prompting, more reliable mechanisms, additional on-line transaction support, telephone aid stations adjacent to the machine and a general enhancement of the product appearance and capabilities.

As can be seen in Table 1, the ATM user interface modules (from Figure 1) became more user-friendly and allowed a transaction to be much more personalized while still providing a standardized, automated service.

The user became more machine-literate and the 24-hour convenience of the ATM finally overcame many of the early obstacles to usage. Regulations were being eased with respect to ATM installations and high-density

Table 1. 20-Year Technology Shifts

Module	1968	1988	Impact
Display	fixed message, rotating drum	programmable CRT	personalized messages
Card Reader	read only, single track	read/write multiple tracks	various card types usable
Keyboard	fixed function labeled keys	alpha/numeric programmable	personalized input
Dispenser	envelopes of three bills fixed $ amount	regular bills, multiple denominations	personalized output
Communications	proprietary message format async mode	ANSI standard messages/format bisync/SDLC	transaction speed, bank interchange

deployment created an atmosphere of increased utility for the user. Extensive deregulation during the 1980s created another positive environmental setting wherein various institutions formed formal interchange alliances that permitted sharing of ATM facilities both in-state and across state lines. Today, there are two national interchange networks, CIRRUS (operated by MasterCard) and PLUS (associated with VISA), that provide ATM access worldwide for participating bank members.

Today, there are more than 70,000 ATMs installed that process more than 400 million transactions monthly (Felgran, 1984). In spite of these numbers, the national average is that only 33 percent of the potential users, actually use ATMs regularly. The machine utilization is only 7% of capacity on the installed base. The transaction costs are between $.20-$.30 and are typically 50% less than a similar teller-initiated check cost for withdrawals. Some institutions have implemented fee schedules for ATM usage but in a recent study by Touche-Ross, not a single bank surveyed reported that installed technology was profitable (Vandervelde & Vargo, 1983). In spite of this, there are indications that the top banks in the industry will spend another $45 billion on technology during the next five years (Soloman, 1986). ATM installation will account for a substantial portion of this investment.

Meanwhile, check volume has not decreased, but its current growth rate of 5 percent is estimated to be less than half the growth projected for a non-ATM environment (BEI, 1986). Teller replacement has not taken place as once expected but essentially the teller growth rate is negligible and can be attributed to ATMs (Soloman, 1986). While the original premise for installing ATMs has not yielded the results that were once proposed, this product has been instrumental in avoiding some of the growth in costs projected for the banking industry had they not been introduced. This would imply that there is a message in this particular product evolution that should be considered.

THE LESSONS

The ATM story suggests several lessons for high technology product implementation that can be summarized in the following rules.

1. *Effective:* Assure that the technology is capable of delivering the actual product/service as specified in the original plan to a designated potential user that exhibits some demand characteristic for the product being implemented.

2. *Maintainable:* When the technology is untried, make sure that the support systems are capable of maintaining the product in an operable condition with the desired up-time performance. This is particularly severe

when the equipment must operate in an unattended mode and interface directly with a customer.

3. *Reliable:* When the product/service requires existing system enhancements or upgrades, make sure that the operating factors enable consistent delivery. Once user education/training has been successfully accomplished, the product must continue to operate in the manner originally prescribed.

4. *Usable:* There should be sufficient education/training of both internal and external personnel to ensure a high degree of support for the project, particularly in the early stages of development. This must be to a level of detail that allows initial and ongoing utilization of the product/ service at a frequency necessary to demonstrate success.

5. *Efficiency:* Once all of the other elements have been addressed satisfactorily, an effort can be made to streamline the system. This requires a sufficient level of quantification of operating parameters to know where, when, what and how changes are to be made. The interaction of the system with other external and internal systems must be studied and modeled if at all possible. Modifications must be made on a selective basis to ascertain the cause-effect relationships and the magnitude of the shift.

THE FUTURE OF ATMS

The current installed base of ATMs is generally considered to effectively saturate the market, especially when shared networks are added to the equation (Zimmer, 1986). The fixed-cost nature of ATM deployment would suggest that the majority of the costs have been incurred and possibly expensed or at least capitalized (Murphy, 1983). The original goals of ATM introduction have been realized to an extent but not to the level initially proposed (Coats, 1984). The strategic orientation extolled by Boyd (1973) for all bank products was considered but during the implementation phase, the environment has shifted to a large degree. The future of ATMs is closely linked to new EFTS delivery systems, particularly retail point-of-sale (POS) (Frazer, 1985). The wide-scale proliferation of POS systems is expected to effectively replace future ATM implementation and has the possibility of displacing transaction volume as well. Both ATM and POS systems are based on debit transactions that have the potential of real-time processing. This aspect, in conjunction with the other productivity promises of EFTS, may help the financial services industry to cope with the tremendous environmental changes envisioned for the next decade (Stevens et al., 1986). Deregulation is a precursor to the global changes that will effect the industry in both structural and economic arenas (Roth & Vandervelde, 1988).

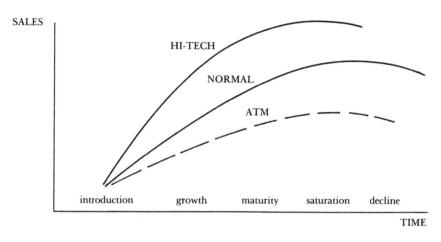

Figure 2.   Product Life Cycle

The business case for EFTS has been well documented relative to processing efficiencies and cost reduction. The marketing aspects of increased customer convenience and market positioning have been effectively pursued by many institutions. The need now is to combine these factors into a strategic plan that will more fully utilize the excess capacities of these facilities and services. This is a reasonable opportunity based on the noted underutilization of ATM capabilities on an aggregate basis in the United States. There is more than a 75% growth potential with existing facilities and customer bases, even with both of these increasing at a known rate. Several banks have experimented with pricing policies that encourage ATM use plus augment transaction income. This has been done by the shared networks for the past five years and been effective in cost containment. However, each financial institution has unique opportunities related to their particular market conditions and these must be considered on a case-by-case basis (Carter, 1982; Finch & Haynes, 1988).

Vendors of ATMs have been successful in utilizing the technology in a variety of other products designed for self-service operation. These include automated rental car check-ins (AVIS Wizard), airline ticket dispensers (American and Southwest), and automated fuel dispensing systems (ARCO and MOBIL). This has essentially extended the product life cycle into other similar delivery operations using the same basic functional modules.

This leads to one final perspective that must be considered: the traditional product life cycle characteristics. The general shape of this curve is shown in Figure 2 with the appropriate stages labeled.

Table 2. Product Obsolescence Chart

Product	Cost ($)	Memory	Characteristics
IBM 360	500,000	64-128K	batch oriented, requires software development, input was punch cards, output was cards and tape, bulk storage was low density multi-platter disk ... all requiring high levels of environmental control (computer rooms) with local air conditioning and dedicated power backup.
			PROCESSOR SPEED: 4MHZ (8 BIT) LIFE CYCLE: 20 years ++
IBM PC (8086)	5000	256-IMB	package software, single user extensive on-line capability, input direct keyboard, output to high density diskette or resident hard disk, highly transportable, room ambient environmental requirement
			PROCESSOR SPEED: 8MHZ (8 BIT) LIFE CYCLE: 5 years
IBM PC (286)	4000	512-5MB	same plus larger hard disks and multi-processing, faster and more reliable.
			PROCESSOR SPEED: 10MHZ (16 BIT) LIFE CYCLE: 3 years
IBM PC (386)	3000	1-10MB	same plus faster, more power etc.
			PROCESSOR SPEED: 20MHZ (32 BIT) LIFE CYCLE: 2 years (est.)

It is characteristic of high technology products that they are often replaced or enhanced rather quickly in the marketplace and this trend seems to be increasing rather than stabilizing. ATMs exhibited a rather flat slope up to the Maturity/Saturation stage and this resulted in several of the original companies in the business to seek other more profitable products. The one company dedicated to ATM manufacturing, Docutel, has ceased to exist even after being sold to Olivetti. Today, others, including Diebold, IBM, NCR, and Fujitsu, consider ATMs as purely an ancillary product and focus primary research and development elsewhere within their product lines. The message indicated by this is that high technology products introduced to a market might want to exhibit a steep slope through the Introduction/

Growth stages as noted by the dashed line in Figure 2. This would serve to generate larger sales revenues early on in the cycle in order to gain better cost-recovery characteristics for the product. A comparison of another familiar high technology product line demonstrates the rapid rate of obsolescence currently being experienced in this business. This is presented as Table 2.

This same process can be seen in a host of other product lines including printers (dot matrix to laser), telephones (dial to tone), aircraft (propeller to rocket), and televisions (rotary dial/black & white/small screen/monaural to digital remote/color/large screen/quadrophonic stereo) and others.

CONCLUSION

The earlier mismatch between supply and demand in the banking industry as evidenced by the introduction of the ATM is a matter of historical record. The lessons identified would suggest that each institution must address their specific opportunities from a technical systems perspective relative to the delivery capability and the effect on other banking products and services. A concurrent consideration must be made of the human aspects, both internal (employees) and external (customers) to the organization and the relative impacts of any new technology. When the preliminary assessments are concluded, an extensive effort to communicate the nature of the changes is necessary that translates into massive education and training at all levels of potential interface with the system.

The final consideration is that a given technology can evolve on an incremental basis and provide new opportunities that should be factored into the strategic plan on a continuous basis. The key concept here may be *evolution* rather than *revolution*. The ATM in 1970 was revolutionary and had problems, from both technological and marketing perspectives. In general, the market today has a strong customer orientation that is fueled by Reaganomics, consumer activists and focused attention to product quality. High technology products tend to have high price elasticity characteristics in the early stages. The microwave and VCR are prime examples of this. In both cases, there was little demand for a $1000 product but heavy demand at $300.

Unfortunately, the paradox is that the quick high technology product life cycles often require a short-term, tactical approach for implementation in a global environment stressing long-term, strategic planning. This is all the more reason to establish a firm foundation of product implementation decision-making rules as suggested herein. A quality product designed to accommodate a known customer need can remain at the apex of Maturity/ Saturation in the life cycle. This is where profits are most achievable.

Various companies and product/services have been consistently in this position. Honda automobiles, American Airlines, Hewlett-Packard computers, Maytag appliances and Sony electronics are but a few representatives. The secret is not particularly mysterious. Each of these companies appears to follow the rules laid out here for new product introduction. Other products and services represent counter-examples: ATM's; Pontiac Fiero; and People Express Airlines are but a few. Most violate Rule 1, but also go on to be suspect for all five during their life cycle. In summary:

> Rule 1 EFFECTIVE
> Rule 2 USABLE
> Rule 3 RELIABLE
> Rule 4 MAINTAINABLE
> Rule 5 EFFICIENT

The deregulated environment in the United States demands that we consider the fine balance between the explicit and implicit attributes of all products and services. Only as we can effectively match the supply side (delivery capabilities) to the demand (customer needs) are we able to achieve and sustain a competitive advantage. This is what is necessary to compete effectively in both domestic and global business. The current trade deficit suggests there is room to grow—combine the opportunity, the tools and the desire and we can move confidently into the next decade and beyond.

REFERENCES

Abell, D.F., & Hammond, J.S. (1979). *Strategic market planning.* Englewood Cliffs, NJ: Prentice-Hall.

Bank Earnings International. (1986). Checks, EFT, and the American consumer: 1984 versus 1985. Atlanta: BEI Publishers.

Benton, J.B. (1977). Electronic funds transfer: Pitfalls and payoffs. *Harvard Business Review, 55*(4), 16-32.

Berry, L.L., Zeithaml, V.A., & Parasuraman, A. (1985). Quality counts in services, too. *Business Horizons, 28*(3), 44-52.

Boyd, J.H. (1973). Bank strategies in the retail demand deposit markets. *Journal of Bank Research, 4*(2), 111-121.

Buffa, E.S. (1984). *Meeting the competitive challenge.* Homewood, IL: Dow Jones-Irwin.

Carter, M.G. (1982). An integrated approach to EFT and retail service delivery. *Journal of Retail Banking, 4*(2), 1-13.

Chase, R.B. (1981). The customer contact approach to services: Theoretical bases and practical extensions. *Operations Research, 29*(4): 699-706.

Coats, P.K. (1984). Electronic funds transfer networks: Modeling their impact on bank service goals. *Computers and Operations Research, 1,* 415-426.

Felgran, S.D. (1984, January-February). Shared ATM networks: Market structure and public policy. *New England Economic Review*, pp. 44-61.

Finch, P., & Haynes, R.M. (1988, March). Research isolates deposit gains from EFT technology. *Bank Systems and Equipment*, pp. 58-59.

Fitzsimmons, J.A., & Sullivan, R.S. (1982). *Service operations management*. New York: McGraw-Hill.

Frazer, P. (1985). EFTPOS: Issues and insights. *Journal of Retail Banking*, 7(2), 1-8.

Haynes, R.M. (1987). Technology in the service sector: Lessons to be learned from electronic banking. *Proceedings of the Western Decision Sciences Institute*: 7-9.

Lipis, A.J., Marschall, T.R., & Linker, J.H. (1985). *Electronic banking*. New York: Wiley.

Long, D.G. (1982). The business case for electronic banking. *Journal of Retail Banking*, 4(2), 14-21.

Long, R.H. (1974). Impact of technological change on bank products and customers. *Journal of Bank Research*, 5(3), 137-142.

Mayer, M. (1974). *The bankers*. New York: Random House.

———— (1984). *The money bazaars*. New York: New American Library.

Murphy, N.B. (1983). Determinants of ATM activity: The impact of card base, location, time and place of the system. *Journal of Bank Research*, 14(3): 231-233.

Page-Jones, M. (1980). *The practical guide to structured systems design*. New York: Yourdon Press.

Roth, A.V., & VanderVelde, M. (1988). *The future of retail banking delivery systems*. Rolling Hills, IL: Bank Administration Institute.

Sasser, W.E. (1976). Match supply and demand in service industries. *Harvard Business Review*, 54(8), 133-140.

Soloman, G.M. (1986). Strategic implications of ATM's: Why haven't all the tellers gone? *Journal of Retail Banking*, 8(3), 43-51.

Stamps, D. (1985, March). When to call in automation consultants. *Computers in Banking*, pp. 28-32.

Stevens, R.E., Martin, R.T., Carter, P.S., & Cogshell, D. (1986). A comparative analysis of users and non-users of ATM's. *Journal of Retail Banking*, 8(1, 2), 71-78.

VanderVelde, M., & Vargo, D.J. (1983). *ATM cost model*. Rolling Hills, IL: Bank Administration Institute.

Wheelwright, S.C., & Hayes, R.H. (1985). Competing through manufacturing. *Harvard Business Review*, 63(1), 99-109.

Zimmer, L. (1986, May). The future of ATM products and services. *Bank Administration*, pp. 21-28.

A REGIONAL CULTURE PERSPECTIVE OF HIGH TECHNOLOGY MANAGEMENT

Joseph W. Weiss and Andre Delbecq

Geographic culture influences organizational behavior and attitudes in sometimes hidden but observable ways. The aim of this paper is to elaborate on a perspective for studying the influence of regional culture on the management of high technology computer firms.

International studies demonstrate that country culture influences and explains managerial attitudes, roles and work styles through social values (Hofstede, 1980; Laurent, 1983; Haire, Ghiselli, & Porter, 1966). Hofstede showed that national culture explained more differences in workplace values than did organizational position, person's age, gender or profession. Child's (1981) findings indicated that while organizations in different countries are converging on large scale dimensions such as structure and technology, at the individual level people in organizations maintain their distinctive national cultural values, which are reflected in the workplace. These country-level cultural studies provide a basis for arguing the uniqueness of geographically value based behavior in the workplace.

Recently, studies have explored the extent to which regional cultures within nations influence management attitudes and ways of doing business. Kahle's (1986) study helped define national U.S. regions and dominant value sets within these boundaries. Weiss (1988) and Weiss and Delbecq (1986) have contributed a framework for linking regional characteristics to organizational practices. Rogers and Larsen (1984) provide a descriptive study of the distinctive environmental characteristics of Silicon Valley and how these impact work in computer companies. Gregory's (1983) interview study identified elements of professional engineering cultures in Silicon Valley.

A regional theory of management based on social values and environmental characteristics is at the developmental stage; there is a continuing need for conceptual and empirical studies to systematically articulate and test a regional perspective within and across industries. This paper reports on results from an earlier, single industry study with the aim of advancing this perspective.

CONCEPTUAL BASIS OF THIS STUDY

Regional culture is defined here as shared beliefs, attitudes and values about space, time, work and leisure, which are influenced by the history, economics, politics, social traditions and customs of a local geographic area. This definition borrows from and extends other definitions of culture by Schein (1984, 1985) and Triandis (1972).

We argue that regional culture influences organizational behavior and attitudes through social values that members bring from their nonwork milieu (Kahle, 1986) and through a range of local environmentally conditioned characteristics such as climate and institutionally conditioned customs and practices (Weiss & Delbecq, 1987).

Both macro- and micro-organizational dimensions can be influenced by geographic regional values and characteristics. Strategy, structure, choice of products, determination of product life cycles and type of technologies employed may be as regionally conditioned as workplace communication, managerial and leadership styles and personnel practices. We argue that these micro and macro management dimensions are related; for example, executives' and organizational members' values, beliefs and perceptions about strategy, market expectations, competition, structure, performance and internal organization determine, in part, the culture, policies and procedures of the firm.

RESEARCH AIMS, DESIGN, METHODS

The aim of this study is to identify and compare top level executives' perceptions and reported beliefs about internal and external organizational practices from a regional perspective. Mature, high technology computer firms that are well established in California's Silicon Valley and Massachusetts' Routes 128/495 were selected from lists provided by the Massachusetts Council on High Technology and the American Electronics

Association. Seasoned executives were sought who were experienced with and could report on the relationships between their respective regional culture and their firm's management.

California and Massachusetts were selected for this study because these regions are the high technology R&D centers of this country. Regionally the two areas are distinctly different historically, culturally and climatically (Garreau, 1981).

This study, which is part of a larger project (Weiss & Delbecq, 1987) is basically exploratory. The novel nature of our inquiry suggested a qualitative design and method. Because our goal was to generate information rather than test assumptions (Van Maanen, Dabbs, & Faulkner, 1982), we used both open-ended questions and asked structured questions in order to elicit information.

The study design is cross-sectional, within a single industry in two geographically separate regions. The data is perceptual and self-reported. Consequently, the conclusions are associational and not causal.

The interview questions asked executives to comment on and compare the following research probes, which are partially based on Rogers and Larsen's (1984) study: workplace formality/informality; risk-taking and entrepreneurship; leadership styles; strategic orientation of firms; managerial workforce characteristics; preferred managerial reward structures; workplace communication and networking. This type of qualitative methodology was successfully used by Gregory (1983). The interviews lasted from one and one-half to two hours. All were tape recorded and transcribed verbatim. Recurring themes were identified by four judges. We then summarized and tabulated these findings into percentages that are reported in another section of the paper.

The interviewers were Dr. Joseph Weiss, Associate Professor of Management at Bentley College in Waltham, Massachusetts, and Dr. Andre Delbecq, Dean at the Leavey Graduate Business School, Santa Clara, California.

Interviewees in the Silicon Valley sample included John Sculley at Apple Computer, Robert Lorenzini and Brad Wait at Siltec Corporation, Irwin Federman at Monolithic Memories, Kenneth Oshman and Gibson Anderson at Rolm, William Terry and William Flaherty at Hewlett-Packard and Robert Fuhrman at Lockheed. Paul Wythes, the general manager of Sutter Hills, a venture capital firm, was included. These executives were in their forties and their average stay with the company was 18 years. Five had either lived or worked on the East Coast. Four attended college in the East. Changes in positions and companies since these interviews were conducted have occurred, as is the case with the New England sample.

Interviewees in the New England sample included Ken Olsen at Digital, John Poduska from Apollo, Joe Hensen at Prime, Jim Berrett who was at

Computervision, Mike Anderson at Nixdorf, Richard Spann and Ross Belson from Adage, Bob Miller who was at Data General, Ben Holmes at Hewlett-Packard, and Ash Dahod from Applitek. Andrew Taylor, a partner at Testa, Hurwitz & Thibeault (a reputable, established Boston legal firm that also deals with venture capital) was included.

RESULTS

The findings indicate significant perceived regional differences between cultures in Silicon Valley and in Massachusetts. These differences were also believed by the majority of executives surveyed to be manifested in the organizational workplace. Table 1 summarizes beliefs and perceptions expressed by the Silicon Valley executives.

Silicon Valley Sample

As can be observed in Table 1, responses indicate strong perceptions that there is greater formality in East in terms of policies, procedures and dress (9 of the 11 questioned supported this query). Eight of the executives believed there is a greater risk-taking attitude in Silicon Valley firms. Eight believed communication in the workplace is less open in the East. Seven believed it is more difficult to be innovative in the East. There were strong perceptions that supported the belief that Silicon Valley is more R&D driven, with an emphasis on entrepreneurship. Seven of the 11 surveyed believed startups are easier in Silicon Valley than in Massachusetts.

Regarding the high technology company work forces, seven of the eleven believed Massachusetts employees are motivated more by rewards that promote stability, namely pensions and longevity with the company. Six believed that there is less labor mobility in the East. Five stated that "firms in the West create jobs for people. The East fills jobs with people." Only one respondent believed there was a difference in the productivity level between coasts.

As can be seen from Table 1, there was disagreement on several items and several respondents expressed no opinion on several items.

New England Sample

Table 2 summarizes responses from the Massachusetts sample. All respondents believed that New Englanders are more formal and conservative in the workplace than are employees in Silicon Valley computer firms. Eight of the eleven believed New Englanders are more family oriented and value stability. Seven believe New Englanders are less flamboyant personally and

Table 1.   Silicon Valley Sample: Executive Responses
to Regional Differences on High-Tech Management:
Route 128 and Silicon Valley
$(N = 10)$

Perceived Differences	Agree		Disagree		No Expressed Opinion	
	No.	%	No.	%	No.	%
Greater workplace formality in the East (Procedures, Policies, Dress)	9	90	—	—	1	10
Greater risk-taking attitude and activity in Silicon Valley	8	80	—	—	2	20
Communication in the workplace is less open in the East	8	80	—	—	2	20
It is more difficult to be innovative in the East	7	70	1	10	2	20
Greater focus on entre-preneurship in the West	8	80	—	—	2	20
Greater orientation on research and develop-ment in the West	9	90	—	—	1	10
The workforce in the East is more interested in stability and pensions	7	70	—	—	3	30
Greater use of stock options as compensation in the West	6	60	1	10	3	30
There is less labor mobility on the East Coast	6	60	—	—	4	40
Firms in the West create jobs for people. The East fills jobs with people	5	50	2	20	3	30
Startups are easier in the West	7	70	—	—	3	30
Productivity of the work-force is different in the East than in the West	1	10	4	40	5	50

Note: Some items do not total 100% due to rounding.

Table 2. Massachusetts Sample: Executive Responses
to Regional Differences on High-Tech Management:
Route 128 and Silicon Valley
$(N = 11)$

Perceived Differences	Agree		Disagree		No Expressed Opinion	
	No.	%	No.	%	No.	%
New Englanders are more formal and conservative in the workplace	11	100	—	—	—	—
Changing jobs and turnover and "burnout" are greater in the West	8	73	—	—	3	27
New Englanders are more family and stability oriented	8	73	—	—	3	27
Long term orientation of strategy and personnel practices in the East	7	64	1	9	3	27
New Englanders are less flamboyant personally and professionally	7	64	—	—	4	36
Greater orientation toward end-users and customer solutions in New England	7	64	1	9	5	45
Startups are easier in the West	6	55	2	18	3	27
Higher cost of living in the West makes relocation of New Englanders difficult	5	45	1	9	5	45
Greater trust in verbal negotiations in the East	4	36	7	64	—	—
Venture capitalists support client firms longer in New England	4	36	3	27	4	27
Networking among CEOs: more formal structured in New England	9	81	2	19	—	—

Note: Some items do not toals 100% due to rounding.

professionally than are their West Coast counterparts. Nine of the eleven
believed networking among CEOs is more structured in New England.

Eight respondents stated that changing jobs, turnover and job burnout are more prevalent among the Silicon Valley high technology workforce than employees in Massachusetts. Five also expressed the belief that Silicon Valley's higher overall cost of living makes relocation of New Englanders there difficult.

Seven respondents of the sample believed there is a greater orientation toward end-users and customer solutions in New England; one disagreed, and three expressed no opinion on this item. Similar to the Silicon Valley independent survey, six in this sample believed startups are easier in the West than in Massachusetts.

Four executives believed venture capitalists support client firms longer in their startup phase in New England than in Silicon Valley. And four stated that there is greater trust in verbal negotiations in the New England than in Silicon Valley. These perceptions were added to the survey by respondents in this sample.

Other Findings

Results from open-ended interviews supported and extended the findings reported above. Themes from the content analysis are summarized in Table 3.

Silicon Valley

Silicon Valley executives characterized high technology management in that region as valuing and rewarding risk-taking activities. Decisions are believed to be based on intuition with individually oriented activities also being highly valued. Mobility and job-hopping are not believed to be punished but are understood by those CEOs who advanced to their positions by moving to more opportune openings. Networking outside the workplace is expected and enjoyed by most managers, according to our interviews. Secrecy was generally seen as suspect, except for certain competitively sensitive information.

The short-term planning and product life cycles in Silicon Valley are seen as both a cause and effect of the highly competitive environment and market driven firms. Also, this region's experience with the success of low-end technological products (the personal computer and video games) has influenced strategic decisions in terms of extreme time compression of getting an idea from the drawing board to the market. Most believed and expressed pride in the fiercely competitive but free spirit that existed in Silicon Valley's computer companies.

The following excerpts from Sculley, Oshman and Terry exemplify major themes summarized above:

Table 3.   Basic Regional Differences Between Firms

Silicon Valley	Route 128/495
Risk taking at almost any cost	Innovation through calculation
Short-term product life and planning cycle	Long-term planning
Nonconsensual decision making; intuition oriented	Group orientation with the brass signing off;
Decentralized	Centralized
Mobility: go for it; share in the pay-off company	Team first,
Job-hopping: part of the game	Loyalty to the corporation
Networking	Networking
Informal	Formal product networking
Market driven	Engineering driven
Cutting edge competition	Technological interdependence

Sculley (Apple): Silicon Valley offers a free form approach. I'd be really surprised if the next great industry emerged from the East Coast. I think it's more likely to come from a place that has no traditions. There are no villages. There are just shopping centers. One day a company is written about in the business news and acclaimed as phenomenal. Six months later it's gone. It doesn't exist. It's not the people who disappeared. It's just that that particular new idea has disappeared. Another new idea will be emerging in another company.

Oshman (Rolm): The genesis of Silicon Valley lies in a business style which is entrepreneurial. Companies in Silicon Valley and their managements are characterized by an open-mindedness regarding the future, a welcoming of change, a belief in trying things to see if they work, experimentation. This is achieved by relying on delegating to people in a decentralized management style, a reluctance to depend on consultants or staffs for important business decisions, and a positive value toward innovative approaches.

Terry (Hewlett Packard): When I think of the West, I think of individuals who are dynamic! Willing to take risks! That's the critical characteristic of Silicon Valley.

Massachusetts

The Massachusetts executives characterized high technology firms very differently from their California counterparts. Innovation through calculation, cost consciousness, long-term planning, group and team approaches were themes that emerged from these interviews.

Six of eleven executives reflected on the history of this area and were aware that this region has passed through several industrial revolutions (textiles, shipbuilding, whaling and machine tool industries). Several attributed the conservative outlook of the workforce to the New England cultural environment and to the climate. Most praised the loyalty of their workforce and their work ethic.

The majority interviewed also believed in the long-term perspective of their missions, which emphasized product networking, an integrated systems approach and establishing interdependence among products. This theme was different technologically and strategically from the Silicon Valley sample.

The following excerpts from Olsen, Poduska and Holms exemplify major themes summarized in this sample:

Olsen (DEC):	Well, one thing is never to admit you're successful because then you're always in danger. My theory is that if you are very bold at risk taking in the business divisions, then you must be cost conscious financially. We've always been careful financially. We like to have money raised before we start projects. We like to have it so that we don't have to worry about hard times and problems, then we're not at risk of losing everything if things don't go the way we planned. This also means that if we don't make the return on equity that we would otherwise, we won't be ridiculed publicly.
Poduska (Apollo):	There is a great sense of community, honor, family, values, town spirit in New England. There is a growing sense of association with Europe in the sense that people find out what their backgrounds and cultures are … There's a sense of permanence in New England.
Holms (Hewlett Packard):	You get a lot less of 'Gee, let's go for it.' You get a lot more of 'Gee, let's study it, do you really want to do that, we've never done it that way,' to the extent that sometimes it's reasonably discouraging.

CONCLUDING COMMENTS

The executives surveyed in Silicon Valley and Massachusetts reported significant regional differences between the cultures inside and external to their high technology management. If CEOs' and top level executives' perceptions and beliefs influence, reflect and/or reinforce strategy, procedure and policy, then the profiles portrayed of high technology management in Silicon Valley and Massachusetts call for further examination.

The New England cultural context suggests a more formal, conservative, stodgy, controlled environment. As productive, effective and efficient as companies in Silicon Valley, Massachusetts firms appear less tolerant of maverick individual decision-making styles. There is less tolerance of job-hopping and mobility across firms, more expectations of company loyalty and dedication from employees. There is strategically a more long-term, systems networking approach. In this cultural context, employees are perceived as expecting security and longer term commitments from their employers.

The Silicon Valley cultural context suggests a more individualistic, entrepreneurially driven culture in which the short-term is the accepted norm for careers and for product planning and life cycles. Loyalty is neither expected nor delivered if individual opportunity exceeds company demands. Monetary rewards and stock options satisfy fast-track managers in computer firms in this region. Start-up firms frequently come and go, as do their employees. The workplace intensity is a reflection of the quickly changing environment, which is market and technology driven.

Managing Regional Values in the Workplace

Our preliminary findings support Kahle's (1986, p. 43) research which reported on social values that are distributed across Bureau of Census regions. Kahle found the following statistically significant value differences between New England and the Pacific regions: New Englanders valued self-respect, being well-respected, security and sense of accomplishment more than did westerners. Westerners valued warm relationships with others, self-fulfillment, and fun-enjoyment-excitement more than New Englanders.

Managing workplace values means managing regional values of employees. Regional value differences surface in the workplace in the way people communicate, organize their time, space and workplace, in the way networking occurs, in motivations, expectations and rewards. Silicon Valley managers may be challenged more to create opportunities for self-fulfillment and excitement; Massachusetts managers may have to create opportunities for employees to feel accomplishment and respect.

Managing Strategy and Structure in Regionally Different Cultures

Our findings also indicate that CEOs in Silicon Valley and Massachusetts who manage computer firms differ in their perceptions of choice and use of structure and strategy. As described in an earlier section of the paper, strategy in Silicon Valley is believed to be more market than engineering driven and has been influenced as much by consumer products as by industrial commercial demands. Silicon Valley executives also believe "less structure is best" and rely on very loosely coupled, individualistic decision-making styles.

Massachusetts executives preferred teams and loyalty in the workplace over maverick oriented entrepreneurship. Strategy and structure in these contexts appear to be related to regional cultural and environmental characteristics. To implement long-term strategies with conservative, stable business customers, Silicon Valley firms may recruit New England CEOs and executives, as did Apple with Sculley. To encourage innovative brainstorming, New England firms may transfer and hire Silicon Valley talent, as did Data General and Hewlett Packard.

Regional Culture, Performance and Productivity

While respondents in our samples perceived little or no differences in productivity and performance between Silicon Valley and Massachusetts firms, the question arises, "If performance is the same in both regions, why is regional culture and environment an issue?" First, it is questionable whether performance is the same. Naroff and Hill (1982) found that high technology companies in the Boston area exceeded counterparts in Silicon Valley in financial performance. These results may be related to regional characteristics; the question is open to study. Secondly, turnover statistics in the computer industry have shown Silicon Valley ranging from 35 to 50 percent and higher (Rogers & Larsen, 1984), while turnover in New England computer firms has been reported between 17 to 25 percent. Executives in both our samples generally believed turnover to be higher in Silicon Valley. These unstable statistics raise the question of whether turnover costs are higher in Silicon Valley. Third, executives in our New England sample generally believed that the human costs of working in Silicon Valley were higher in terms of burnout, fast-paced life styles, lack of community and social support systems. However, executives in our Silicon Valley sample believed that the adventure, risk and possible high return on investment from entrepreneuring was worth the effort given by employees. Human costs associated with work may be as much a product of expectation levels and regional values as of technological and industrial variables. Managing turnover and mobility in Silicon Valley computer firms would seemingly require different managerial values and skills than Massachusetts firms would require.

While this study and the larger project on which it is based have definite limitations, as stated earlier, the goal has been to generate information which argues for a regional perspective of the firm. Organizations are admittedly multicultural—they are products of national, international, corporate and occupational cultural forces. Organizations are also influenced by regional and local cultural and environmental contexts. This is not to say that every firm is influenced in the same way by its regional culture and environment. A regional view does, however, provide a complementary analytic perspective for examining and comparing external influences on industries and companies. Social values serve as a starting point for identifying regional cultural differences. A region's economy, technological resources, climate, markets, labor demographics and industrial history are also reflected in and are part of its culture. This exploratory study identified East and West Coast regional cultural differences through reported executive perceptions and beliefs. Further studies are needed which empirically test differences we have conceptually raised.

Since this study, there have been significant market and industry changes. However, the basic tenets and underlying regional characteristics found in this study remain intact.

REFERENCES

Child, J. (1981). Contingency and capitalism in the cross-national study of organizations. In L.L. Cummings & B.M. Staw (Eds.), *Research in organizational behavior* (Vol. 3, 303-456). Greenwich, CT: JAI Press.

Garreau, Joel. (1981). *The nine nations of North America.* New York: Avon.

Gregory, K.L. (1983). Native-view paradigms: Multiple cultures and culture conflicts in organizations. *Administrative Science Quarterly, 28,* 359-376.

Haire, M., Ghiselli, E. E., & Porter, L.W. (1966). *Managerial thinking: An international study.* New York: Wiley.

Hofstede, J. (1980). *Culture's consequences: International differences in work related values.* Beverly Hills, CA: Sage.

Kahle, Lynn. (1986). The nine nations of North America are the value basis of geographic segmentation. *Journal of Marketing, 50,* 37-47.

Laurent, A. (1983). The cultural diversity of western conceptions of management. *International Studies of Management and Organizations, 13*(1-2), 75-96.

Naroff, J.L., & Hill J. (1982). *The effect of location on the performance of high technology firms.* Paper presented at the Meetings, The Regional Science Association, Pittsburgh, PA.

Rogers, E.M., & Larsen, J.K. (1984). *Silicon Valley fever.* New York: Basic Books.

Schein, E.H. (1984). Coming to a new awareness of organizational culture. *Sloan Management Review, 25*(2), 3-16.

_____ (1985). *Organizational culture and leadership: A dynamic view.* San Francisco, CA: Jossey-Bass.

Triandis, H.D. et al. (1972). *The analysis of subjective culture.* New York: Wiley-Interscience.

Van Maanen, J., Dabbs, J.M., & Faulkner, R.R. (1982). *Varieties of qualitative research.* Newbury Park, CA: Sage.

Weiss, J. (1988). *Regional culture, managerial behavior, and entrepreneurship: An international perspective.* Westport, CT: Greenwood Press.

Weiss, J., & Delbecq, A. (1986). High technology cultures and management: Silicon Valley and route 128. *Group & Organization Studies, 12*(1), 39-54.

PART II

GLOBAL SETTINGS FOR HIGH TECHNOLOGY COMPETITION

PATTERNS OF COOPERATIVE COMPETITION IN GLOBAL TECHNOLOGY INDUSTRIES

Srinivasan Balakrishnan and Mitchell P. Koza

No well reasoned analysis of high technology business would be complete without an assessment of the impact of globalization on business policy. Today, such diverse industries as semiconductors, automobiles, aircraft, copiers, robotics, machine tools, foundry products, telecommunications and financial services are global. Globalization of business is so widespread that Levitt (1984) argues that it is the most salient feature of modern business.

Consider the value chain of AT&T's personal computers. The design and development stage of AT&T's PC6300 is located in the United States. The Central Processing Unit (Intel 8088) is also made in the United States. The RAM chips are sourced in several countries, including Japan, Malaysia and Mexico, while the disk drives are imported from Singapore. The final assembly is carried out under a joint venture with Olivetti in Italy. Finally, the AT&T monitors are made in Japan. The PC6300 is marketed on a worldwide basis; it is a product of a global industry.

Also, consider the telecommunications business. In the early part of the twentieth century, before the Communications Act of 1934, the competitors of The Bell System were all U.S. companies. Almost all of The Bell System's revenues were from the U.S. market. The operations of The Bell System's manufacturing subsidiary, Western Electric, were entirely domestic. However, today, following the 1982 breakup of the old Bell System, AT&T

expects to receive 20-30 percent of its revenues from foreign markets and has several international strategic alliances, many with its competitors. Today, telecommunications is a global industry.

What are the distinctive characteristics of global technology industries? What are the sources of competitive advantage? What are the organizational forms likely to predominate as additional industries globalize? These questions raise fundamental issues in both business policy and industrial organization.

Several frameworks have been developed to analyze issues related to globalization. Bartlett and Ghoshal (1987), analyzing the movement to the "transnational" company, propose that globalization requires firms to employ multi-dimensional strategies that integrate the criteria of efficiency, responsiveness and ability to exploit learning. Prahalad and Doz (1987) examine the tensions for firms needing to balance the potentially conflicting demands produced by the local and global environment. However, an important issue that requires further research is the strategies of firms competing in global industries.

In this paper, we examine the characteristics of global industries, paying close attention to the implications for competitive strategy and industrial organization. We argue that the important strategic imperative in these industries is global sourcing of capital, technology and labor. We further argue that the firms in global industries prefer strategic alliances, such as joint ventures, partial ownership, licensing and syndicates for accessing capital, technology and labor inputs. The preference for such strategies derives from imperfections in the input markets and the need for responsiveness to local government and private interests in controlling the operations of the global firm. As a consequence of global sourcing and strategic alliances, multinationals increasingly look like supranationals, with the nationalities of these corporations losing their meaning.

THE STRUCTURE OF GLOBAL COMPETITION

International trade itself is not a new phenomenon. Rather, it is as ancient as the flourishing trade between the Sumerian city of Ur and the Indus valley city of Harappa in 2000 B.C. However, the evolution of the modern day multinational corporation occurred almost entirely during the twentieth century (Stopford & Wells, 1972; Wilkins, 1974; Williamson, 1981).

Wilkins and others contend that the multinational is primarily an American phenomenon, at least until the 1960s. Several factors contributed to the domination of the global business environment by the American multinationals. The most important factors that led to U.S firms' supremacy were:

1. World War II and the "industricide" in Europe and Japan;
2. the size and the integrity of the American markets;
3. the pressure for mechanization because of a relatively smaller American labor force; and
4. a series of organizational and managerial innovations in American business (Chandler, 1977; Servan-Schriber, 1968).

The international component of American business during this period is classified mainly into three types of operations: domestic production for off-shore markets, off-shore sourcing of raw materials for domestic production, and off-shore production for off-shore marketing. The literature on foreign direct investment and multinational corporations (MNCs) referred primarily to the last two types of operations.

Typically, overseas operations were organized as wholly owned subsidiaries or divisions. The overseas subsidiaries usually were monitored by a skeletal division at the headquarters, mostly on the basis of the bottom line performance of the subsidiaries. The international operations were conducted independently; synergies among the businesses were seldom exploited. The technologies involved were either simple, as in the case of raw material sourcing operations, or were well developed and mature (Vernon, 1966). Bargaining power favored the U.S. firms, with Europe and Japan attempting to catch-up after World War II.

The structural characteristics of today's global industries differ from the structural characteristics of industries in which the American multinational (or multidomestic as Hout, Porter, & Rudden [1980] call it) form was predominant. Unlike the extractive or mature industries of the multinational era, the global industries are often characterized by technologically intensive products and emerging technologies. Rapid and unpredictable technological changes, coupled with ballooning R&D costs and uncertain demand, make these industries high stakes games. Strategic problems are often compounded by experience effects, switching and other buyer related costs that require a firm to be the early entrant in such industries. Not surprisingly, the emerging industries often experience high levels of entry and exit. Most firms entering such high stakes, high risk industries must adopt a global market perspective.

Mature industries also are affected by rapid technological progress. Innovations in process technologies have resulted in increasing scale economies in many industries. Globalization of markets is also helped by increasing standardization and homogeneity of products, particularly technologically intensive products. Cultural and national differences have little influence on the demand for such products.

At a more macro level, the global industrial environment also sustained several recent changes. The completion of the post war reconstruction of the Japanese and Western European economies facilitated the achievement of a parity of firms from these countries and their American competitors. Research and development and the capacity for technological innovation is no longer vested only in the United States. The diffusion of technology and manufacturing skills has extended beyond Japan and Western Europe. Many newly industrialized countries like Brazil, India, Mexico, South Korea and Taiwan compete successfully for a significant share of gross world product. Besides the global diffusion of technology, progress in transportation and communication technologies has also helped to achieve more efficient coordination of the flow of goods and services, thereby facilitating global integration of manufacturing operations.

With the diminished "need for protectionism" in many countries, barriers to trade and capital movements have been significantly lowered in recent years. At both the Kennedy Round and the Tokyo Round of the GATT (General Agreement on Trade and Tariffs), the United States was successful in persuading other (developed) nations to liberalize imports and move toward free trade. Following the "Nixon Shock" in 1971 and the international monetary crisis of February, 1973, an agreement was reached to do away with the fixed exchange rate regime. This marked the beginning of the floating exchange rate regime and with it an increased volatility of the currency markets. The importance of the dollar as the currency of world trade has also diminished since then. With better communication systems, the efficiency of the international capital markets also seems to have improved considerably in recent years.

Finally, although protectionist policies and frequent intervention in the currency markets gave way to freer trade, governments' role in business has not become one of disinterested observer. The energy crisis and the consequent balance of payment problems led the governments of many countries to actively promote the global competitiveness of their respective industries, with carefully formulated industrial policies. Therefore, it is debatable whether government intervention in the markets has increased or decreased.

It may be useful to differentiate between regulatory and facilitatory intervention. We include in regulation, tariff and nontariff barriers to trade and restrictions on repatriation of capital. Facilitation includes such examples as MITI's industrial policy and the coordinated intervention in the currency market by the United States, Japan and West Germany, to accomplish what was, in effect, a devaluation of the dollar. In recent years, governments have played the facilitator role, promoting the global competitiveness of its industries.

Thus, the global competitive environment is characterized by several unique features.

1. *The shift in the composition of world trade toward more technologically intensive products.* Semiconductors, very large scale

integration (VLSI), satellites, computers, robotics and biotechnology are only some of the industries currently global in scale.

2.   *The increasing scale economies in R&D and manufacturing.* Today, for example, the minimum efficient scale of an auto plant is over a million vehicles produced annually, dramatically up from just a short decade ago.

3.   *The global diffusion of technology and manufacturing skills.* Several developing countries including, but not limited to, Taiwan, South Korea and Mexico, now possess the technological infrastructure and labor force necessary to appeal to global firms.

4.   *Less friction in the transborder movement of goods and services.* Deregulation by national governments, reductions in import quotas and standardization of production make global industries increasingly competitive. Indeed, the unification of Europe in 1992 will be a watershed for issues related to globalization.

5.   *The increasing role of governments in promoting national champions.* The role of MITI in promoting Japanese firms' involvement in the semiconductor industry is only the most well known example of the value for domestic firms of a nationally coherent industrial policy.

STRATEGIC IMPERATIVES IN GLOBAL INDUSTRIES

Perhaps the single most important aspect of today's global industries is that competing firms will have to view the world as a single market (Levitt, 1984). The necessity for such a global perspective derives from three strategic imperatives that confront firms competing in global industries.

The first strategic imperative in global industries is the need for *global sourcing of manufacturing and marketing inputs.* Worldwide diffusion of technology and manufacturing skills, and progress in transportation and communication technologies allow several alternative ways of configuring the components of the value added chain. Cost-quality based competition implies that firms will have to adopt the most efficient configuration. Often the most efficient configuration means a complex network of operational facilities located in different countries. For many products, technology is also sourced on a worldwide basis.

The global sourcing imperative is not restricted to manufacturing labor. Overseas R&D is often a requirement for developing new products and processes most efficiently. Licensing agreements often include grant-back provisions, which give licensors rights over the results of R&D at the overseas licensee's facilities. Such grant-back provisions signal the licensors' expectation of preemptive innovation by the licensees.

Sourcing of capital is also being done on a global scale. For example, 80% of 50 of the world's largest firms' stocks are listed and traded in at least two stock exchanges located in different countries (*Euromoney*, 1984). The Eurobond market has remained a significant source of debt financing for more than a decade. As long as the international financial markets are not perfectly integrated, gains from global sourcing of capital cannot be ruled out.

The second strategic imperative in global industries derives from the need for efficient global sourcing of labor, technology and capital. The national constituencies that are characteristic of global industries produce *tension for firms seeking to meet both local and global demands* (Prahalad & Doz, 1987). Governments are interested in increasing the value added in their respective countries. The industrial policies of the governments aimed at improving the competitiveness of their targeted industries are designed to achieve this national goal. Firms, on the other hand, must develop strategies that can successfully negotiate between these sovereign interests of governments and the interests of the rest of their globally dispersed stakeholders.

Modern business history is filled with examples of local governments seeking to keep a factory open in order to preserve and promote employment, while the global interests of business may dictate plant closing. On the positive side, the local government may also encourage multinational investment through tax reliefs, subsidized loans and grants. These arrangements may be designed to accomplish several aims of the government such as regional development, technology transfer and stimulating competition in the local industry. The global firm, however, will have to examine such proposals carefully for the proposal's impact on the firm's global strategic position. What may be locally attractive may not be as attractive when the global consequences are taken into account.

The third strategic imperative derives from the *increased volume and scale economies in R&D and manufacturing*. Increasing sales volume may enable a firm to move down the learning curve faster and gain cost advantages. With the lowering of trade barriers, a firm that restricts its operations to the domestic market, therefore, is vulnerable to competition from firms with a wider market base. Penetration of foreign markets is necessary, to realize scale and volume economies. This is particularly true of firms from smaller countries where the domestic market is thin. Nevertheless, with the intensified competition from foreign firms in the U.S. market, U.S. firms must also extend their operations beyond their domestic market to sustain their volume based cost advantages. Share wars will be over global and not domestic market shares. Global market shares become critical when products are standardized, buyers are better informed and fairly homogeneous and when competition is on the basis of quality-adjusted cost.

How is strategy to be understood in an environment with these three imperatives? The competition in these industries is based primarily on quality-adjusted costs that produce the imperative for efficient global sourcing and organization of the value added chain of each competing firm. The multiple national constituencies, on the other hand, have local economic and strategic interests. The firms competing in global industries are adopting a variety of organizational strategies designed to manage the dual demands of global strategy and national responsiveness.

ORGANIZATIONAL FORMS FOR GLOBAL INDUSTRIES

Williamson (1975) identifies two primary mechanisms for organizing economic transactions: markets and hierarchies. Both of these forms of industrial organization have received a great deal of attention (Chandler & Daems, 1980; Ouchi, 1980; Rugman, 1980; Teece, 1982).

Surprisingly little attention, however, has been paid to the intermediate forms of industrial organization. Intermediate forms of industrial organization are particularly interesting because few industries are organized into either a pure market or hierarchy. Firms routinely enter into joint ventures with suppliers, negotiate with governments continuing access to markets and develop agreements producing stable distribution networks. These intermediate forms are strategic alliances, which are the sine qua non of modern industrial organization. They are a necessary means of linking actors within a global industry. Strategic alliances are valuable because they provide some of the stability of hierarchical modes of organization and some of the efficiencies of the market-place, but, significantly, without many of the costs entailed in either market or ownership strategies.

We identify three generic strategies for attaining strategic alliances: contracts, joint ventures and multinational ownership.

1. *Contracts* are agreements into which two or more parties enter entailing mutual rights and obligations. Contracts may embody extensive legal documentation. Typically, contracts are negotiated at arms length, are limited in scope and pertain to a single transaction, such as those between suppliers and firms. However, contractual agreements between two parties may entail substantial constraints on a firm's operating position.

2. *Joint ventures* are business activities in which two or more parties agree to start up a new company. Parties to a joint venture agree to share equity involved in the new venture and equitably allocate rewards of the venture. The firm in which the joint venture is vested is a separate entity from the parent companies, with its own administrative organization, accounting system, and the like. Typically, parties to a joint venture will each assume seats on the joint venture's board of directors and share control

of the joint venture. A joint venture has the advantage of allowing a firm to diversify into a new line of business without engaging in a potentially costly acquisition (Balakrishnan & Koza, 1988a; 1988b).

3. *Multinational ownership* is the most recent of the organizational forms. Multinational ownership is a strategy in which a firm diversifies its stock offering across several nations. Multinational ownership has the advantage of allowing the firm to arbitrage in the imperfectly integrated global equity markets. At the same time, the salience of domestic and local demands on the firm are reduced. While the available data indicate that a significant portion of debt financing is done through the Eurobond market, systematic collection of information on multinational stock listing and trading, and the global distribution of equity began only recently.

Strategic alliances occur as a variety of legal arrangements. Leasing, long-term contracts, licensing agreements, buy-back arrangements and partial ownership are some of the strategic alliance forms currently favored by global industry firms. Additionally, strategic alliances may combine several of the these legal arrangements in a hybrid organizational form (Powell, 1987). While some parties to the alliance may be linked by long term contract, other parties to the alliance may be linked through a license or joint venture. Indeed, strategic alliances with multiple partners are currently appearing in several industries, including computers, microsoftware and financial services.

Table 1 compares the incidence of several forms of strategic alliances among the 50 largest global companies. In 1974, the 50 firms reported just 19 international joint ventures, gave 15 licenses, received 9 licenses, participated in 32 joint development efforts and held 1380 overseas subsidiaries. However, by 1984 the 50 largest global companies reported 29 international joint ventures, gave 68 licenses, received 31 licenses, participated in 90 joint development efforts and held 1832 overseas subsidiaries. Of course, these figures only represent the number of these activities formally entered into and reported to the trade and popular press. However, it is safe to infer from the data that global firms are actively pursuing strategic alliances and that these strategies are likely to increase as additional industries globalize.

Table 2 summarizes the results of an analysis of the number of international stock exchanges on which the 35 largest publicly held global firms in 1984 were either listed or traded in 1974 and 1984. In 1974, the average number of international stock exchanges on which the 35 world's largest firms' stocks were traded, but not listed, is only .14. However, by 1984 the 35 firms were pursuing unlisted trading on .57 international exchanges, with one firm trading on 12 international exchanges. When the pattern of listed trading is examined the results are more dramatic. In 1974 the average

Table 1.   Patterns of Cooperative Competition Among the
50 Largest Global Firms in 1984

	1974	1984	Increase (%)
International Joint Ventures	19	29	53
Licenses Given	15	68	353
Licenses Received	9	31	244
Joint Development	32	90	181
Overseas Subsidiaries	1380	1832	33

Source: F&S Annual Indices (1974, 1984).

Table 2.   Patterns of Equity Trading in Foreign Markets

No. of Stock Exchanges Range	Number of Firms			
	Listed 1974	Trading 1984	Unlisted 1974	Trading 1984
0	10	6	33	29
1-3	14	9	1	4
4-6	3	3	1	1
7-9	7	13	0	0
10-12	1	4	0	1
Total	35	35	35	35
Maximum	12	12	4	12
Minimum	0	0	0	0
Mean	3.06	4.96	0.14	0.57

Sources: Moody's Manuals (1974, 1984).

number of international exchanges that the 35 firms were listed and traded on was 3. However, by 1984, the number of international exchanges jumped to almost 5. Indeed, by 1984, 20 of the 35 firms were listed and traded on at least 4 international stock exchanges. Although multinational ownership strategies are relative newcomers to the global scene, the flurry of new issues listed in several exchanges around the world, indicates their increasing importance.

Strategic alliances are uniquely adapted to the strategic imperatives in global industries. In global industries information on buyers and sellers is often scarce and unreliable. The infrastructure for efficient transactions— organized markets, laws governing contractual rights and obligations, arbitrage and dispute settlement procedures—is not extensive, introducing a variety of transaction costs. Global sourcing is a recent phenomenon. Consequently, the rules of the game are still unclear. The need for rules is so apparent that "strategic alliance" are now the latest buzz words in global business. In forming strategic alliances, the intermediate organizational forms seem to offer the needed flexibility. Flexibility is required in global industries for providing a firm with the ability to exploit current opportunities while preserving its responsiveness to new information on the alliance partners and unanticipated changes in market conditions and government policies.

THE EMERGENCE OF THE
SUPRANATIONAL ENTERPRISE

The complex network of joint-ventures, licensing and other contractual relationships among the buyers, suppliers and competitors in global industries has led to the emergence of a new form of organization, the supranational enterprise (SNE). With capital, revenues and profits generated through several strategic alliances with firms from countries other than its home country, the SNE's country of incorporation has little significance. Strategic decisions in SNEs are made through negotiations and bargaining with its joint venture and licensing partners. Control over its operations is diffused through the network of international relationships. With multinational listing and trading of its stock, the ownership of the SNE's assets is global.

The SNE is a response to the new challenges of global industries. Competitive pressures require a global strategy aimed at minimizing quality-adjusted cost. The SNE accomplishes this through an efficient value chain configuration that takes advantage of the imperfections in the input markets. Simultaneously, the SNE preserves the flexibility to respond to necessary changes in the value chain configuration by pursuing strategic alliances with other SNEs and national firms. Its network of joint ventures and licensing agreements, and distributed ownership facilitate effective management of the tensions created by multiple national constituencies.

The sociopolitical implications of the SNE could be far reaching. National governments may find their flexibility reduced because of a decreasing ability to regulate the operations of their constituent firms. As additional industries globalize, government regulatory effectiveness in these industries may also decline. Additionally, the emergence of supranationals may require substantial revisions in antitrust policy. Currently, antitrust theory is based on the expected anticompetitive implications of cooperation among firms. However, cooperation may be the only way firms may participate in global industries. Governments will have to balance the anti-competitive implications of cooperation among firms against the possible efficiencies of these arrangements. Finally, SNEs may have a profound influence on labor. American and Western European labor may find its bargaining position with management compromised, and its standard of living reduced, because firms may employ foreign labor. While the social and political implications of SNEs are difficult to predict, it is safe to say that these implications will be a watershed for social and economic policy.

CONCLUSION

In sum, global industries produce distinctive strategic imperatives for firms. These strategic imperatives include need for global sourcing of capital, technology and labor. We argued that the firms in global industries would prefer strategic alliances such as joint ventures, partial ownership, licensing and syndicates. These organizational forms are uniquely adapted for firms wishing to access internationally dispersed capital, labor and technology inputs. The preference for such strategies derive from the imperfections in the input markets and the need for responsiveness to local government interests. As a consequence of global sourcing and strategic alliances, multinational firms increasingly look like supranational firms. The nationalities of supranational firms may be losing their significance.

ACKNOWLEDGMENTS

Conversations with several individuals were helpful in developing the ideas presented in this paper, including Jose de la Torre, Bill Ouchi, and Dick Rumelt. Financial support for this research was provided by the United States-Japan Friendship Commission and the UCLA Pacific Basin Study Center.

REFERENCES

Balakrishnan, S., & Koza, M.P. (1988a). *Information asymmetry, market failure, and joint ventures: Theory and evidence* (Working paper). Curtis L. Carlson School of Management, University of Minnesota, and INSEAD, Fontainebleau, France.

———— (1988b). *Organizational costs and a theory of joint ventures* (Working paper). Curtis L. Carlson School of Management, University of Minnesota, and INSEAD, Fontainebleau, France.

Bartlett, C. A., & Ghoshal, S. (1987). Managing across borders: New strategic requirements. *Sloan Management Review, 28*(4), 7-17.

Chandler, A.D. (1977). *The visible hand: The managerial revolution in American business.* Cambridge, MA.: Belknap Press.

Chandler A.D., & Daems, H. (Eds.). (1980). *Managerial hierarchies.* Cambridge, MA: Harvard University Press.

Euromoney. (1984, June). London: Euromoney Publications.

Hout, T., Porter, M.E., and Rudden, E. (1982, September-October). How global companies win out. *Harvard Business Review,* 98-108.

Levitt, T. (1984). *The marketing imagination.* New York: The Free Press.

Moody's Industrial Manual. (1984). New York: Moody's Investors Service.

Moody's Transportation Manual. (1984). New York: Moody's Investors Service.
Moody's Public Utility Manual. (1984). New York: Moody's Investors Service.
Moody's International Manual. (1984). New York: Moody's Investors Service.
Ouchi, W. (1980). Markets, hierarchies and clans. *Administrative Science Quarterly, 25,* 129-141.
Powell, W.W. (1987). *Hybrid organizational arrangements: New form or transitional development?* (Working paper). Stanford, CA: Center for Advanced Study in the Behavioral Sciences, Stanford University.
Prahalad, C.K., & Doz, Y.L. (1987). *The multinational mission: Balancing local demands and global vision.* New York: The Free Press.
Predicasts F&S Index United States. (1974). Cleveland: Predicasts.
Predicasts F&S Index United States. (1984). Cleveland: Predicasts.
Predicasts F&S Index International Annual. (1974). Cleveland: Predicasts.
Predicasts F&S Index International Annual. (1984). Cleveland: Predicasts.
Rugman, A.M. (1980). Internationalization as a general theory of foreign direct investment: A re-appraisal of the literature. *Weltwirtschaftliches Archiv, 16,* 365-379.
Servan-Schriber, J.J. (1968). *The American challenge.* New York: Atheneum.
Stopford, J.M., & Wells, L.T. Jr. (1972). *Managing the multinational enterprise: Organization of the firm and ownership of subsidiaries.* New York: Basic Books.
Teece, D.J. (1982). *A transaction cost theory of the multinational enterprise* (Working paper No.65). University of Reading, Reading, England.
Vernon, R. (1966). International investment and international trade in the product cycle. *The Quarterly Journal of Economics, 53,* 190-207.
Wilkins, M. (1974). *The maturing of the multinational enterprise: American business abroad from 1914 to 1970.* Cambridge, MA: Harvard University Press.
Williamson, O.E. (1975). *Markets and hierarchies.* New York: The Free Press.
————— (1981). The modern corporation: Origins, evolution and attributes. *Journal of Economic Literature, 19,* 1537-1568.

PERSPECTIVES ON INTERFIRM, GLOBAL AND INSTITUTIONAL STRATEGY:
INTERNATIONAL COMPETITION IN HIGH TECHNOLOGY

Gerardo Rivera Ungson

During 1981-1982, Japanese semiconductor firms hoisted a competitive challenge to their U.S. competitors: they introduced enormous quantities of the 64k RAM at sharply reduced prices. When the prevailing market price for the device was $25-$30, Fujitsu offered $15. Still reeling from the effects of the recession, U.S. firms tried to fight back with lower prices, but to no avail. By the end of 1981, prices had dropped to $7.75, with several Japanese firms quoting prices as low as $5.00. In time, Japanese firms were able to garner almost 70 percent of the U.S. market, heralding their emergence as viable global competitors in VLSI (Very Large Scale Integration) devices. The Japanese were able to mount such a competitive onslaught by capitalizing on the advantages derived from supportive government policies, national procurement policies within their industrial groups, favorable tax policies and a highly trained and motivated work force—institutional advantages that were not as extensively shared by their U.S. competitors (The Semiconductor Industry Association, 1983).

The opening vignette suggests that competitive strategies of firms are not determined by market and technological factors alone, but by incentives or disincentives provided by the institutions under which these firms operate. In this chapter, we develop two arguments. The first is that competitive strategies of multinational firms often reveal comparative advantages that arise from institutional settings within which they compete, but that the importance and consequences of these linkages have not been fully specified. A second argument is that extant representations of corporate strategy, whether expressed in terms of interfirm or global rivalry, might not be adequate for capturing the specific linkages between strategy and institutions.

The particular setting in which we illustrate these arguments is the international rivalry between Japanese, U.S., and European firms in semiconductors. Competition in this industry is replete with trade controversies, protracted debates on protectionist policies and outright investigations of alleged thefts and illegal incursions into proprietary products and materials. On the surface, Japanese strategies aimed at achieving market dominance are not altogether different from what has occurred in other industries such as steel, consumer electronics, automobiles, motorcycles, and others (Borrus, Millstein, & Zysman, 1983). What disturbs corporate officers and governmental officials, however, is that a similar pattern appears to be occurring in semiconductors—an industry that is considered to set the pace and extent of future development in informational technology.

Even so, present controversies obscure a critical point: the fact that Japanese success in their industrial policies and corporate strategies extends across different industries, and not any particular industry, suggests the presence of enduring institutions that create competitive advantages for Japanese firms in international competition. In this sense, competition between Japan, the United States and the European Economic Community (EEC) can be considered to be as much an issue about supportive institutions as it is about appropriate corporate strategy.

This chapter is organized in five parts. The first describes the nature of competition in high technology, and how high technology industries are different from traditional capital-intensive industries. The second part discusses the pattern of international rivalry in high technology, with an emphasis on how Japanese firms have been able to change, if not dictate, the competitive rules within the semiconductor industry. The third part documents some of the responses made by U.S. firms and evaluates the relative success of these responses. The fourth examines the adequacy and capacity of extant theories of strategy in explaining the lack of success of U.S. responses. The fifth part discusses the relationship between institutions and strategy, and presents implications for the study of strategic management.

DEFINING HIGH TECHNOLOGY

Defining high technology has been a bit problematic because the term has been broadly used to describe technologically-related and emerging industries. For example, industries such as steel and ice-making were as much high technology industries at the turn of the century when new technological processes for producing these products were being introduced. Even so, we argue that there are particular characteristics of industries that we term as "high technology" that differentiate them from traditional capital-intensive industries (i.e., steel, metal, automobiles), or from the simple introduction of new technological processes (i.e., steel, ice-making at the turn of the century).

High technology industries are primarily driven by changes in technology that permeate all facets of the organization (Porter, 1980; Riggs, 1983). At the time of their inception, the transistor and the integrated circuit literally rendered existing technologies obsolete, and, in so doing, radically changed the bases of competition in the industries in which these products were used (Riggs, 1983). While capital-intensive industries face similar challenges in introducing new technologies into their products, changes are nearly not as extensive nor as revolutionary as they are in high technology.

High technology industries are also distinguished from other industries in terms of growth rates, technological diffuseness and internal structures (Ungson, 1988). Technologically-driven industries, such as semiconductors, computers, electronic connectors, electronic measurement and instrumentation, telecommunications and consumer electronics, constitute the fastest-growing industries in the United States for the period 1971-1987. The semiconductor industry is the fastest growing sector with a compounded annual growth rate of 33% over this period. Despite some glitches in demand, the year's forecast for many of these products remains good; the editors of *Electronics* (January 7, 1988) project data processing to grow by 28%, software by 21%, communications by 9%, instrumentation by 9%, CAD/CAE by 29%, and semiconductors by 19%.

Moreover, high technology firms generally offer products and services that have very short product life cycles. The period of time between innovation and product delivery is relatively short, three to five years, with two years being not at all uncommon (such as in emerging computer-aided design, i.e., CAD work stations) and seven years being extremely long (such as administrative applications software). In contrast, the product life cycle of dishwashers and steels extend from 12 to 15 years (Kotler, 1985).

Relatedly, product innovations in high technology create new markets when placed into commercial applications. Dubbed the "crude oil of the 1990s," semiconductors have, in turn, created new applications for products and markets that have led to very rapid growth in computers, connectors, instruments, agricultural machinery, electronic banking, satellite-based communications, consumer electronics and consumer products. As further miniaturization of microelectronic circuits occurs, new markets and applications are likely to develop. In this context, the pervasiveness of high technology products distinguishes them from other consumer and industrial products.

High technology industries are also different from traditional industries in that they employ a large number of scientific personnel (Shanklin & Ryans, 1984). This results in more intensive and varied demands for technical proficiency than one would see in traditional industries. And because of their rapid growth, high technology firms are characterized in terms of fast-track, entrepreneurial cultures. People work long hours and tend to be younger and more ambitious compared to their counterparts in traditional industries.

PATTERNS OF COMPETITION BETWEEN JAPAN AND THE UNITED STATES IN HIGH TECHNOLOGY

Historically, U.S., Japanese and European high technology firms have competed in distinctively different ways that have led to the pattern of their strengths and vulnerabilities. Since the discovery of the transistor in 1948, the United States has been regarded the technological leader and the economic power in high technology. U.S. firms, notably Intel and Texas Instruments, pioneered the technological breakthroughs in both the product and process designs of integrated circuits—a process that was facilitated in part by early Pentagon funding (Reid, 1984; Okimoto, Sugano & Weinstein, 1984). Technological innovation was enhanced by the structure of a "Silicon Valley," which combined the synergistic benefits of abundant venture capital, a cluster of high technology firms, and close university-firm linkages. Even to this day, a "Silicon Valley" has not been as successfully duplicated in Japan and Western Europe, although there is no lack of effort by the Japanese in this endeavor (Tatsuno, 1986). The creation of new products and services, such as peripherals, components, data communications, and others, resulting from these innovations was easily accommodated by a large and relatively affluent domestic market. Therefore, huge domestic demand paved the way for even more innovations.

Because U.S. trade policymakers believe that markets should allocate resources efficiently according to the rules of the world trading system, the

United States has been a relatively open market for both Japanese and European semiconductor products, although European manufacturers have not been as much of a threat to U.S. firms as the Japanese (Finan & LaMond, 1985). The ability of U.S. semiconductor firms to maintain their technological and economic leadership is presently being tested by Japanese firms. Historically, Japanese firms had relied on both U.S. and European firms for licensing new products, a practice that earned them a reputation of being "free riders" in the market. However, the Japanese have used their strengths in low cost manufacturing to successfully overcome their weaknesses in product innovation, while exploiting both the financial resources of U.S. firms and the U.S. trade policy of keeping the U.S. market open to foreign competition (Borrus, 1988).

Until very recently, Japanese firms have been able to sustain a presence in the world market by offering lower priced products. At present, the Japanese have leveraged their strategic position by becoming leading manufacturers in the lucrative semiconductor memory market and aggressive competitors in more complex products, that is, microprocessors and standard logic circuits. Their ability to do this stems not only from their traditional strength as low cost manufacturers, but also from the incentives and financial support derived from supportive government-business relationships and other institutions (Abegglen & Stalk, 1986; Borrus, 1988; Johnson, 1985).

The context in which the supportive relationship between government and business firms in Japan facilitates competitive strategies has been well-documented (Borrus, 1988), and has become a contentious issue in U.S.-Japan trade relations. Generally, Japanese firms, particularly those that are "targeted" by Japanese ministries such as MITI, enjoy such benefits as financial assistance, generous tax breaks, favorable loan terms, research and development support, export aid and access to technical and market information (Borrus, Millstein, & Zysman, 1983; The Semiconductor Industry Association, 1983).

Through various "targeting" methods, generally known as "administrative guidance," the Japanese place strategic emphasis on key industries, which leads to a more coherent strategy for promoting exports. Unlike U.S. trade policymakers, who construe the world market as subject to policies that promote efficiency in resource allocation, Japanese lawmakers regard their market in terms of a "development state," and have restricted the entry of foreign competitors accordingly.

The competitiveness of European firms cannot be addressed without considering the problems caused by the fragmentation of the Community market and the consequences of not being able to develop a truly European common market. Historically, European nations in the EEC have not as extensively cooperated in matters that would have enhanced their strategic positions. Europeans have provided more Nobel prize winners in information technology than the rest of the world put together (English, 1985). In addition, they have pioneered many significant products such as the videotape recorder (now dominated by the Japanese), the digital audio tape, and, by some accounts, even the personal computer. Yet, the Europeans have failed in the commercialization of these products, areas in which the United States and Japan have excelled.

Some of the underlying reasons would be sheer managerial conservatism and strategic myopia (Mackintosh, 1986), although Europeans have always had to deal with the vagaries of a divided community—fragmented standards, parochialism in the selection of vendors, undue promotion of "national champions," and so forth. For example, Phillips has to supply over 100 different types of television sets to meet the different European standards; Germany and the United Kingdom have adopted slightly different forms of PAL and France SECAM; a stereo television broadcast has yet to be established (English, 1985).

These are serious competitive disadvantages when competing against the Japanese or the United States. Fragmentation impedes European industries, notably high technology, from capturing the kind of industrial economies of scale enjoyed and exploited by their trading partners, the United States and Japan, with their huge domestic markets. This disadvantage is particularly evident in consumer electronics, where economies of scale are essential to recover huge investment costs. By failing to capitalize on economies of scale, European firms have not been able to exploit the pricing mechanism to trigger large volume turnover. Jeelof (1988) estimates that the EEC loses at least $250 billion a year as a result of market barriers that impede productivity and competitiveness.

ELEMENTS OF RIVALRY BETWEEN JAPANESE AND U.S. SEMICONDUCTOR FIRMS

The pattern of international competition in semiconductors can be distinguished in time as comprising two phases: prior to 1977, when the U.S. firms dictated the bases of competition, and post-1977, when such bases were changed by the nature of Japanese entry-strategies. Since U.S. and Japanese firms are the key actors here, our discussion will focus on rivalry between them during these periods. The European case is deferred until the last section of this chapter.

Basis of Rivalry, Prior to 1977

Finan and LaMold (1985, p. 164) argue that prior to 1977, competitive success in semiconductors was based on four factors: consumer acceptance of product design, availability of second-source suppliers, aggressive pricing and credible delivery acceptance. The structure of the semiconductor industry could be described as a continued series of product offerings with relatively short life cycles. At the early stage of each successive product offering, competition focused on product development as several firms would compete to have their product design accepted as the industry standard. Mostek's design of the 16k dRAM is one example of a clear favorite. Once a favorite was selected, other firms would typically enter the race as second-source producers, and compete on the basis of price, marketing and distribution, quality and reliability (Finan & LaMold, 1985).

Basis of Rivalry, After 1977

The Japanese entry into the 64k dRAM market in the late 1970s to the early 1980s changed the competitive rules in the industry. Since the complete picture of the Japanese assault on the dRAM market has been extensively reviewed in other published sources (Borrus, Millstein, & Zysman, 1983; Okimoto, Sugano, & Weinstein, 1984; The Semiconductor Industry Association, 1983), we simply present the fundamentals of the competition here. Briefly, Japanese firms utilized their strengths in low-cost manufacturers of the product to aggressively attack the U.S. market and exploit the financial constraints experienced by U.S. firms during recessionary periods. Our opening vignette highlighted competition between Japanese and U.S. firms in the case of 64k dRAM market. The success of the Japanese is even more significant when one considers that they successfully employed the same strategy in attacking the 256k dRAM and the 1 MEGA-RAM markets that they presently dominate (McClean, 1986).

The Japanese entry strategy was based on a build-up of memory production capacity, which was ensured, in no large part, by government measures aimed at protecting the domestic market. Part of the strategy has also been explained by the financial structure of the Japanese firm. Since Japanese firms tend to carry large fixed costs owing to high interest rates and fixed wages, they are compelled to price at a level to cover their high fixed costs, even if such prices are disproportionately lower than world market prices (Abegglen & Stalk, 1985; Ungson, Bird & Steers, 1988).

The success of the Japanese ushered in new competitive parameters—an emphasis on prices and timely delivery. Instead of the conventional emphasis on research and development, competition had shifted to becoming a low cost producer, a strategy that was enhanced by the Japanese strengths in manufacturing and process refinement. As part of the Japanese emphasis on better handling equipment, air purifying techniques, comprehensive clean room measures and well-trained personnel, Japanese products were regarded not only as lower priced but with reliable high quality as well (Okimoto, Sugano & Weinstein, 1984).

The Adverse Impact of Japanese Entry-Strategies

In changing the competitive rules of the game, Japanese firms have affected U.S. semiconductor firms in a number of adverse ways. Generally, they have minimized the traditional strengths of U.S. firms in product development in favor of process development in which they excel. McKenna, Cohen and Borrus (1984) have described the Japanese action as "disrupting the reinvestment cycle" of U.S. firms. The reinvestment cycle refers to particular periods in time when earnings obtained from the sale of a standard product are "recycled" back to the production of a newer product. Early development of a product consists of product definition, laboratory designs, prototype development and the design of tools and machines. On the average, it would take four years to move the product from its developmental stage to its sale in the market. As the product approaches maturity, the costs of the product are reduced through production refinement and automation, and revenues for the firm start to accrue. Overall, a greater proportion of industry capital is spent on costly equipment in order to establish a competitive position for volume marketing (Borrus, Millstein, & Zysman, 1983).

Product maturity corresponds to the time in which an industry standard is selected, in which case the semiconductor firm is able to recoup some of its investment in the early growth stages of the product. Like many other products, internal funds derived from the sale of the standard product (e.g., the 64k dRAM) are used to finance new products (e.g., 256k dRAM). For a highly competitive industry such as semiconductors, it is crucial for the firms that this cycle is maintained, since more research and development eventually leads to better products. For example, more complex chips have created new applications in computer peripherals, analytical testing instruments, laser testing applications, software products, and so on.

Japanese firms disrupt this reinvestment cycle by entering the market at the beginning of the maturation period, or about the time when U.S. firms are ready to recoup some of their initial investment through volume production. For reasons discussed earlier, Japanese firms can enter the market at a *lower* price, even if they compete at a later date as followers in terms of the technology. In doing so, they have lengthened the pay back cycle for U.S. firms; instead of the three-five year pay back period, U.S. firms would then expect a delay up to seven years (McKenna et al., 1984).

From here, other adverse consequences can follow. The success of the Japanese in pursuing this strategy places an enormous burden on U.S. firms to compete head-to-head with the Japanese as full-line manufacturers, specialize in more advanced products that are regarded to be less vulnerable to Japanese pricing strategies or to simply leave the market altogether (Borrus et al., 1983). Another response has been protectionist: lobbying the U.S. Congress to pass import quotas on incoming Japanese semiconductors into the U.S. market. The Semiconductor Trade Agreement reached between Japan and the U.S. to specify and limit the prices of semiconductors reflects this effort.

Strategic Responses to Japanese Entry-Strategies

Several studies indicate that U.S. firms have responded to the Japanese in a number of ways (Borrus et al., 1983; Okimoto et al., 1984; The Semiconductor Industry Association Report, 1983; Ungson, 1988). Firms such as AMD, Hewlett Packard, and Eaton Corporation have attempted to reduce product-development activities, or shorten the length of time between product inception and its introduction to the market. They have used a variety of methods, such as product campaigns, decision support systems, impact analysis and organizational development to achieve this objective. When successful, there is less pressure for these firms to finance the next generation of the product or new process improvements, given the relative shorter period of product and process development.

Another strategy, pursued by Texas Instruments, Mostek, Motorola and AMI, has been to differentiate their products to avoid early standardization and to delay the maturation of the product. Differentiation involves the tailoring of 256k dRAM, for example, to meet the speed, power and data access capabilities of multiple users. By differentiating their products and coopting multiple end-users at the start, U.S. firms have gambled that they can obtain sufficient leverage to maximize returns and still take advantage of volume markets in the long run.

Still another popular strategy is to forge strategic alliances with Japanese, and, on occasion, with European firms. The motivation behind these alliances are partly strategic (e.g., LSI Logic provides Toshiba with technology, and Toshiba supplies the wafer fabrication), and partly defensive (e.g., Intel's attempt to have the Japanese adopt its 2704 EEPROM to forestall Japanese reverse engineering) (Johnston, 1984). The theoretical argument underlying alliances is provided by Ohmae (1985), who sees the shortening of product-development activities as minimizing the traditional practice of second-sourcing and off-shore production, thus eliminating "first-mover" advantages and creating the need for greater collaboration through joint ventures and triads.

Assessing the Effectiveness of U.S. Strategic Responses

Any evaluation of U.S. strategic responses has to be viewed in terms of a transition. In the shifting tide of competition, the Japanese have stepped up their investment in the United States, while the United States, now more aware of the Japanese strategic emphasis on semiconductors, has responded by building factories in Japan. The efforts by Texas Instruments, Motorola, Intel and Fairchild provide testimony to this observation (Okimoto et al., 1984, p. 75). Henceforth, the cross-investments have blurred national boundaries, making it difficult to evaluate the effectiveness of particular strategies.

Even so, an emerging picture is that the U.S. responses discussed in the previous section have met with mixed success. While U.S. firms have, in fact, been able to reduce product-development times, this has not deterred the Japanese in their efforts to further reduce development times for process refinement. With the competitive emphasis having shifted to timely delivery of quality products, the rate of product introductions for both U.S. and Japanese firms are just about the same (Gregory, 1984). Such responses have prompted some researchers to closely examine the "corporate cultures" that underlie research and development activities in Japanese and U.S. firms (Gregory, 1984). While some key differences have been identified, it is not clear which system is superior in coming up with new products or processes that are aligned with overall competitive success.

For related reasons, it is difficult to evaluate the effectiveness of product differentiation strategies. For one, differentiation *did not* forestall the Japanese from entering the market, but might have motivated them to enter it even sooner! The Japanese assault on the 64k dRAM, 256k dRAM, and, at present, the 1 MEGA RAM markets, in which they have pioneered both product and process developments, represents a clear departure from their stereotyped role as followers (Borrus et al., 1983).

However, the success of the Japanese is muted if one accepts the alternative scenario that efforts by U.S. firms to promote differentiation might have engendered a closer relationship with their (domestic) end-users, leading to further consolidation within the entire industry (Borrus et al., 1983). Since greater miniaturization of complex circuitry, meaning, CAD/CAE designs, provides opportunities for end-users to develop proprietary designs for their products, it is argued that end-users would prefer to develop collaborative ties with U.S. semiconductor firms, rather than the Japanese or the Europeans, whom they consider to be long-term rivals in their line of work. The synergies derived from such a consolidation would swing the competitive balance back to research and development—areas in which U.S. merchant firms and smaller firms still enjoy an advantage relative to their foreign competitors. Therefore, even while conceding the lucrative memory market to the Japanese, U.S. firms might have much to gain as the industry consolidates.

Strategic alliances are terms to describe the present, and it is too early to evaluate their effectiveness. Indeed, many theoretical arguments, particularly those made by Ohmae (1985), have been advanced to support the cause of alliances. Yet, there is emerging evidence that the problems in managing strategic alliances might be more significant than the problems they were conceived to have solved (Reich & Mankin, 1986). Experiences in joint ventures indicate that after the relationships were dissolved, former partners became fierce competitors (Reich & Mankin, 1986).

REASSESSING CONVENTIONAL THEORIES OF STRATEGY

Conventional theories of strategy emphasize competition between firms operating in similar markets or industries (Porter, 1980). In terms of an international context, these theories have been recently reformulated to encompass multidomestic and global industries (Porter, 1986). Multidomestic industries consist of essentially domestic industries that are not linked together in any systemic fashion to allow for advantages derived from a comprehensive global strategy. Any competitive advantages derived by the firm tend to be anchored on comparative advantages of a particular country (e.g., lower labor costs in Korea). Some examples provided by Porter (1986) include retailing, consumer-packaged goods, distribution, insurance and consumer finance.

At the other end of the spectrum are global industries, that is, a series of interlinked industries in which rivals compete against each other in some worldwide fashion (Porter, 1988). Since these industries are linked, it is possible to configure specific activities within the firm to capitalize on the synergies afforded by these linkages. Competitive advantage of firms would rest on their abilities to do this, and not necessarily on country-specific benefits. Industries exhibiting this pattern include semiconductors, steel, commercial aircraft and television sets.

Several factors accelerate the evolution of multidomestic industries into global ones. On the demand side, converging market and technological forces lead to large, concentrated and global industries. In the case of semiconductors, the growing preference by buyers for more standardized products that could be sold at lower prices on a worldwide basis established its global status. Similar arguments can be made for the steel, consumer electronics and automobile industries, although these products have not fully extended into the European market on account of restricted policies by the EEC. The global nature of semiconductors can be contrasted with telecommunications, which still represents a national market on account of differing technical standards.

Porter (1986) also discussed how international strategy changes the meaning of comparative advantage. He rejected the traditional view of comparative advantage that is based on factor endowments, and proposed that a firm's competitive advantage is derived less from where activities are performed than from how it performs them on a worldwide basis. Therefore, competitive advantages derive from cost leadership and differentiation strategies that are inextricably linked to a firm's activities. Government policy, in this framework, influences these activities through tariffs, nontariff barriers and nationalistic purchases.

Porter's framework is helpful in explaining the relative success of the Japanese semiconductor firms against the U.S. firms, but it does not provide the full story. While we are much in agreement with Porter's formulations, our differences with him lie in the *emphasis* we place on the ability of governments to influence firms' global strategies in international competition and the *specificity* in which institutions might facilitate, accommodate or hinder the accomplishment of these global strategies. At the minimum, we doubt that the Japanese competitive strengths in semiconductors can be fully explained in terms of strategy alone. In the cases of Korea, Taiwan, Singapore and other rapidly-developing countries, their success appears to be grounded in favorable and facilitating institutions (Bradshaw, Burton, Cooper, & Hormats, 1988). We had earlier argued that the success of the Japanese extends to a wide variety of industries, suggesting the presence and force of underlying institutions, and not simply indigenous factors favoring one particular industry. To the extent that strategy and institutions are related, we now turn attention to examining how institutional changes might impact international high technology competition in the future.

THE INSTITUTIONAL CONTEXT OF GLOBAL STRATEGIES

Several observers have noted that the competitive landscape confronting Japanese, U.S. and European firms has been changing in fundamental ways. Mergers, takeovers and divestitures continue to reshape the structure and competitiveness of key industries. Stock market fluctuations have added volatility, uncertainty and new imperatives for financial performance. Meanwhile, Japan, Korea and newly-industrializing countries have accelerated the pressure on traditional leaders, such as the United States, West Germany and Great Britain, to shift from manufacturing to service economies, despite the adverse consequences implied in these efforts (Cohen & Zysman, 1987).

To place the relationship between strategy and institutions in perspective, we now contrast the institutional environment faced by high technology firms in worldwide competition during two periods: from 1970-1980, and from 1980 to the present time.

The Institutional Environment, 1970-1980

The institutional environment faced by U.S., Japanese and EEC high technology firms from 1970 to 1980 pertain largely to market factors that propelled market demand for semiconductors in each of these geopolitical areas. While the demand for semiconductors in the United States was primarily oriented to computers, defense and industrial products, the demand in Japan was largely spurred by consumer electronics and computers. This difference resulted in an R&D product bias by U.S. firms, and an R&D process bias for the Japanese. Both U.S. and Japanese firms had accelerated their investment in semiconductors and plant and equipment, but with an important institutional difference. Investments by U.S. firms were largely firm-oriented and therefore subject to the vagaries of bust-and-boom periods. Contrariwise, Japanese firms were partly financed by governmental institutional houses and did not have the pressures for profitability that had beleaguered their U.S. counterparts.

The major thrust of Japan's efforts to contribute to semiconductors was the well-publicized program for industry-government cooperation in VLSI research. Associated companies included NEC, Toshiba, Hitachi, Fujitsu and Mitsubishi. Research and development laboratories were staffed by engineers from all five companies. As a result of this project, over 1,000 patents were issued, and about 460 technical papers were published—a remarkable organizational success (Okimoto, Sugano, & Weinstein, 1984).

In general, the decline of traditional industries in Europe has forced many European governments to support these industries in order to retain people in the work force. To a large extent, the best articulated industrial policy within the EEC relates to agricultural competition, that is, Common Agricultural Policy (Hall, 1986). However, there is a growing awareness that these practices and policies are not sufficient to enhance the competitiveness of a wider array of industries, and that new industrial initiatives are necessary (Ungson & Van Dijk, 1987). Initiatives such as ESPRIT (European Strategic Programme for Research in Information Technology), ECRC (European Computer Industry Research Center), EUREKA, and RACE (Research on Advanced Communications in Europe)—all directed at enhancing competitiveness in high technology—have all been widely publicized, although the levels of investment do not particularly match well against comparable U.S. and Japanese investments (Brandin & Harrison, 1987).

The Institutional Environment, 1980-Present

Perhaps the most prominent among these institutional changes is the appearance of various forms of networks: strategic alliances, joint ventures, interlocking networks and cross-licensing agreements inhabit the competitive landscape. Despite the prominence of these networks, few authors have yet to link them to competitive strategies (Gerlach, 1988; Ohmae, 1985). We argue that networks represent a significant change in institutions that heralds the emergence of new competitive rules for high technology industries in general, and for semiconductors in particular.

In the case of the United States, we see the emergence of several "national research projects," a form similar to what the Japanese institutions had supported in an earlier period. Among these projects include: the Defense Advanced Research Projects Agency (DARPA), a project that involves the management of basic research and advanced technology in industry, universities and private organizations, with an emphasis on computer technology; the Strategic Computing Initiative (SCI), which emphasizes new materials and fabrication techniques; the Strategic Defense Initiative (SDI); and a host of other projects. Looming in the background would be giant consortia, such as Sematech (Semiconductor Manufacturing Technology Initiative) or SRC (Semiconductor Research Center), that allegedly provide additional vehicles for enhancing competitiveness in manufacturing competencies and product/process innovation.

On the surface, these and other factors favor the technological leadership of the United States in high technology. High technology firms will continue to reap the benefits of an outpouring of venture capital into Silicon Valley, while other places strive to become "another" Silicon Valley (e.g. Austin, North Carolina Triangle, Boston, Minnesota, etc.). The emergence of new markets resulting from more VLSI (Very Large Scale Integration) applications provides the incentive for entrepreneurial firms to join the industry. Some industry analysts have argued that the consolidation in the industry, such as the trend toward system development, will continue to favor U.S. semiconductor firms, partly because end-users would be reluctant to give proprietary designs to foreign competitors (Borrus, Millstein, & Zysman, 1983). Should smaller U.S. firms, in fact, fade or become merged with larger ones, it is uncertain whether large-scale alliances and consortia such as Sematech and SRC would ultimately provide the appropriate structure in which to extend the stream of new product innovations. Even so, scale of investment and collaborative structures have emerged as key factors in international high technology competition.

Japan faces a slightly different environment. It has stepped up investment in MITI Laboratories and NTT's electrocommunication laboratories. At present, the Japanese government has organized and financed efforts to develop the Fifth Generation Computer Project that aims to break new ground in artificial intelligence. Possible spinoffs include a typewriter mechanism that can react to human speech and an automatic translating machine. If successful, these will give Japan a distinctive edge over its rivals. Finally, Japan has sought to create innovation and entrepreneurship through its "Technopolis Concept," a rather audacious project to build a network of nineteen high technology cities based in Japan that are partly patterned after Silicon Valley (Tatsuno, 1986).

It has been suggested, however, that Japan's success may result in its own undoing. Japanese semiconductor firms now dominate the standard memory market, and are gearing up to competing with U.S. firms in the more advanced circuit chips, telecommunications and supercomputers. Japanese firms, now popularly referred to as "kaisha," tend to be large, aggressive, and competitive—ingredients that prepare them for global competition (Abegglen & Stalk, 1985).

Japan's key problem is slower economic growth which has occurred at a time when it had become dependent on export trade to fuel its growth, and when other countries, notably the United States and Europe, are starting to erect protectionist measures. Slower growth has placed a heavy burden on the government to consider the costs and the consequences of rapid economic growth. Compared to other industrial countries, Japan lags behind in social security and welfare spending (Lincoln, 1988). A future policy issue is whether Japan's gains in high technology and other industries are worth the price that has to be paid in terms of insufficient institutional development.

Simply stated, Europe needs help to catch-up and remain competitive with the United States and Japan. Visionaries of a united Europe point to a total of 323 million people in the trading community—a figure that dwarfs the population of Japan (122 million) and the United States (244 million), and makes the EEC the largest trading block in the world, with more than 40 percent of all foreign trade. The combined gross domestic product of the Community in 1987 was $4.2 trillion, almost equal to that of the United States ($4.4 trillion), and considerably larger than the combined total of Japan, South Korea, Taiwan, Hong Kong and Singapore ($2.7 trillion).

Unfortunately, the elegance and intellectual appeal of this argument does not brush away the political obstacles that prevent its realization. European integration, or a truly united market, means the elimination of regional protection and other impediments to a free market. A simple laundry list of changes discloses a herculean task: 300 legal changes are needed to dissolve barriers to trade between EEC countries; up to 100,000 trade barriers and technical regulations have to be overhauled; and operating standards that deal with information transfer and telecommunications have to be harmonized to reduce the duplication of effort for research and distribution projects. Jeelof (1988) has outlined additional changes in the Community that would facilitate a fully integrated Europe: the establishment and adoption of a strong European monetary system, the use of "reciprocity" as the basis for a European position in international trade and investment, the development of an acceptable EEC Social Policy and the widespread support of various management training and educational programs. For high technology firms within the EEC to achieve technological parity with their world competitors, a necessary condition is a truly common market that provides a favorable and supportive climate that is comparable to their competitors.

CONCLUSIONS

Following the characterization of Johnson's (1985) analysis of industrial policymaking, we argue that a cross-national comparison of institutional factors offers an important element in evaluating a firm's competitive advantage. We argue that competitive strategies of firms are inextricably linked to the larger institutional context in which these policies are developed. For U.S. firms to succeed, it is important that they recognize the intricacies of their institutional environment. The task of U.S. managers and policymakers should be to carefully examine the national institutions that generate and sustain corporate strategies of their competitors, and to determine how a restructuring of their own institutions might lead to competitive advantages. This will require them to develop a picture not only of where present institutions are leading them but where present or new institutions *should* lead them. The challenge is to promote appropriate changes in these institutions without altering their basic character. Such changes may well be the key to determining whether future relationships between firms in other countries will be ones of greater competition and cooperation, or of decreased competitiveness and submission.

REFERENCES

Abegglen, J.C., & Stalk., G. Jr. (1985). *Kaisha: The Japanese corporation.* New York: Basic Books.
Borrus, M. (1988). *Competing for control.* Cambridge, MA: Ballinger.
Borrus, M., Millstein, J., & Zysman, J. (1983). *Responses to the Japanese challenge in high technology.* Berkeley, CA: Berkeley Roundtable on the International Economy, University of California, Berkeley.
Bradshaw, T., Burton, D., Cooper, R., & Hormats, R. (1988). *America's new competitors: The challenge of the newly industrializing countries.* Cambridge, MA: Ballinger.
Brandin, D., & Harrison, M. (1987). *The technology war.* New York: Prentice-Hall.
Cohen, J., & Zysman, J. (1987). *Manufacturing matters.* New York: Basic Books.

"Electronics." (1988, January 7). *The Year In Review*, pp. 29-31.

English, A. (1985). Tracking European inventions. *Euro-Asia Business Review, 3*(3), p. 18-25.

Finan, W., & LaMond, A. (1985). Sustaining U.S. competitiveness in microelectronics: The challenge to U.S. policy. In B.R. Scott & G.C. Lodge (Eds.), *U.S. Competitiveness in the World Economy*, (pp. 77-175). Boston, MA: Harvard Business School Press.

Gerlach, M. (1988). Business alliance and the strategy of the Japanese firm. *California Management Review, 30*, 126-142.

Gregory, G. (1984). The Japanese propensity for innovation: The case of electronics. *Euro-Asia Business Review, 3*(3), 17-22.

Hall, G. (1986). *European industrial policy*. Kent, Great Britain: Croom Helm.

Jeelof, G. (1988, October 28). *Europe 1992: A Phillips perspective*. Paper presented at the University of Oregon.

Johnson, C. (1985). The institutional foundations of industrial policy. *California Management Review, 27*, 59-69.

Johnston, M. (1984). Chip wars. *Esquire, 102*(3), 85-93.

Kotler, P. 1985. *Marketing Management*. Englewood-Cliffs, NJ: Prentice-Hall.

Lincoln, E.J. (1988) *Japan: Facing economic maturity*. Washington, D.C.: The Brookings Institute.

Mackintosh, I. (1986). *Sunrise Europe: The dynamics of information technology*. Oxford: Basil Blackwell.

McClean, W. (Ed.). (1986). *Status 1986: A report on the integrated circuit industry*, Scottsdale, AZ: Integrated Circuit Engineering Corporation (ICE SCOT).

McKenna, R., Cohen, S., & Borrus, M. (1984). International competition in high technology. *California Management Review, 2*, 15-32.

Ohmae, K. (1985). *Triad power: The coming shape of global competition*. New York: The Free Press.

Okimoto, D.I., Sugano, T., & Weinstein, F.B. (1984). *The competitive edge: The semiconductor industry in the U.S. and Japan*. Stanford, CA: Stanford University Press.

Porter, M. (1980). *Competitive strategy*. New York: The Free Press.

————(1986). *Competition in global industries*. Boston, MA: Harvard Business School Press.

The Semiconductor Industry Association. (1983). *The effect of government targeting on worldwide semiconductor competition: A case history of Japanese industrial strategy and its costs for America*. Cupertino, CA: Author.

Reich, R.B., & Mankin, E.D. (1986). Joint ventures with Japan give away our future. *Harvard Business Review, 64*(2), 78-86.

Reid, T.R. (1984). *The chip*. New York: Simon & Schuster.

Riggs, H. (1983). *Managing high technology companies* Belmont, CA: Wadsworth.

Shanklin, W., & Ryans, J. (1984). *Marketing high technology*. Boston: Lexington Books.

Tatsuno, S. (1986). *The technolopolis strategy: Japan, high technology, and the control of the 21st century*. New York: Prentice-Hall.

Ungson, G.R. (1988). *Developing flexible infrastructures: Responding to the Japanese challenge in high technology*. Working paper, Graduate School of Management, University of Oregon.

Ungson, G.R., & Van Dijk, N. (1987). Concurren in de postindustriele semeleving: de Verenigde Staten, Japan en Europa [High Tech in the U.S., Japan, and Europe]. M & O Tijdschrift voor organisatie-kunde en sociaal beleid, 41c, jaardang [M & O Journal of Organizations and Culture], 41: 378-389.

Ungson, G., Bird, A., & Steers, R. (1988). *Institutional foundations of corporate strategy* (Working paper). Eugene: Graduate School of Management, University of Oregon.

BUILDING DEVELOPING COUNTRIES INTO THE STRATEGY AND MANAGEMENT OF HIGH TECHNOLOGY FIRMS

John D. Daniels

Firms find more opportunity for their high tech products in industrial countries than in developing countries (LDCs), whether seeking additional markets or more competitive means of production. This is because of such factors as market size and similarity, the ease of transferring technical information, the ability to gain additional technology and the low emphasis of price as a competitive weapon for these products. Yet there are emerging situations that warrant more attention to LDCs, including some market inhibitions in industrial countries, selective LDC sourcing opportunities and the need by high tech firms to gain cost advantages.

SCOPE OF THE PAPER

There are many advantages and nuances of foreign operations that are common to both high and low tech firms as well as to their operations in both industrial countries and LDCs. This paper will concentrate on those operations by high tech firms in LDCs that are different in substance or by degree from those of other firms in LDCs or from high tech firms' operations in industrial countries.

For purposes of this paper, high technology companies are those with a high percentage of scientific and technical personnel and sophisticated new technology, not only for the purpose of creating new products but also for developing new markets (McCarthy, Spital, & Lauenstein, 1987). Although various arbitrary measurements are often used to classify firms as high tech, the distinctions are not that clear in practice. Not all products of high tech firms are new or comprised of sophisticated technology, nor are the components that make them up. Likewise, many firms from industries not normally considered to be high tech have certain high tech products and components within their product lines. Since the difference is by degree, this paper will occasionally make a distinction between high tech products and high tech firms.

The scheme of the paper is as follows:

1. brief examination of the reasons for high tech foreign operations, making some general contrasts with foreign operations for other firms and products;
2. a review of how high tech characteristics cause different opportunities, obstacles and adjustments between LDCs and industrial countries; and
3. a short discussion of the overall outlook for business by high tech firms in industrial versus developing countries, with emphasis on some emerging opportunities and niches in LDCs.

OBJECTIVES OF FOREIGN OPERATIONS

The two primary objectives of foreign operations are to expand markets and to acquire resources in the form of products or better means to produce them. High tech firms are no different from other firms in this respect. In looking at the specifics of why firms find it advantageous to sell abroad or acquire product capabilities abroad, some differences exist between high tech products and those that rely more on nontechnical entry barriers, such as capital or marketing intensity. The differences also manifest themselves in the use of different means of handling foreign business among different products, such as exporting versus licensing (United Nations Center on Transnational Corporations, 1987).

For example, capital intensive products tend to compete more on the basis of price. Furthermore, these products can gain sharp cost reduction through longer production runs brought about by additional export sales to foreign markets. Because cost reduction is such an important consideration for these firms, their foreign technology acquisitions tend to be for processes rather than for new product capabilities. The sale of new high tech products,

Table 1. Benefits of Foreign Operations for High Tech Products

Sales	Benefits*
1. Gain scale economies	L
2. Extend product life cycle	H
3. Use excess capacity (product, capital, human resources, etc.)	L
4. Inhibit competitive entry	H
5. Gain higher return than at home (tax, PLC, incentives, competitive environment)	L
6. Maintain domestic customers	L
Resource Acquisitions	
1. Process technology	L
2. Product technology	H
3. Cheap or specialized labor	L
4. Raw materials	L
5. Capital	L

Note: *High = H; Low = L.

however, is much less dependent on price; thus other factors are more influential in the foreign sale or production of these products. Although this paper will not elaborate on all the possible differences, Table 1 does show various advantages of foreign operations and the usual relative importance of these for high tech products. These will, of course, vary somewhat by firm and product-specific conditions.

As the high tech products mature, the competitive needs change. If the high tech firm is to compete with some more mature products (perhaps necessary to gain the cash flow for the next generation of products), it must adopt the practices of the capital intensive or marketing intensive firms.

LDC DIFFERENCES

Table 2 shows the major factors differentiating sales of high tech products to developing countries.

Product Fit

Innovative product characteristics are the primary basis of competitive advantage for high tech firms. Products are developed in response to observed market needs, most likely what is found in the high tech firm's domestic market. This should not imply, however, that all countries want or need the same capabilities. For example, we have seen differences with

Table 2.   Foreign Operations for High Tech Products
LDCs vs. Industrial Countries (ICs)

Characteristics		*Differences*
A.	Product	A.1 Fits LDC conditions less well.
B.	Government Sales	B.1 More bargaining strength in IC to require local production.
		B.2 Need for financing in LDC.
		B.3 LDC decision makers lack of sophistication
C.	Industrial Sales	C.1 More staff support to transfer to LDC.
D.	Protection of Technology	D.1 Nonpatented more easily lost in IC.
		D.2 Patented more easily lost in LDC.
		D.3 Long lead time favors concentration strategy to ICs first.
		D.4 Short lead time favors diversification strategy and early entry to LDC.
E.	Off Shore Production	E.1 To share high cost of developmental risk in IC.
		E.2 To reduce production cost in LDC.
F.	Technology Acquisition	F.1 More likely in IC.
		F.2 LDC primarily modification than creation and more suited to other LDC needs.

defense sales; for example, the range for missiles and aircraft need to conform to a country's location relative to its likely enemies.

What does this mean as far as LDCs are concerned? Because almost all new technology originates in industrial countries, the observed characteristics for which the new technology is developed are likely to fit the needs of industrial countries better than the needs of LDCs. This has made assimilation of new technology more difficult and expensive for LDCs, inasmuch as products often have to be modified before they can be efficiently used. The most common types of modification are in response to the use of different raw materials, the scaling down of plant size, the need to diversify the product mix, the use of simpler and lower capacity machinery and the need to stretch out the capacity of existing equipment (Teitel, 1984). Even when LDC markets are protected from external competition, firms operating therein find the need to modify equipment to the LDC conditions in order to compete in external markets. It is often alleged as well that technology uses too much capital and too little labor in relation to LDC market cost conditions.

Even when a firm designs a high tech product for a so-called global market segment and alters its domestic product characteristics to conform to the global standard, there is apt to be more response to the needs of industrial countries than of LDCs. After all, the former have more purchasing power and more knowledgeable experts to give opinions. Although there are some international organizations, such as ICAO, which include LDCs as members and set minimum worldwide specifications, most organizations, such as the Eurodata Foundation in telecommunications, represent only industrial countries.

Government Sales

Probably no sales have been more dominated by government than highly technical, complex types of products in the telecommunications, electronics and computer industries. This is because the major customers (postal, telegraphic and telephone administrations) are usually government-owned; and all defense establishments are in the public domain. The sales are particularly sensitive because of their size and strategic importance. The size of orders frequently exceeds $100 million; therefore, the impact on the balance of payments, growth and employment is substantial. The strategic implications are even more pervasive. Although this environment exists within developed as well as developing countries, the necessary corporate response differs between the two because of relative bargaining strengths, because of different levels of sophistication of decision makers, and because of many LDCs' desires to diversify their dependence.

In selling to other industrial countries, one is apt to come in to direct competition with local firms. Direct government subsidies of the local computer, electronics or telecommunications industry is practiced by many countries, including the United Kingdom, France, Italy, Germany and Japan. Of the United States R&D undertaken in the area of radio, television, and communications equipment and components, approximately 70% is undertaken by U.S. government agencies. In most cases aid is designed to foment research and development, so that these domestic industries might keep pace with these rapidly advancing fields.

Even where the competition is not direct, the industrial countries have capabilities of becoming potential suppliers. These domestic capabilities, coupled with their high purchasing power, have given strong bargaining power to industrial country governments, which want to share in the production benefits. It is difficult today to make any large high tech sales to them without considerable participation of their local firms. This participation includes the development of consortia to bid on contracts, joint ventures, coproduction agreements, offset agreements, local content requirements, and so on. These arrangements necessitate costly negotiations with other firms, complexities of transferring technology to other organizations, and more difficulty in managing because of various corporate objectives, languages and cultures (Lorange, 1986; Rugman, 1981).

Furthermore, the particular combination of companies is apt to differ from one country to the next. Although the firms in these situations are exhorted to keep prices to a minimum, cost and productive efficiency are often less important than local participation in order to secure contracts.

Developing countries have not had the same degree of bargaining power. Undoubtedly, the most important factor in selling to them, other than the technology itself, is the ability to arrange financing. This is complicated by the fact that reference selling (the bringing of prospective government purchasers into contact with a previously satisfied foreign customer) is a common selling method for large contracts in LDCs. Since various nationalities of firms were likely to have been involved in building the reference product or project, a duplication of the product or project means working again with a group of firms from different countries. This multinational sourcing is also compatible with LDCs' desires to diversify their high tech dependencies among different industrial countries. However, this usually necessitates government-to-government financial assistance from more than one source, thus further complicating the financial arrangements. Of late there has been some increase in efforts by LDCs to try to finance at least part of purchases through various barter arrangements.

One of the factors that might be a harbinger to an increased bargaining power of LDCs is that most large scale high tech systems are already in place in industrial countries, so that sales to them are more likely to be for modifying existing systems. LDCs, in turn, need entire new systems and usually want to jump to the latest technology, even in areas where they have no experience.

Governmental agencies in the industrial countries generally have a fairly clear-cut concept of specifications prior to dealing with producers. The agencies are staffed with technocrats who feel confident in dismantling technology packages in order to combine equipment, processes or components from numerous origins. In many of the developing countries, however, firms have found that agencies frequently do not develop detailed plans and specifications on their own. At their own expense, some firms have put together planning studies to aid government development projects in the hopes that they can either insert specifications tailored to their own capabilities or that they will obtain preferential treatment in the contract award if the plan is accepted. For example, this approach helped N.V. Philips get a $3.1 billion contract in Saudi Arabia (Flanigan, 1978). Yet this approach is costly and incurs the risks that a country will ultimately award a contract to another firm anyway.

Once negotiations begin, the process can be very frustrating in many developing countries. The many levels of bureaucracy are staffed with people who are not fully cognizant of technological processes and alternatives. Delays may be inordinately long, and communications may be slow. In spite of widespread reports in the 1970s that developing countries wished to disassemble technology packages in order to better their bargaining positions and to lower their costs, their ability to do this has been minimal. In fact the trend in the 1980s has been toward more comprehensive package deals, which include training, maintenance and infrastructure development concomitant with the primary product sale. This trend has further enhanced the use of bids by a consortia of companies, including many that are represented by firms from different countries. Another trend has been for companies to diversify so as to be able to offer a more complete line of products and services when making such bids.

Industrial Sales

Not all high tech sales are to governments, nor are they all of the magnitude of the big projects referenced above. Many are of manufacturing equipment, systems and processes to turn out new products or older ones through new means. These occur through various international forms (e.g., exports, licensing, turnkey), all requiring the transfer of specific skills on how to operate, service and repair what is being sold. The more complex and specialized the sale, the more likely the buyer is to need highly educated engineering specialists in order for a transfer to be performed efficiently.

This transference is usually more difficult in LDCs. There are fewer engineers per capita. Of those available, fewer are likely to be trained in the needed specialties, being general engineers rather than electrical or textile engineers. Furthermore, equipment cycles tend to be much longer in LDCs because of smaller markets and the difficulty of financing new purchases; therefore, there is a "leap-frogging" among generations of equipment so that the knowledge transfer has to come in large rather than small increments. As a consequence, the high technology seller must spend much more time in effecting transfers to LDCs than to industrial countries. Not only is this costly, it is an added drain on the scarce personnel who are fully knowledgeable of the technology in the high tech firm at the early stage of sales.

Developing countries could opt for older or less complex models, which may be cheaper to acquire, more proven and more congruent to their employment needs. They sometimes do; but the tendency is to jump to the latest technology, even in areas where they have no experience. The recent emphasis on export led development models has enhanced the use of the most advanced production equipment, since this equipment is perceived as helping to assure the uniform quality needed to stimulate exports (Daniels & Robles, 1983).

Protection of Technology

Millions of dollars can be used in the development of technology; improper protection of this asset could lead to limited use by the developer worldwide and therefore to limited profitability. Patents are a major means of protection, as are industrial secrecy programs that make copying difficult without access to the high tech firm's facilities. Some high tech products would be easy to copy if it were not for patent protection. Some others would be very difficult, regardless of patent protection. The nature of the product and the lead time over competitors influence what types of protection strategies are undertaken.

Technological protection also influences the form of operation undertaken and the sequence of foreign countries to enter. Ultimately, a firm may gain a sizable presence and commitment in most countries of the world; however, there are different paths to reach that position. Firms seldom have the resources necessary to move everywhere in the world with a full commitment all at once. The commitment of human, technical and financial resources to one locale may result in delaying or even foregoing projects in other areas. One theory, the imitation lag, is to go first to those countries whose firms are most likely to be competitors, thus inhibiting early competitive entry (Stobaugh, 1969). If the firm assesses that its lead time over competitors is long, the order of entry may be combined with a concentration strategy, that is, moving only to one or a few foreign countries until there are very strong involvements and competitive positions there, meaning, a high market penetration with wholly owned operations as opposed to external agreements, such as licensing. Later the move can be into other countries (Ayal & Zif, 1979). Ordinarily, a concentration strategy would lead firms to go first to other industrial countries. This is because local firms in industrialized countries have more technical capabilities that can be mobilized for competitive entry and because their domestic market sizes are more likely to entice them to compete. Such a strategy of internalizing operations is particularly useful in delaying competitive entry even longer because it is generally conceded that external arrangements help technological recipients to close their technological gaps faster than when relying only on their internal R&D. However, the decision to follow a concentration strategy must consider the firm's market position and country-specific situations as well.

For example, IBM still resists sharing technology through joint ventures and licensing, and can sequence its country entries of most new high tech products without much risk of losing markets to competitors; this is because of its dominant position in size and technological reputation. But even IBM has had some notable exceptions, such as the necessity to divest in India and the requirement of a joint venture in Mexico. Sperry Univac, on the other hand, has not had the same negotiating power. Although its managers realize that joint ventures might build foreign competitors' capabilities, this consideration is outweighed by the advantage of local identities that help in getting foreign government contracts (Daniels & Grafenberg, 1981).

ITT has taken another tack. It has been very reluctant to enter into joint ventures in the developed world because of the fear that competitors' positions would be improved. ITT has been willing to do so in the developing world, in places such as Mexico and Brazil, when it was the only way to get the business. Its willingness to transfer technology to LDCs in this manner is based on its fair certainty of being able to maintain a technological lead over its local partners who don't have a massive research and development effort.

Opposite to a concentration strategy is a diversification strategy, in which companies move rapidly into most foreign markets, gradually increasing their commitments within each of them. This could be done, for example, through a liberal licensing policy for a given product so that there are sufficient resources to gain initial widespread expansion. The companies may eventually increase their involvement by internalizing activities that they initially had contracted to other firms. Such a strategy is particularly warranted when the competitive lead time is short in many markets and where the resource commitment for developing each is high.

The easier it is to copy a product once it is developed, the shorter the potential lead time over competitors. As discussed above, patents are a means of protecting against competitive entry; however, some countries (primarily LDCs) offer haphazard patent protection or none at all. There are, of course, other barriers that retard the entry of high tech competitors; however, some industries have to rely heavily on patent protection. Pharmaceutical firms, for example, are among the largest R&D spenders and the most dependent on patent protection. Because of the nature of chemical compounds and the need to divulge virtually all information about product content in order to gain governmental approvals to market new drugs, competitors could easily copy if it were not for patent protection. Since weak patent protection decreases the competitive lead time, a firm may need an earlier entry into those markets that offer little protection. This may be done either by entering certain LDC markets ahead of industrial country markets or by using a diversification strategy. A good illustration of entering an LDC market too late is Pfizer's introduction of feldene, an antiarthritic drug, in Argentina. Five Argentine firms preempted Pfizer by introducing generic copies into the market (Harvey & Ronkainen, 1985). Getting into such a market early, even by licensing, creates less incentive for another firm to copy the product. It also offers some added legal protection, because the first firm into the market may sometimes be given local rights. Furthermore, the company can police the activities of imitators.

There are, of course, hybrids of the concentration and diversification strategies—for example, moving rapidly to most markets but increasing the commitment in only a few. It is undoubtedly becoming easier to build commitments rapidly in many markets because high tech firms have already developed sales and/or production arrangements in many countries. Country specific startup problems are minimized, and any excess capacity may be diverted to the new products.

Off Shore Production

New high tech products have traditionally relied primarily on home country production (Lutz & Green, 1983; Mullor-Sebastian, 1983). Foreign production has taken place as the technology has become diffused, usually as a means to hold markets that had been developed through exports. Since price is not an important competitive characteristic of the new high tech product, there has been little compulsion to shift that production abroad. As long as a firm has been the market share leader, it has been assumed that it would usually have a cost advantage by moving down the experience curve at its original production location. Much of this line-of-reasoning is undergoing change, and the changes affect operations in industrial countries and LDCs differently.

One of the trends has been the tendency of high tech firms to introduce new products at home and abroad almost simultaneously. A reason is that many projects are too large for any single company to handle. This has been apparent in the development of new aircraft and weapon systems. From the inception of a project, companies from different industrial countries agree to take on the high cost and high risk of development work for different components needed in the final product. Afterward a lead company buys the components from the firms that did a part of the developmental work. This system of rationalized production among cooperating companies in different industrial countries is further enhanced by the need to sell final output to governments that insist on local production of some portion of the value added.

In contrast, foreign production in LDCs is taking place as a means of early cost reduction, so that competitors will less likely become significant when the high tech products mature. High tech firms can now more easily procure components in LDCs almost from the inception of a new product because of having production arrangements already in place. Unlike the component transfer among industrial countries, the imports from LDCs are usually low in technology, even though they are used in high technology products. The classic example of this has been the semiconductor industry which moved offshore in the 1960s to take advantage of low labor costs for the packaging phases of the manufacture. The feasibility of using LDC production locations has been stimulated by transportation efficiencies as well as by tariff reductions through the General Agreement of Tariffs and Trade (GATT), the Generalized System of Preferences (GSP) and the Caribbean Basin Initiative.

More rapid and extensive foreign sourcing in LDCs is also taking place more quickly because of a realization that labor cost differences may be more important than cost reductions that occur because of moving down the experience curve. Xerox, for example, now moves to foreign procurement more rapidly than in the past. In the early 1980s Xerox did not forecast the speed with which price competition would become an important consideration. As the market share leader in copiers, the company was further along the production learning curve than competitors and was therefore complacent that other copier manufacturers could not match its cost and price structure. This led to a slowness in moving to cheaper labor-cost production locations in developing countries where competitors set up operations before Xerox (Adkins, 1983).

Technology Acquisition

High tech firms not only transfer technology abroad, they also acquire it. Technology acquisition is important for adding complementary products, particularly those that give sales advantages through the offering of complete systems and those that enable existing products to be improved. Because of the competitive implications, it is not surprising that many firms are establishing mechanisms whereby they may increase the likelihood of gaining advantages before their competitors.

One of the most used mechanisms has been the establishment of company units to monitor journals, patent registrations and technical conferences (Svirdov, 1981). This combined monitoring helps assure that the company is made aware of new developments, thereby enabling decision makers to decide whether to ignore the innovations, counteract them through in-house developments, or establish an operational link with the individuals or organizations that are apparently leading the field. A second mechanism is to develop formal links with academic and other research organizations at home and abroad so as to determine possible breakthroughs before they are publicized in professional journals. A third means is to increase visibility through participation in trade fairs, the distribution of brochures and contacts with technical acquisition consultants. This visibility may encourage innovators to think of one's firm rather than another when they seek out clients. A fourth is the establishment of cooperative research projects with foreign firms, thereby gaining scale benefits and the use of personnel from other organizations. Finally, a company may set up part of its research and development activities in foreign countries in order to utilize foreign talent that would not likely immigrate to the company's home country (Karlin & Anders, 1983; Ronstadt & Kramer, 1982). For example, physicists at IBM's Swiss research facility have twice won the Nobel prize.

Almost all of this activity is centered in industrial countries, not surprising since LDCs have much less innovative capability. There are fewer scientists and engineers per capita; and a smaller portion of the smaller GNPs are spent on research and development. Although high tech firms are still leery of developing future competitors in industrial countries by transferring technology to them, the need to gain technology from those same firms is often overriding. The result is a growth in cooperative linkages in industrial countries, such as joint venture research facilities and cross licensing agreements, but not in LDCs.

Of the technological development in LDCs, most is centered on by-products of manufacturing activity rather than the result of specific R&D programs (Teitel, 1984). In other words, the developments tend to be modifications of imported technology, rather than creation of new technical information. Since these modifications are geared to the conditions of LDCs, such as smaller scale production or the use of different material inputs, there is rarely an applicability in industrial countries. When modifications are developed by subsidiaries of multinational firms, there are some efforts to diffuse the technology to subsidiaries in other LDCs (Montaña, 1981).

There are also numerous case studies of technical developments by domestic firms within LDCs. A common thread among these is that the firms lack the linkages, resources and market knowledge to diffuse the technology internationally on their own. For example, Grupo Industrial Alfa (Mexico) developed a method of producing steel by direct reduction, thus bypassing the high capital cost of blast furnaces. To transfer this patented technology to new plants in other countries would require substantial on-site personnel and construction assistance. Alfa lacked personnel that could be spared as well as foreign construction experience. Alfa had to transfer its know-how to four foreign engineering firms—West Germany's GHH-Sterkrade, Japan's Kawasaki Heavy Industries and the United States' Pullman Swindell and Dravo. Those firms in turn acted as agents on behalf of Alfa and constructed steel plants in such countries as Brazil, Venezuela, Indonesia, Iran, Iraq and Zambia (Dravo agrees, 1980).

EMERGING LDC SITUATIONS

Continued Industrial Country Emphasis

Most international attention by high tech firms will undoubtedly continue to center on industrial countries in the foreseeable future, especially in the so-called triad powers of the United States, Western Europe and Japan (Ohmae, 1986). From a sales standpoint, the industrial countries account for most of the market, particularly if purchasing power is equated in hard currencies rather than payment in some type of barter arrangement. Furthermore, high tech products are generally higher on industrial countries' ranking of product priorities. Barring another abrupt shift in income distribution, such as occurred because of 1970s' oil prices, this situation will remain static.

There will undoubtedly be a shrinking of the lead time between high tech firms' first product introductions and their sales to LDCs. This is due, for example, to greater spillover of information about new products, to the haphazard patent protection in many LDCs, the emergence of newly industrialized countries whose firms have increased capabilities and the existence of competitors' foreign subsidiaries that can draw on their home country resources. These conditions will place more pressure on rapid sales expansion and make prolonged product life cycles more difficult to achieve through the sequencing of countries.

From the standpoint of sourcing new products, pressures to rationalize production among industrial countries in order to secure governmental sales are likely to be more important than pressures to save costs by producing in LDCs. This is in spite of efforts at the GATT Montevideo Round to gain freer trade on governmental purchases. The transfer of production to LDCs for the more mature products could even slow because of new perceived risks involved. One such risk is the possible rescission of trade preferences. This occurred in late 1986 against Chile because of its labor practices and in 1987 against four other LDCs (South Korea, Taiwan, Hong Kong and Singapore) that have been "too successful" at tapping the U.S. market. In 1988 Malaysia reversed its prohibitions against collective bargaining to maintain its trade preferences with the United States; however, this action made Malaysia much less attractive as a sourcing location by international high tech firms. Another factor is the increased realization that LDC firms might also become competitors for mature products more rapidly when they have served as suppliers to high tech firms, such as has Samsung from South Korea. Furthermore, if the technological concept of using robots in flexible factories becomes a reality, cheap labor inputs will be much less important.

Product Modifications

Although most high tech purchasers in LDCs prefer the latest technology, equipment is often modified to fit their needs. Although some of these needs are country-specific, many changes have utility in other LDCs as well. The high tech firms from industrial countries may therefore be able to develop profitable means of helping to modify equipment and selling modification technology once it is developed. In an increasingly competitive world, the advantage of fitting equipment more closely to clients' needs would seem to make good sense in spite of the hullabaloo about global standardization.

Market Needs

As discussed earlier, LDCs have less high tech in place; thus the need is for whole systems rather than for modifications. In addition, the problems of LDCs are so great and so diverse that they may necessitate very large and very different technical approaches to those that are developed for industrial country markets.

As solutions are in place for some problems in industrial countries, there may be little alternative except to confront LDC needs if some firms wish to stay primarily in high technology products for their competitive advantages. Pharmaceuticals are a good example since all the major firms are heavily committed to LDCs, but have allocated very little of their R&D efforts to those health problems found almost exclusively in LDCs. Until the emergence of AIDS, the companies had found pharmaceutical solutions to virtually all contagious diseases in the industrial part of the world. Although they increased their efforts toward finding solutions to noncommunicable health problems, there has, nevertheless, been a decrease in the number of compounds under research and the number in preclinical R&D (Erickson, 1985).

R&D in LDCs

One of the striking occurrences in recent years has been the growth in the number of doctoral science and engineering degrees granted to foreigners in the United States. More than 40 percent of engineering Ph.D.s and more than 20 percent of those in the physical sciences and mathematics are now granted to foreigners. Nationals of LDCs are growing as a portion of the foreign students, especially those from Taiwan, Korea and India. So far, United States high tech firms have been able to utilize a large portion of this talent by gaining permits for them to work in the United States. The continuation of this high talent immigration is always in doubt, given political pressures. There may be further opportunities to utilize this talent through the development of additional specialized research facilities to be located in LDCs.

LDC Sourcing/Financial Arrangements

One of the biggest problems facing many of the developing countries today is their high external debt. This has furthered a reluctance of high tech firms to invest within those countries for fear that capital restrictions will be too stringent on their operations. Increasingly, it looks as if debt-equity swaps by large international bank lenders will play an important role in any type of solution to the debt problem (Wise, 1988). These swaps may present opportunities for high tech firms to develop imaginative arrangements with the large banks that are owed money by LDCs. Simplistically, the banks could convert their loans for equity ownership in new operations within LDCs. These would produce for high tech firms from industrial countries. The high tech firms would not have to put up capital, but could receive compensation through licensing and management contracts. At least a portion of the output of components or finished products could then be sold abroad to generate the hard currency needed for payment to the high tech firms and for dividends to the bank owners.

REFERENCES

Adkins, L. (1983). What happened to Xerox? *Dun's Business Month, 121,* 56-60.

Ayal, I., & Zif, J. (1979). Marketing expansion strategies in multinational marketing. *Journal of Marketing, 43,* 84-94.

Daniels, J.D., & Grafenberg, A. (1981). International high technology sales to governments: A comparative analysis. *Foreign Trade Review, 16,* 9-29.

Daniels, J.D., & Robles, F. (1983). Perceived industrial innovation advantage and export commitment. *Journal of Business Research, 11,* 363-378.

Dravo agrees to market type of plant for Grupo. (1980, September 30). *Wall Street Journal,* p. 38.

Erickson, T.J. (1985). The next decade in pharmaceuticals. *Business Quarterly, 50,* 79-82.

Flanigan, A. (1978). The mystery of the vague specifications. *Forbes, 21,* 39-40.

Harvey, M.G., & Ronkainen, I.A. (1985). International counterfeiters: marketing success without the cost and the risk. *Columbia Journal of World Business, 20,* 37-45.

Karlin, K., & Anders, G. (1983, October 5). Importing science. *Wall Street Journal,* p. 1.

Lorange, P. (1986). Human resource management in multinational cooperative ventures. *Human Resource Management, 25,* 133-148.

Lutz, J.M., & Green, R.T. (1983). The product life cycle and the export position of the United States. *Journal of International Business Studies, 14,* 77-94.

McCarthy, D.J., Spital, F.C., & Lauenstein, M.C. (1987). Managing growth at high-technology companies: a view from the top. *Academy of Management Executive, 1,* 1.

Montaña, E. (1981). *Exportaciones de technologia de la industria quimica privada de Mexico* [Technology exports of the Mexican private chemical industry]. Washington, DC: InterAmerican Development Bank/World Bank.

Mullor-Sebastian, A. (1983). The product life cycle theory: Empirical evidence. *Journal of International Business Studies, 14,* 95-106.

Ohmae, K. (1986). Becoming a triad power: The new global corporation. *International Marketing Review, 3,* 7-20.

Ronstadt, R., & Kramer, R.J. (1982). Getting the most out of innovations abroad. *Harvard Business Review, 60,* 94-99.

Rugman, A. H. (1981). *Inside the multinationals: The economics of internal markets.* New York: Columbia University Press.

Stobaugh Jr., R.B. (1969). Where in the world should we put that plant? *Harvard Business Review, 47*, 129-136.

Svirdov, F.A. (Ed.). (1981). *The role of patent information in the transfer of technology.* New York: Pergamon Press.

Teitel, S. (1984). Technology creation in semi-industrial economies. *Journal of Development Economics, 16*, 39-61.

United Nations Centre on Transnational Corporations. (1987). *Technology corporations and technology transfer: Effects and policy issues.* New York: United Nations Centre on Transnational Corporations.

ADAPTIVE SYSTEMS AND TECHNOLOGICAL DEVELOPMENT WITHIN THE JAPANESE POLITICAL ECONOMY

Allen L. Brown and Gregory A. Daneke

Much of the foreign interpretation of Japanese management is either one sided—with more recent emphasis on success factors—or one dimensional. The soft areas such as decision making, training and employment practices are treated in isolation from the hardware or technology issues, such as equipment production processes and industrial engineering. Another deficiency is that specific firm level types of factor—human resource strategies or marketing issues—are isolated from broader industrial goals and public policies.

—McMillan (1985, pp. 16-17)

Theorizing about the process of, and the conditions for, innovation is an academic growth industry. There is by now quite an accumulated body of propositions: about the difference between generic and a nongeneric technology, about criteria for the 'maturity' of a technology, the different trajectories of product and process innovations, the nature of the product cycle, and so on. Most of these propositions are couched in an ahistoric form: they are not specific to time or place, or to a type of social structure.

—Dore (1987, p. 125).

Despite admonitions of this type, and numerous descriptive as well as prescriptive characterizations of Japanese management, studies continue to fall prey to a sort of "forest and trees" problem. That is, they explore either the forest or the trees, yet fail to fully appreciate the process of forestation. This is not merely a "process vs. products" problem; but rather, a tendency to isolate either actions or interactions, ignoring patterns of mutual causality. In particular, several studies have failed to grasp the complex web of synergistic interactions between strategic management, technological innovation, and the broader sociocultural system in Japan. Dating back to Meiji restoration, when Japan began absorbing western technology and the Samurai began turning themselves into a respected class of bureaucratic generalists, the Japanese have developed a political economy that supports technological innovation. In one sense, Japan is still a feudal rather than a capitalist society, in which systems of vassalage have gradually given way to mutual cooperation. In turn, these patterns provide institutional support for rapid commercial adaptation and/or experimentation.

Drawing upon extensive case studies of Japanese corporate planning (e.g., Daneke & Brown, 1987; Imai, Nonaka, & Takeuchi, 1985; Jaeger & Baliga, 1985; Kagono, Nonaka, Sakakibara, & Okumura, 1985; Takanaka, 1986) and more general appraisals of Japanese industrial organization (Dore, 1986; 1987; Gresser, 1984; Johnson, 1982; Okimoto, 1986; Ouchi, 1984), this discussion attempts to explain why the objectives, structures and decision-making processes in large Japanese firms are more "evolutionary" in nature than those of major U.S. companies, even the most innovative. A brief discussion of this type cannot hope to do justice to the vast complexities; however, as an agenda for further research, it might illuminate a few interesting domains.

Generally speaking, Japanese innovators feature an "adaptive systems" (see Appendix) approach to organizational management that depends upon a strong sense of overall vision and long-term organizational and societal objectives. These visions are shared throughout organizations by means of strong corporate cultures and group decision-making processes. Contrary to conventional wisdom, these shared visions do not constrain but rather enhance opportunities for adaptive responses to changing environmental contingencies. A more fluid set of structural and managerial imperatives emerge from these broad goal alignments. Moreover, Japanese organizations are less hierarchical and more flexible than most U.S. companies. Decision-making processes are less formalized and rely upon strong group behavior, an emphasis on production systems and a long-range perspective towards change. This greater emphasis on long-term decisions reflects the importance given to human resource development policies, as opposed to the predominant emphasis placed on short-run financial performance in most U.S. firms. This orientation results in approaches to strategic management that are much less analytical and comprehensive.

STRUCTURE, VALUES AND STRATEGY

In Chandler's (1962) classic analysis of organizational strategy, he demonstrated that the structure of an organization tends to follow its strategies for growth. In contrast, the strategies of modern Japanese companies are often driven by prevailing structural and behavioral conditions. The predominance of lifetime employment practices, long-term performance appraisals, strong sets of shared values and group decisionmaking help contribute to organizational strategies that place great emphasis on long-term objectives, manufacturing innovations and human capital or knowledge development.

Many of the unique interorganizational features of the Japanese industrial system play important roles in determining the patterns of strategic management of Japanese firms. Most notably, organizational strategies are influenced by close bank-business relations in Japan that contribute to less perceived financial risks (Okimoto, Sugano, & Weinstein, 1984), the predominance of relational subcontracting networks for coordinating market transactions (Dore, 1983), cooperative government-business relations (Johnson, 1982), joint R&D efforts (Doane, 1984), strong industry associations that facilitate the sharing of information, and large general trading companies that manage international trading activities (Ouchi, 1984).

Visionary Management and Human Resource Development

As Gresser (1984) suggests, the key to understanding the adaptation and innovation of Japanese industries is their shared vision of a knowledge intensive society. However, knowing where they are going does not necessarily commit them to one way of getting there, it merely orients organizations toward long-term development. This curious orientation is visionary without depending on rigorous long-term planning exercises. Complex analyses and quantitative techniques, such as the use of computer models, simulation or decision analysis, play a much less important role in the management of Japanese companies (see Lauenstein, 1985; see also Hayes & Abernathy, 1980).

In Japan, long-term visions serve as a compass rather than a map; and incremental and participatory processes develop these visions into detailed strategies. Group consensus building provides opportunities for discussion and debate between various divisions where integrated long-range strategies are developed. These also reflect broad organizational objectives identified by top management (Takanaka, 1986). This approach does not require outguessing the future. Japanese corporate leaders display a great deal of skepticism about the ability to make accurate predictions. Since one cannot predict all contingencies, the best generic strategy is to intensify the human capital.

The prevalence of lifetime employment, despite its restriction primarily to full-time male employees, reinforces the long-term perspective of Japanese management. Workers are selected quite carefully with the notion that they represent a critical long-term resource for the company. Lifetime employment also coincides with less labor mobility, strong bonds between workers that can be cultivated over the years on the job or after work while blowing off steam at the local bars, and relations between management and workers that are based on mutual dependence (Nakane, 1973).

In addition to lifetime employment, Japanese companies have developed extensive training programs and compensation systems that are aimed at promoting long-term employee development. By incorporating widespread on-the-job training and the use of job rotations, Japanese companies have cultivated employees with multifunctional skills that contribute to a much broader, comprehensive view of the organization and interrelationships that exist within the company. They also seem to be more willing to take on tasks that are beyond their formal areas of expertise and tend to be less specialized than their fellow workers in the United States.

Compensation systems for Japanese workers are typically based on seniority, although merit also plays an important role (Clark, 1979). Financial rewards tend to be separated from individual performance, and instead are tied to the long-term performance of the company as a whole, with much less disparity between the wages of the top and lower level workers. Increased global competition and the aging of the Japanese work force have put pressures on many firms to modify the use of compensation systems that are linked to the length of service with a company. A study by Takanaka (1986) found that seniority-based wage and promotion systems have declined in prominence during recent years. While in 1981 about 63% of company wage systems were tied to seniority factors, the frequency had declined to about 49% by 1984.

In a similar vein to the prominence of lifetime employment, Japanese firms have also cultivated long-term reciprocal relations with suppliers and distributors. These relationships are based on mutual trust and obligation and provide great flexibility for companies by allowing them to share the risks associated with major investments (Dore, 1983). Unlike U.S. companies, there is less vertical integration in the factory and more reliance on subcontracting. Many Japanese firms have adopted what Asanuma (1986) refers to as a "two-vendor policy" that relies on the use of both in-house and subcontracted supplies so as to provide greater flexibility and reduce the need to make use of subcontractors as "capacity buffers."

De-emphasizing Financial Management

The financial perspective of Japanese firms also differs markedly from that of U.S. companies. Concerns for short-run profitability are overshadowed by primary objectives of long-term organizational growth and survival. Less emphasis is placed on short-term financial efficiency, partially due to a greater reliance on debt financing and cooperative bank-business relationships. Debt financing requires lower rates of return than equity financing in the United States and the terms of payment tend to be more negotiable (based on how well a company performs). In addition, Japanese shareholders are more supportive of long-term growth since dividends are highly taxed while capital gains are not (Abegglen & Stalk, 1985).

Objectives of growth and survival lead to aggressive strategies for expanding market shares, regardless of the short-run costs, by developing resources in anticipation of growing demands, rapidly developing new products and adopting extremely competitive pricing policies. While these strategies may be viewed as risky by some U.S. firms, they have aided the Japanese in growing at a tremendous pace. As a result, Japanese industries are clearly dominated by larger firms.

The desire for increased market shares has thrust Japanese companies into a reliance on increased exports. They stress the need to "import to survive, export to import." However, Japanese firms are typically very careful in selecting in which markets they choose to compete. In order to assure continued excellence, they attempt to "stick to the knitting" and stay close to their customers (Peters & Waterman, 1982). When the going gets rough, Japanese firms work together to leverage their strengths rather than rely on mergers and acquisitions to provide artificial solutions to deep-seated problems.

When analyzing markets, Japanese companies are extremely aggressive at gathering competitive intelligence. Lifetime employment and long-term relations with suppliers and dealers help contribute to a better understanding of customers and competitors. Marketing decisions tend to be based on information gathered directly from retailers and customers rather than from general market surveys. A classic example was the introduction of the Walkman by Sony despite market research that suggested that consumers would not purchase a tape recorder that couldn't record.

The Efficiency Response

Despite the significant commitments outlined above, Japanese companies have displayed an ongoing ability to adapt relatively quickly to change. These reactions tend to incorporate a strategic, long-term perspective that views sudden unforeseen changes as opportunities to improve the structure and performance of Japanese firms. Historically, crisis situations have served as important incentives for companies to operate more efficiently and helped boost their competitive positions. Following a period of devastating war, the Japanese were driven to catch up with the industrialized nations and followed a strategy of modernization supported by concentrated effort to increase exports. After tremendous successes in this area, oil shortages in the 1970s provided firms a new impetus to replace older, energy-intensive technologies and again reduce overall costs of operations.

More recently, Japanese companies have been coping with a crisis known as endaka—the high valuation of the yen. Many firms have buckled down once again and taken actions to reduce production costs even further. Many companies have cut the pay of their managers. For example, Hitachi and Nissan sliced 5% off the salaries of management and 10% off those of its directors. Others have shifted their product and marketing strategies to higher value-added goods, such as the arrival of the Acura line of cars from Honda and the focus on higher priced audio products at Sansui. Even more significantly, a growing number of firms are moving production facilities to the United States, Europe and Southeast Asia. Some predict that nearly 40% of Japan's export-related production will be overseas by 1990 (e.g., Borrus, 1986). The strategic nature of these decisions is reinforced by the fact that, despite the crisis of a high value yen in Japan, most companies have not cut their R&D spending. In the face of this crisis, they recognize the critical importance of continuing long-term efforts that could eventually lead to valuable innovations.

THE COOPERATIVE CULTURE

The development of Japanese industry has a history of strong cooperation between the government and business sectors. While direct government support for industry was much more active in the 1950s and 1960s, Japanese government agencies still play a vital role in orchestrating industrial development in Japan. American scholars, especially those influenced by the neoclassical economic perspective, often depict Japan as a planned economy; yet, this is extremely misleading. Here again, the adaptive systems perspective may be extremely useful in illustrating the very subtle patterns of cooperative planning, which totally defy models of centralized or comprehensive planning. Japanese government agencies serve to merely maintain long-term societal visions. One such agency is the Ministry of International Trade and Industry (MITI). Despite being the smallest of Japan's ministries, MITI has historically commanded extensive influence upon industrial management and economic development in Japan. During the 1950s and 1960s, MITI enjoyed its greatest power through control of foreign exchange and technology imports. It has also played a key role in helping steer investments towards strategic or targeted industries in the Japanese economy.

More recently, MITI's influences on the management of Japanese industry have stemmed from its use of "administrative guidance," which is rooted in the broad authority to work as diplomats in negotiating agreements. MITI often plays a pivotal role in building consensus for policies drawn up as a result of discussions and informal meetings with industry leaders and financial institutions. The agency communicates directly with various companies through active industry trade associations. In many cases, the specific policies that are developed are less important than the information sharing, discussions and cooperative relationships that are cultivated during the process of developing them. Johnson (1982) provides a detailed discussion of how MITI's administrative efforts helped guide the development of the Japanese steel and computer industries.

Another of MITI's important contributions to the management of Japanese companies has been the publication of its annual "long-range vision" of the nation's industrial development. The first such report was published on the heels of the oil crisis in 1974 and it set the tone for an historic shift towards the development of energy-efficient and knowledge-intensive industries in Japan. Once again, the development of these visions (10-year forecasts) is a collaborative venture and the process of getting companies to think about their long-range direction is probably more important than the actual report itself. In recent years, MITI has also helped facilitate the development of national research objectives and helped administer and finance cooperative industry-government efforts aimed at meeting these objectives.

The Innovation Emphasis

Beyond basic survival, the great advantage of the adaptive-systems approach is its emphasis on innovation. Innovation typically conjures up images of new technologies and new products. However, as the Japanese have successfully demonstrated, some of the most important innovations are based on new social systems and new processes—such as production techniques, distribution systems and marketing arrangements.

A distinction is often made between breakthrough or "revolutionary" innovations, and those that might be termed incremental or "evolutionary" innovations. The conventional wisdom is that the Japanese have been extremely successful at developing evolutionary innovations while the United States has excelled in the areas of revolutionary innovations. Indeed, history seems to suggest that the Japanese have thrived on the basis of creative imitation and the adaptation of breakthrough innovations imported from other countries (most notably the United States). Research shows that from 1953 through 1973, Japan accounted for only about 5% of a total of 500 breakthrough innovations worldwide, while the United States accounted for 63% (Okimoto, 1986).

It may be convenient to hypothesize that evolutionary forms of strategic management in Japanese firms are better suited to the development of evolutionary innovations than they are to stimulating the development of breakthrough innovations. However, despite Japan's legacy in developing incremental innovations, there are increasing signs of a move towards increased development of breakthrough innovations. In support of this notion, it might be pointed out that Japan now has the largest number of patents issued on an annual basis (Uno, 1984).

The Dynamics of Innovations

This level of success stems from strategic mechanisms that are more attuned to the dynamics of innovation. Conventional descriptions of innovation often imply an orderly and sequential process that goes from research through development to manufacturing and marketing. However, industrial innovation is really a dynamic and integrative process that can be viewed from a systems perspective. Kline (1985) has developed a "linked chain" model that focuses on the integrated nature of innovation. In this model, the central pathway for innovation consists of five major phases—market finding, synthetic design (which includes invention, preliminary design and simulation), detailed design and testing, redesign and production and distribution and marketing. The key to successful innovation lies in the various feedback loops that provide iterative mechanisms for integrating the work associated with these different stages. In addition, research plays an important role in augmenting the reservoir of knowledge that supports the work of synthetic design, while the resulting development of new products often loops back to prompt new forms of research. As a result, the most useful research work is typically performed in close coordination with the other stages of the innovation process rather than in an isolated laboratory setting.

Drucker (1985) identifies seven primary sources of opportunity for innovation—the unexpected; the incongruity; innovation based on process needs; changes in industry or market structure; demographics; changes in perception, mood and meaning; and new knowledge. While Drucker acknowledges the potential role of "new knowledge" or research in sparking selected innovations, he observes that the vast majority of innovations are tied to changes in the market. From the perspective of the linked-chain model, these opportunities can be viewed as driving forces behind the process of "market finding" and the feedback links in the chain. The Japanese have been extremely adroit at enhancing the operation of these feedback loops through various social innovations, such as the development of consensual decision-making processes, quality control circles, strong supplier-user relations and job rotations between functions and divisions of firms that help cultivate a better understanding of the interrelationships between the various stages of innovations.

Efforts to increase the degree of integration within Japanese firms appear to coincide with higher levels of uncertainty in the environment. These often result from a high dependence on imported raw materials, severe competition between firms and the rapid acceptance of new technologies in Japan. Studies of organizational performance by Lawrence and Lorsch (1967) found that in more dynamic and uncertain environments, there is a greater need to incorporate devices for enhancing organizational integration. As levels of uncertainty increase, decisionmaking becomes more widely dispersed throughout a company and lateral relationships are developed so as to enhance integration (Galbraith, 1977).

While a more integrated process of innovation may have negligible or even negative impacts on the development of breakthrough innovations, such an approach is more likely to provide a breeding ground for more selected innovations to come to fruition. For example, closer cooperation between a company's R&D manufacturing and marketing staff is more likely to bring about new products that are easier to manufacture and more desired by customers. Moreover, greater shared values, understandings and decision-making processes encourage groups to be more sensitive to and supportive of the need for change that are necessary to promote the cooperative development of a desired innovation. U.S. companies tend to use "bureaucratic" control systems, which rely primarily on quantitative information and adherence to standard operating procedures that can often thwart innovation. On the other hand, this type of approach does support a diversity of perspectives that may be critical for breakthrough innovations. Jaeger and Baliga (1985) have analyzed the Japanese approach to organizational control and they refer to it as "cultural control." This perspective places emphasis on the strong sets of shared values, or corporate "culture," within Japanese companies. Imai, Nonaka and Takeuchi (1985) refer to a similar process of subtle control as "self-control," or control through peer pressure.

Efficiency Response and Process Innovation

The adaptive efficiency of Japanese firms is, of course, the result of conscientious process as well as product innovations. Process improvements require organizational learning and cooperative group problem solving that allow for new ideas to be modified and adopted from the bottom up in an iterative fashion. Such process innovations are especially important in industries where complex products, such as electronics and automotives, are assembled in rapid fashion with multistage, high volume production facilities.

A greater emphasis on process innovation in Japan is reflected in the importance placed on production-oriented strategies and the strong influence wielded by production departments (as opposed to finance departments in the United States). Human resource policies also support process innovation by promoting people in operations to top management positions in many Japanese companies.

Japanese success in process innovation is exemplified by systems of flexible manufacturing that predominate in Japan. Studies have shown that Japanese companies favor production technologies that are more nonroutine, such as individually ordered production and production in small lots, while U.S. companies accept more production in large lots (Kagono, Nonaka, Sakakibara, & Okumura, 1985). These systems rely on flexibility in volume, mix and start-up requirements. Reliance on subcontractors and part-time labor can help provide flexibility in volume. Modular, batch-flow production systems allow the mix of several products in the same assembly line that are supported by multiskilled employees. In addition, development groups work in parallel on products to achieve the best approach (Bolwijn & Brinkman, 1987). Such techniques have helped reduce the time needed to shift manufacturing from one product to another.

Much has been written about Japan's innovations in process engineering known as "just-in-time" production (Hall, 1983; Schoenberger, 1982). This technique was developed by Toyota Corporation in the early 1960s and has spread widely throughout Japan. In recent years, there have been growing efforts to adopt similar techniques in U.S. companies. However, the success of JIT in Japan is tied to the prevalence of strong subcontractor relations. The relative absence of long-term subcontracting relationships in most U.S. firms make it less likely that these techniques can be easily adopted in U.S. industries.

JIT is actually a system of process innovations aimed at reducing the level of inventories so that the components and raw materials that go into manufacturing a product become available just when they are needed. These inventory reductions are supported by manufacturing techniques that include reduced machine setup and changeover times, the production of small batches, levelized production schedules and the control of production process through the use of kanban—production order cards that are part of a demand-pull system that specifies how much should be produced at one stage in a production process to meet the needs of a following stage.

JIT production techniques work in conjunction with other techniques in Japan that facilitate flexible manufacturing and quality control efforts that allow for the production of a more diverse product line with higher quality at a reduced cost. They are extremely important for reducing overhead costs and are, therefore, especially applicable to machinery and electronics industries where overhead costs are a major component of total product costs.

The capital investments associated with these process innovations are relatively small. In fact, JIT relies on the maximum utilization of workers accompanied by investments in abundant, relatively simple and lower cost machinery (Abegglen & Stalk, 1985). By limiting the amount invested in expensive and more specialized types of machinery, there are greater opportunities for innovation (Hambrick & MacMillan, 1985). Despite committing less capital resources to JIT production processes, the Japanese still invest over twice the amount of capital per worker in their manufacturing sector than does the United States (Landau & Hatsopoulos, 1986).

This capital intensiveness is augmented by unique Japanese financial systems. Longer term outlooks on financial investments help support innovative projects that may carry a higher degree of short-term risk than a company would accept if it had a greater concern for short-term profitability. In general, the process of capital budgeting in Japanese firms evaluates risky projects while assuming discount rates of about 10% (Hodder, 1986). These rates compare with levels of up to 30% in U.S. firms and may provide a greater incentive for innovation in Japanese companies.

Societal Learning and Innovation

Since human resources are viewed as the most valuable and scarce resource in Japan, an emphasis on multilearning organizational capabilities encourages greater organizational flexibility so that companies can achieve technological innovations in the midst of a rapidly changing environment. From the perspective of the employees, there must also be a system for rewarding, or at least not penalizing, their efforts to innovate. Since many Japanese companies provide guaranteed lifetime employment and tie individual performance appraisals to the long-term success of the entire company, there may be more acceptance of risk-taking in these firms. This form of appraisal does not penalize those who attempt to experiment yet fail many times before eventually succeeding. Maidique and Zirger (1985) observed that "learning-by-failing" is an important component of product innovation based on irregular patterns of learning and unlearning. Hence, the success of a new product cannot be judged adequately based on short-term financial criteria since "failure" in these terms may actually breed important innovations that benefit the company in the long term.

In complex technologically-based industries, successful innovations depend upon the work of technically skilled employees. The reservoir of technically proficient persons is much larger in Japan than in the United States. Moreover, prevailing labor practices in Japan result in the retention of innovative ideas within firms where they can be built upon by the organization, because researchers are not likely to break off and start their own companies. The reduced level of entrepreneurial start-ups in Japan is further constrained by a dearth of venture capital. Decreased level of labor mobility restricts the flow of ideas outside of larger companies and may restrict the cross-pollination of knowledge that helps contribute to the process of innovation. On the other hand, there is more emphasis placed on cooperation between firms in Japan for efforts involving basic research. Industry associations play a more active role in promoting the spread of information and facilitating the development of joint R&D. In a detailed study of Japanese innovation in the steel industry, the role of such associations was highlighted as an important component in the development of successful innovation (Lynn, 1982).

The R&D Society

While overall levels of support for R&D in Japan and the United States are nearly equivalent, more detailed comparisons should account for differences in the cost of capital, salaries for researchers and levels of automation. In general, the largest companies in Japan spend about 40% more of their revenues on R&D than the largest U.S. companies. Indeed, Japanese corporations provide about 75% of the R&D support in Japan compared with only about 50% of total R&D support in the United States (Abegglen & Stalk, 1985). The greater role of government support for R&D in the U.S. focuses primarily on military applications and these investments have taken on an increasingly narrow focus, which makes them less and less adaptable for commercial spin-offs. In the United States, much greater emphasis has been placed on cooperative research efforts between industry and universities. However, unlike government-business cooperation in Japan, these projects provide more targeted results for specific firms rather than industries as a whole.

In Japan, the principal emphasis of government support for R&D has been for commercial application and development of the civilian economy. This commercial emphasis of Japanese government investments in R&D has supported cooperative government-business projects. These cooperative efforts offer the advantage of spreading the costs, technical expertise and risks associated with R&D among the parties that participate. Doane (1984) provides a detailed analysis of the important role of interfirm cooperation for supporting basic and applied research in Japan. Rubinger (1985) analyzes the higher level of cooperative research efforts between automobile manufacturers and parts suppliers in Japan than in the U.S.

One of the most successful cooperative research projects in Japan was a $200 million effort in VLSI research. This pioneering effort lasted over four years, from 1976-1980, and it was the first cooperative basic research effort based on the creation of a joint research institute. The VLSI project was financed 60% by five Japanese companies and the remainder was funded by MITI. MITI's support came in the form of low-interest loans that were to be repaid out of royalties and any profits that result from new products that are developed from these efforts. This project was extremely successful and resulted in 1,000 new patents and the publication of 460 technical papers (Okimoto et al., 1984).

As Japanese firms have grown and become world leaders in many industries, the importance of original innovation has increased and the government has begun to shift its emphasis from that of applied research to more basic research. Similar patterns have been observed in Japan's corporate research. Kagono, Nonako, Sakakibara, & Okunura (1985) analyzed R&D strategies in the United States and Japan and found that U.S. companies allocate more resources to short-term R&D, such as the implementation of existing products and manufacturing processes, while Japanese companies spend more resources on long-term basic research or new product development.

CONCLUSIONS AND IMPLICATIONS

The general perspective provided by these observations is one of large scale societal evolution. While many U.S. firms can and have adopted "adaptive-systems" approaches, they are probably less successful without a supportive milieu. Hybrid systems, uniquely suited to the odd ad-mixture of capitalism, government interventions and heterogeneous cultural influences of the U.S. political economy are certainly possible. Nonetheless, the Japanese system, while unique, may provide valuable clues to such enterprises. The highly integrated strategizing processes of Japan will be difficult to replicate anywhere else in the world, even in other emerging "Pacific Rim" economies. The United States is especially constrained with regard to sociocultural elements, vital to the Japanese approach (see Daneke, 1984).

Within the existing constraints of the U.S. political economy, strategically innovative firms are becoming increasingly rare. In a recent article by Hill, Hitt, and Hoskisson (1988), "declining U.S. competitiveness" is again recast in terms of managerial motivations. Evoking Hayes and Abernathy's (1980) earlier indictment, they suggest that the forces antithetical to innovation have actually intensified.

Furthermore, they specify a modified model of decline (see Figure 1). In their model, they suggest that it is not so much the managerial mindset as it is the financial systems that create corporate myopia. They fail to elaborate, however, on how these debilitating patterns of capital accumulation are a direct reflection of the prevailing political economy and thus deeply embedded within the basic socioeconomic culture of the United States. In his somewhat oversimplified assessment, Dore (1987) boils down numerous differences to the "Confucian" emphasis on cooperation within the Japanese political economy. He summarizes his arguments as follows:

1. 'x-efficiency' or 'production efficiency' is as important as, and probably for explaining differences in national economic performance more important than, allocative efficiency.
2. A sense of the fairness of social and economic arrangements is a crucial precondition for that kind of efficiency.
3. That sense of fairness cannot be achieved in the rough and tumble which results when each actor in the market is encouraged to maximize his own short-term benefits, unconstrained by anything except the hard reality of market forces—not, at any rate, in modern societies, with modern concepts of citizenship and the accompanying rights to be respected and consulted and to receive a minimum level of income and security.

Several scholars have recognized the implications for global competitiveness of the United States' fiercely individualistic (zero-sum-game) political and economic culture (the most outspoken being Reich, 1987; Thurow, 1980). The great debate over the viability of "the entrepreneurial economy" which raged recently in the pages of the *Harvard Business Review* (see Ferguson, 1988; Gilder, 1988), is profound testimonial on an increasing awareness of the problems inherent in the fundamental tenants of advanced capitalism. These problems notwithstanding, one is still left with the desire to call down a plague on both sides of the cooperation vs. competition debate. Recognizing that Japan's growing commercial superiority is a function of the cooperative culture in no way suggests that anything like Reich's notion of "collective entrepreneurship" is near at hand for Western economies. What it does suggest is that scholars and policy-makers must intensify their quest for a system of institutional incentives that expand the innovative capabilities of U.S. firms without necessarily demanding a fundamental change in either macroeconomy or its underlying political and cultural institutions. In the final analysis, an "adaptive systems" approach to technological development must first adapt itself to the existing cultural climate while awaiting gradual institutional evolution.

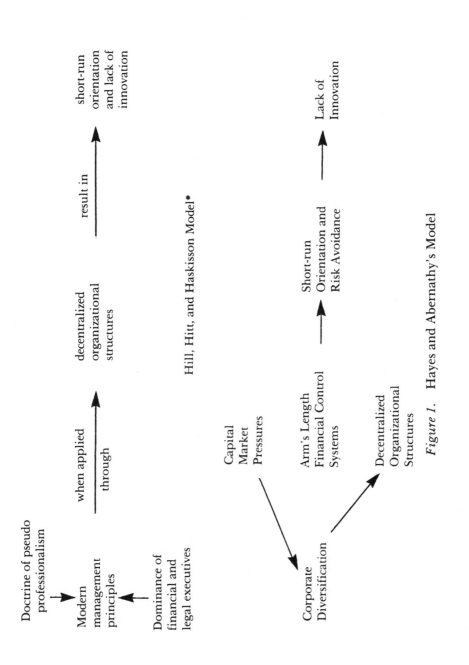

Figure 1. Hayes and Abernathy's Model

157

APPENDIX:
THE EVOLUTION OF AN EVOLUTIONARY
APPROACH TO STRATEGIC MANAGEMENT

Planning, whether at the level of the community or the nation state, rarely conforms to the various conceptualizations applied to it. This is true of both the descriptive and, of course, the prescriptive literature. Nevertheless, the general milieu in Japan, as well as the behavior of individual firms, coincides quite closely with certain conceptualizations found under the rubric of "adaptive-systems." Thus, these concepts provide a highly useful tool to explain strategizing of a type very alien to U.S. practice; yet, quite familiar to planning theorists and students of the various urban and regional planning programs in the United States and Europe.

With specific reference to public sector approaches, Wilson (1980) identified the following alternative schools of thought:

- *Rational Model* (centralized, comprehensive, mechanistic).
- *Incremental Model* (political, marginal adjustments).
- *Mixed Scanning* (situational, combining both of the above).
- *General Systems* (integrative, interactive, goal defining, iterative).
- *Adaptive Learning* (decentralized, participative, futures oriented).
- *Future Hybrids* (a synthesis of general systems and adaptive-learning concepts and methods).

Wilson implies that the list is somewhat chronological, representing distinct epochs. However, if thinking has indeed evolved over time, the process is more dialectic than linear; and all types still exist in practice. Wilson, nevertheless, envisioned the inevitable movement toward his category of future hybrids (or "adaptive-systems") approaches. This transformation of planning activities (both public and private) would be driven by the following forces (paraphrased from p. 290):

1. a need to understand changing social values;
2. a need to develop holistic approaches to complex issues;
3. a need for the future's oriented social learning as a means of reducing uncertainty;
4. a call for increased rank and file participation in the work place and in government;
5. growing concern for personalized interaction in an increasingly depersonalized world (high tech and high touch); and
6. an increasing emphasis on the design function within the evolution of human institutions.

While these forces have intensified, this natural transition has been truncated, at best. In the United States, the adaptive-systems approach remains much more prescriptive than descriptive, especially with reference to corporate strategizing.

Given the general lack of widespread application, conceptual development has also tended to be somewhat languorous to and/or isolated from highly theoretical explorations. Thus, a brief review of early formulations as well as diverse on-going developments may be instructive.

An Adaptive-Systems Approach

The on-going merger of adaptive-learning concepts and planning perspective derived from "general systems" theory is not so much a hybrid as a recognition of common concerns. Not only are the basic concepts complementary, a number of applied theorists have made contributions to both schools. Both theoretical traditions have produced numerous distinct bastard children, of course; but, the unifying concerns of the planning professions tended to focus in a narrow band of overlapping elements.

General systems being, perhaps, the most grandiose of "grand theories," provides a very diverse intellectual tradition—spawning everything from computer science to dynamic global models. Given this diversity, it has meant many different things to different people; but, to planning theorists, it was essentially a handy biological metaphor, used to explain patterns of interaction with changing external environments. Despite its mathematical underpinnings and close proximity to the scientific method, it was also nonmechanistic, nonreductionist, and nondeterministic (see von Bertalanffy, 1974, p. 20). Through its holistic visions, it could incorporate transrational and/or value judgments into its representations of goals-seeking behavior (see Churchman, 1971). In sum, it was an ideal instrument for the purposeful design of human institutions.

Given these lofty aspirations and its inherent conflicts with traditions of logical-positivism, it had pretty much run its course as a leading approach to social inquiry by the late 1960s. Nonetheless, students of planning and management (especially in the public sector) continued to develop tools and strategies derived from basic systems concepts well into the 1970s (see Steiss & Daneke, 1980). Moreover, a variety of these techniques (PERT, CPM, MAUT, etc.) continue to thrive in management science departments and governmental analysis shops. Systems thinking also endured in numerous normative planning formats (e.g., AcKoff, 1974; Emery, 1974; Gross, 1965; Jantsch, 1979). In recent years, esoteric systems theorizing has proceeded in attempts to apply certain advances in biophysics to social evolution (Corning, 1983; Jantsch, 1981).

While not nearly so comprehensive in scope, the "adaptive-learning" approach proved only slightly less ambitious with regard to societal change. Based in theories of educational and environmental psychology, as well as elements of systems thinking, the learning approach accepted fairly severe constraints on human rationality. Moreover, it took a rather phenomeno-logical approach to planning, in which social innovation takes place in small, loose-knit, nonhierarchical, and often adhoc, associations (see Friedman & Hudson, 1974). Its focal point was not upon achieving "steady-state," but rather enhancing adaptability in ever increasingly "turbulent" environments. The role of planning was, in the words of Michael (1973, pp. 281-282), to facilitate "future responsive social learning" and not at all to engage in "societal engineering." To overcome the intense social-psychological patterns of unlearning present in complex organizations, planners must be willing to:

- Live with and acknowledge great uncertainty.
- Embrace error.
- Seek and accept the ethical responsibility and the conflict-laden interpersonal circumstances that attend goal-setting.
- Evaluate the present in the light of anticipated futures, and commit themselves to actions in the present intended to meet such long-range anticipations.
- Live with role stress and forego the satisfactions of stable, on-the-job, social group relationships.
- Be open to changes in commitments and direction, as suggested by changes in the conjectured pictures of the future and evaluations of ongoing activities.

While highly prescriptive in tone, adaptive-learning grew out of elaborate case studies of successful adaptations, in public and private sector enterprise (see Michael, 1973). Furthermore, it drew extensively on observations arising from the burgeoning "organizational development literature." (Argris, 1965; Bennis, 1966; Emery, 1974; Lawrence & Lorsch, 1967; Likert, 1961). Moreover, adaptive-learning concepts were easily blended with various systems design approaches, and was particularly congruent with so-called "contingency theory" (Galbraith, 1977).

If thorough-going synthesis of adaptive and systems approaches is at hand, then it is probably by way of emerging preoccupation with evolutionary perspectives. Evolutionary models are becoming increasingly important in a number of disparate disciplinary perspectives. Systems scientists (Jantsch, 1979), adaptive theorists (Trist, 1981), and organizational studies (Aldrich, 1979), have sought to understand social systems evolve over

Table A.1. Features of Old and New Pardigms

Old Paradigm (U.S. Firms)	New Paradigm (Japanese firms)
The technological imperative	Joint optimization
People as extensions of machines	People as complimentary to
machines	
People as expendable spare parts	People as a resource to be
developed	
Maximum task breakdown, simple narrow skills	Optimum task grouping, multiple broad skills
External controls (supervisors, specialist staffs, procedures)	Internal controls (self-regulating subsystems)
Tall organization chart, auto-cratic style style	Flat organization chart, participative
Competition, gamesmanship	Collaboration, collegiality
Organization's purposes only	Members' and society's purposes
Alienation	Commitment
Low risk-taking	Innovation

time. Meanwhile, various "institutional" and/or "evolutionary" economists have focused on issues of social adaptation for some time (Boulding, 1978); and even a few "mainstream" or neo-classical economists have suggested modifications of the basic "theory of the firm," to incorporate evolutionary dynamics (see Nelson & Winter, 1982).

These evolutionary perspectives provide an especially potent conceptual base for strategic planning, particularly for firms involved in technological innovation. To begin with, they define a new, human resource and research intensive form of industrial organization under the rubric of evolving "social-technical systems." To paraphrase Trist (1981), the new organization paradigm comprises the unique elements listed in Table A.1.

The Evolution of U.S. Strategic Management

Unfortunately, few U.S. firms rely heavily upon this conceptual base. Perhaps the reason for this lack of attention is the level of societal learning and cooperation that such systems demand. In the heterogeneous pluralistic, and mutually combative society, a set of planning and management parameters derived from adaptive-systems might be fool hardy at best. Given antiquated inappropriate perspectives about the nature of planning, corporate strategic activities in the United States evolved into a largely nonplanning system pretty much analogous to Trist's "old paradigm," shown above. Consider the abandonments of the phrase "strategic planning" for the more amorphous term "strategic management" in the academic literature. It is, of course, noteworthy that actual management practices rarely, if ever, correspond to scholarly appraisals, even the fairly mundane intellectualisms common to most business schools.

Strategic planning, as a major corporate activity, began as an attempt to merely expand conventional budgeting and control techniques beyond the customary single-year format, through the use of 5-year projections. In the late 1940s, Von Neumann and Morgenstern introduced the idea of strategic "reacting," (see Bracker, 1980) to more immediate changes in business conditions. Drucker (1961) introduced the modern version of strategic planning, distinguishing between forecasting and planning, and emphasizing the creative dimension of the latter. In the early 1960s, Chandler (1962), a business historian, developed vital perspectives on the centrality of goal formulation and coined the famous apriorism that "strategy determines structure." Throughout the 1960s, strategic planning mirrored the more mechanistic aspects of systems analysis and the "rational comprehensive" approach.

Increased agglomeration in the 1970s brought a number of sophisticated market and financial analysis techniques together to augment continued attempts to outguess the future. Leading business schools and consulting groups championed various "portfolio" approaches. Patent formulas could be used to guide investment decisions between various units and products within poorly integrated corporate structures. However, increasing environmental turbulence quickly brought these formula approaches into ill-repute. *Business Week* ("New breed," 1984, p. 63) reported: "Clearly, the quantitative, formula-matrix approaches to strategic planning ... are out of favor."

Rather than adopt adaptive systems approaches designed for high uncertainty situations, many firms merely withdrew from the process of impacting the future altogether. One of the few beneficial dimensions of this retreat, however, was the diaspora of planning functions into nearly all the nooks and crannies of the organization. In essence, the notion of strategic management implies increased participatory activities and systems in which all line and operations managers are asked to "think strategically." Yet, this concept remains more promise than prospect.

In sum, Hax and Majlut (1984) define the evolution of U.S. corporate strategizing as involving five distinct epochs:

1. Budgeting and financial control;
2. Long-range planning;
3. Business Policy;
4. Corporate strategic planning; and
5. Strategic management.

It remains problematic whether the current epoch is as much strategy as it is management, and management of very limited vision.

REFERENCES

Abegglen, J.C., & Stalk, G. Jr. (1985). *Kaisha: The Japanese corporation.* New York: Basic Books.

AcKoff, R.L. (1974). *Redesigning the future: A systems approach to societal problems.* New York: Wiley.

Aldrich, H.E. (1979). *Organizations and environments.* Englewood Cliffs, NJ: Prentice-Hall.

Argyris, C. (1965). *Organization and innovation.* Homewood, IL: Irwin/Dorsey.

Asanuma, B. (1986). *Transactional structure of parts supply in the Japanese automobile and electric machinery industries: A comparative analysis.* Unpublished paper, Kyoto University.

Bennis, W.G. (1966). *Changing organizations.* New York: McGraw-Hill.

von Bertalanffy, L. (1974). The history and status of general systems theory. In R.L. Ackoff (Ed.), *Systems and management annual.* New York: Petrocelli Books.

Bolwijn, P. T. & Brinkman, S. (1987). Japanese manufacturing: Strategy and practice. *Long Range Planning, 20,* 25-34.

Borrus, A. (1986). Japanese managers alarmed in the land of the rising yen. *International Management, 41,* 58-66.

Boulding, K.E. (1978). *Ecodynamics.* Beverly Hills, CA: Sage.

Bracker, J. (1980). The historical development of the strategic management concept. *Academy of Management Review, 5*(2), 219-224.

Chandler, A.D. (1962). *Strategy and structure.* Cambridge, MA: MIT Press.

Churchman, C.W. (1971). *The design of inquiring systems.* New York: Basic Books

Clark, R. (1979). *The Japanese company.* New Haven, CT: Yale University Press.

Corning, P.A. (1983). *The synergism hypothesis: A theory of progressive evolution.* New York: McGraw-Hill Book Company.

Daneke, G.A. (1984). Why Sam can't plan: Industrial policy and the perils of a nonadaptive political economy. *Business Horizons, 27,* 50-56.

Daneke, G.A., & Brown, A.L. (1987). *A socio-cultural model of Japanese technological innovation* (Working paper). Stanford, CA: Terman Engineering Center, Stanford University.

DeGreene, K.B. (1982). *The adaptive organization.* New York: Wiley.

Doane, D.L. (1984). *Two essays on technological innovation: innovation and economic stagnation, and interfirm cooperation for innovation in Japan.* Unpublished doctoral dissertation, Yale University.

Dore, R. (1983). Goodwill and the spirit of market capitalism. *The British Journal of Sociology, 34,* 459-482.

_____ (1986). *Flexible rigidities: Industrial policy and structural adjustments in the Japanese economy.* Palo Alto, Calif.: Stanford University Press.

_____ (1987). *Taking Japan seriously: A confucian perspective on leading economic issues.* Palo Alto, CA: Stanford University Press.

Drucker, P.F. (1961). *Technology, management and society.* New York: Harper & Row.

_____ (1985). *Innovation and entrepreneurship.* New York: Harper & Row.

Dunn, E.S. (1971). *Economic and social development: A process of social learning.* Baltimore, MD: Johns Hopkins University Press.

Emery, F.F. (1974). Educational planning and strategic innovation. In R.L. Ackoff (Ed.), *Systems and management annual* (pp. 253-281). New York: Petrocelli Books.

Ferguson, C.H. (1988). From the people who brought you voodoo economics. *Harvard Business Review, 66,* 55-62.

Friedmann, J., & Hudson, B. (1974). Knowledge and action: A guide to planning theory. *Journal of the American Institute of Planners, 40,* 2-16.

Galbraith, J.R. (1977). *Organization design.* Reading, MA: Addison-Wesley.

Gilder, G. (1988). The revitalization of everything: The law of the microcosm. *Harvard Business Review, 66,* 49-61.

Gresser, J. (1984). *Partners in prosperity: Strategic industries for the U.S. and Japan.* New York: McGraw-Hill.

Gross, B. (1965). What are your organization's objectives? A general systems approach to planning. *Human Relations, 18,* 195-216.

Hall, W. (1983). *Zero inventories.* Homewood, IL: Dow Jones-Irwin.

Hambrick, D.C., & MacMillan, I.C. (1985). Efficiency of product R&D in business units: The role of strategic context. *Academy of Management Journal, 28,* 527-547.

Hayes, R.H., & Abernathy, W.J. (1980). Managing our way to economic decline. *Harvard Business Review,* 67-77.

Hax, A.C., & Majlut, N. (1984). *Strategic management: An integrative perspective.* Englewood Cliffs, NJ: Prentice-Hall.

Hill, C., Hitt, M.A., & Hoskisson, R.E. (1988). Declining competitiveness: Reflections on a crisis. *The Academy of Management Executive, 2*(1), 51-60.

Hodder, J.E. (1986). Evaluation of manufacturing investments: A comparison of U.S. and Japanese practices. *Financial Management, 15*(1), 17-23.

Imai, K., Nonaka, I., & Takeuchi, H. (1985). Managing the new product development process: How Japanese companies learn and unlearn. In K. Clark, R. H. Hayes, & C. Lorenz (Eds),. *The uneasy alliance: Managing the productivity-technology dilemma* (pp. 337-375). Boston, MA: Harvard Business School Press.

Jaeger, A.M., & Baliga, B.R. (1985). Control systems and strategic adaptation: Lessons from the Japanese experience. *Strategic Management Journal, 6,* 115-134.

Jantsch, E. (1979). *The self-organizing universe: Scientific and human implications of the emerging paradigm of evolution.* New York: Pergamon Press.

_____ (1981). *The evolutionary vision toward a unifying paradigm of physical, biological, and sociocultural evolution.* Boulder, CO: Westview Press, Inc.

Johnson, C. (1982). *MITI and the Japanese Miracle.* Stanford, CA: Stanford University Press.

Kagono, T., Nonaka, I., Sakakibara, A., & Okumura, A. (1985). *Strategic vs. evolutionary management: A U.S.-Japan comparison of strategy and organization.* Amsterdam, The Netherlands: Elsevier.

Kline, S.J. (1985). *Research, invention, innovation, and production: Models and reality.* Stanford, CA: Stanford University Department of Mechanical Engineering.

Landau, R., & Hatsopoulos, G.N. (1986). Capital formation in the United States and Japan. In R. Landau & N. Rosenberg (Eds.), *The positive sum strategy* (pp. 563-606). New York: National Academy Press.

Lauenstein, M.C. (1985). Strategic planning in Japan. *Journal of Business Strategy, 6,* 78-84.

Lawrence, P.R., & Lorsch, J.W. (1967). *Organization and environment.* Boston, MA: Harvard Business School Press.

Likert, R. (1967). *The human organization: Its management and value.* New York: McGraw-Hill.

Lynn, L.H. (1982). *How Japan innovates: A comparison with the U.S. in the case of oxygen steelmaking.* Boulder, CO: Westview Press.

Maidique, M.A., & Zirger, B. (1985). The new product learning cycle. *Research Policy, 14,* 299-313.

McMillan, C.J. (1985). *The Japanese industrial system* (2nd ed.). New York: de Gruyter.

Michael, D. (1973). *On learning to plan and planning to learn: The social psychology of changing toward future-responsive societal learning.* San Francisco, CA: Jossey-Bass.

Nakane, C. (1973). *Japanese society.* Middlesex, England: Penguin.

Nakatani, I. (1984). The economic role of financial corporate grouping. In M. Aoki (Ed.), *The economic analysis of the Japanese firm* (pp. 227-258). North-Holland: Elsevier.

Nelson, R.R., & Winter, S.G. (1982). *Evolutionary theory and economic change.* Cambridge, MA: Harvard University Press.

The new breed of strategic planner. (1984, September 17). *Business Week,* pp. 62-68.

Okimoto, D.I. (1986). The Japanese challenge in high technology. In R. Landau and & N. Rosenberg (Eds.), *The positive sum strategy* (pp. 541-568). New York: National Academy Press.

Okimoto, D.I., Sugano, T., & Weinstein, F.B. (1984). *Competitive edge: The semiconductor industry in the U.S. and Japan.* Stanford, CA: Stanford University Press.

Ouchi, W. (1984). *The m-form society.* Reading, MA: Addison-Wesley.

Peters, T.J., & Waterman, R.H. (1982). *In search of excellence.* New York: Harper & Row.

Reich, R.B. (1987). *Tales of a new America: The anxious liberals' guide to the future.* New York: Vintage.

Rubinger, B. (1985). Technology policy in Japanese firms: Decision-making, supplier links, and technical goals. *Technology in Society, 7*(2/3), 281-296.

Schonberger, R.J. (1982). *Japanese manufacturing techniques: Nine hidden lessons in simplicity.* New York: The Free Press.

Steiss, A.W., & Daneke, G.A. (1980). *Performance administration.* Lexington, MA: D.C. Heath.

Takanaka, A. (1986). Some thoughts on Japanese management centering on personnel and labor management: The reality and the future. *International Studies of Management and Organization, 15,* 17-68.

Takeuchi, H. 1985. Motivation and productivity. In L. C. Thurow (Ed.), *The management challenge* Japanese views (pp. 18-28). Cambridge, MA: MIT Press.

Thurow, L.C. 1980. The zero-sum society. New York: Basic Books.

Trist, E. 1981. The evolution of socio-technical systems. Toronto, Ontario: Ministry of Labour.

Uno, K. (1984). Recent trends in R&D and patents: A quantitative appraisal. In H. Eto & K. Matsui (Eds.), *R&D management systems in Japanese industry* (pp. 113-139). New York: Elsevier.

Wilson, D.E. (1980). *The national planning idea: Five alternative approaches.* Boulder, CO: Westview Press.

PERSPECTIVES OF INTERNATIONAL EXECUTIVES ON INTERNATIONAL TECHNOLOGY TRANSFER ISSUES

Basil J. Janavaras

High tech firms are cognizant of and concerned with international technology transfer challenges and opportunities. Some of the strategic areas identified by these firms include export controls, cultural problems, competition, market share and profitability. However, only a few firms have policies in place that would enable them to be proactive in managing international technology transfers. This paper discusses the perspectives and strategic management responses of high tech firms regarding international technology transfers.

International technology transfer presents opportunities as well as problems for U.S. high tech firms. In many instances, such transfers have been a double-edged sword for U.S. companies. In certain industries, foreign manufacturers have captured nearly the entire market for such products as color televisions, using technology originally developed domestically. John Sculley, the CEO of Apple Computer, in his December 9, 1987 speech before the Commonwealth Club of California, was asked about the threat to the long-term competitiveness of U.S. companies being posed by the international transfer of technology. He cited the U.S. consumer electronics industry to illustrate that licensing technology to gain short-term bottom line results may not be in the best interest of the technology supplier.

Other authorities take the view that technology sharing, which may include coproduction and comarketing of products, is a viable method of gaining access to markets that would otherwise be restricted, such as the People's Republic of China. There are also numerous examples of U.S. firms that have successfully adapted technologies developed abroad. One example is Multi-Arc Vacuum Systems of Minneapolis, which learned of a Soviet technique of hardening drills for longer life and has now become a mid-sized international firm.

U.S. manufacturers are starting to look outside of their own R&D departments for innovations important to their long-term growth. Tim Lavengood of Northwestern University estimates that only 30% of the world's advanced technology will be developed in the United States by 1994, compared with 70% in 1974. Large companies such as DuPont, 3M, Monsanto, Proctor and Gamble, and others have organized departments dedicated to monitoring technological developments worldwide. Small high tech companies that are dependent on technology but have limited resources to devote to R&D are forced to seek licensing arrangements or joint ventures with other countries to remain competitive.

As economic and technological interdependence continues to shrink the world, the debate over international technology transfer issues is sure to continue. Corporate executives are concerned with these issues due to the impact they have on the survival and growth of the high tech firm operating in a highly competitive environment.

PURPOSE

The purpose of this study was twofold: (1) to identify the key international technology transfer issues and (2) to examine the perspectives of international executives and elicit their responses to these issues. The firms targeted for this preliminary study were in the computer, electrical, scientific testing, medical equipment, pharmaceutical and adhesive industries.

The specific objective of this study was to elicit the experience of international executives and examine strategic management responses as practiced by high tech firms. Some of the areas investigated were:

1. policies and strategies of U.S. firms regarding the management of technology transfers;
2. effective methods of technology transfer currently being practiced by U.S. firms;
3. impact of U.S. government export controls on international technology transfer; and
4. the long-term implications of technology transfers on the competitiveness of the firm.

Benefits

It is hoped that the findings of this study will contribute to a better understanding of international technology transfer problems and opportunities faced by all parties concerned. The study should also assist firms and policy makers in developing effective strategies and policies regarding the transfer of technology across national borders. Such policies should aid in the development of a global economic viewpoint which addresses the interrelated nature of technological developments and their impacts in international markets.

METHODOLOGY

The sample for the research study consisted of 131 high tech firms representing six industries: computer, electrical, scientific testing, medical equipment, and pharmaceutical industries. The firms in the selected industry represent a range of sizes and technologies, but the majority were small-to-medium sized in dynamic high tech industries. The mailing list, categorized by Standard Industrial Code number, included all Minnesota international firms within the selected industries. This list was provided by the U.S. Department of Commerce, Minneapolis District Office.

A questionnaire was mailed on November 12, 1987. The questionnaire consisted of a total of 15 questions, 13 open-ended questions and 2 based on rating scales (see Appendix). These questions were designed to elicit qualitative responses based on the practical experiences of the respondents. After a follow-up mailing, 15 companies had returned the questionnaire and 5 interviews had been conducted.

FINDINGS

Definition of International Technology Transfer

The literature suggests that international technology transfer is any form of transmission of technology either between firms or governments or between members of the same organization (such as subsidiaries) over national borders, however no consensus was reached among respondents on the definition of international technology transfer. The following are some of the definitions provided by the executives.

I consider a definition of technology transfer to mean a specification for a product or a material which is passed on to a second party outside of the United

States. Technology could be either commodity technology or leading edge technology.

The exchange of ideas, goods and services in such a fashion as to create a true world market for the item in question. My own experience says that is what has happened and is happening in production of color televisions.

Learning to build a product in the United States without spending millions to develop it. And conversely, teaching foreign producers about technologies which a domestic manufacturer may excel in.

To implant processing technology from the United States into a foreign market, giving the foreign partner a new capability and providing an expanded market for the technology provider.

Selling high tech instruments or systems to the international market.

The transfer of any technical knowledge outside the jurisdiction of the United States to a foreign country.

Method(s) of Technology Transfer

Figure 1 shows the methods the respondent firms are using to transfer technology.

As most of the respondent firms were small to mid-sized, sale of their technological products and/or services was the dominant transfer mechanism. Among the few large respondent firms, licensing was the most important mechanism, followed by joint ventures.

Technology Recipients

The overwhelming majority of respondents were transferring product/ services technology to developed countries. The European countries were the most common destination, followed by the Pacific Rim countries of Japan, Taiwan, Korea and Singapore. Less developed countries were specifically mentioned as destinations only by large firms that took a "developmental" approach to technology transfer.

Technology Transfer Policies

Most respondent firms stated that they do not have a specific international technology transfer policy. Firms responding that they had a policy on international technology transfer had one or more of the following goals in mind:

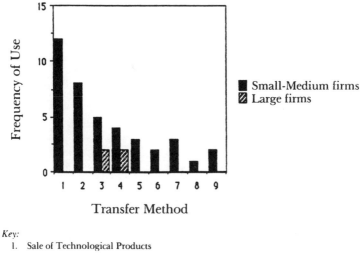

Transfer Method

Key:
1. Sale of Technological Products
2. Sale of Technological Services
3. Licensing
4. Joint Ventures
5. Contract Manufaturing
6. In-House Transfers to Subsidiaries
7. Training Foreign Workers
8. Turnkey Operations
9. Emulation (Technology Being Copied)

Figure 1. Methods of Technology Transfer

- protection of proprietary technology;
- control of competition;
- use of innovative technology developed in other countries to reduce R&D costs;
- use of generic, nonpropriety technology to aid economic development in less developed countries (LDCs); and
- use of a corporate approval procedure for international technology transfer: top management involvement ensures that the project will get the support needed and that it fits into the overall business plan.

The majority of respondents said that they had different technology transfer policies for different regions of the world. Reasons cited for such

Table 1.   Regional Problems and Responses

Problem	LDCs	Developing Countries	Industrialized Countries	Response
Inadequate Training	X	X		Provide Training
Foreign Government Regulations	X	X	X	Comply
Quality Controls Standards	X	X		Stress Quality
Language	X	X	X	Hire Expertise
Local Electrical Codes	X	X	X	Adapt Product
Concept of Time	X			Education About U.S. Business Practices
Exchange Rates	X	X	X	
Servicing Equipment	X	X		Train Dist. to Service or Return Products to U.S. for Service
Stable Power Supply	X			

a regionalized policy structure were concerns about creating additional competition. Others stated that their policy is determined by political and economic conditions in each region. In LDCs, oftentimes local producers lack the ability to market their products. This situation can lead to the U.S. partner being asked to provide marketing for the products produced by the transferred technology.

Regional Problems and Solutions

Table 1 shows the problems experienced when transferring technology and the strategic responses to such problems. Local government regulations and quality control standards were a common problem among respondents. Response to local government regulations was made on a case-by-case basis, as was the response to quality control problems. Responses to the problem of poor training ranged from educating distributors in order to provide local servicing to returning the equipment to the United States for servicing.

LDCs

In general, firms encountered the largest number of problems in transferring of technology to LDCs. Cultural problems such as language, the concept of time and a lack of understanding of U.S. business practices were most common. For joint venture partners, a shared mutuality of objectives was stated as important in achieving success. If both partners were moving toward the same goal, problems could be worked out on a case-by-case basis.

Developing Countries

Once again, training and quality control were mentioned as problems when transferring technology to developing countries. Local government regulation and electrical codes were also cited as problem areas.

The firms responded to these problems by providing support to foreign partners or customers to teach them the technical skills required. In relation to government regulations and codes the unanimous response was to comply with local regulations. One CEO in a computer-related industry describes his company's response:

> Our response to the problems can best be described as a commitment by our firm to its marketplace. We try to understand cultural differences and, in fact, have employed people from various countries to coach us and guide us into our relationships. With regard to the technical skills required to service our product, we generally will be supplying resources directly until such time that the training takes effect and the personnel in other lands are capable. We try to work with the local groups on marketing plans and certainly on quality control issues which involve not only the equipment itself but also the after service and process support required. In the area of process support this seems to be one of the largest issues we have after equipment is placed with customers worldwide.

Industrialized Countries

Once again, cultural differences were mentioned as the most common problem when transferring technology to industrialized countries. Also mentioned were import regulations and tariffs along with governmental health regulations in the case of medical equipment. The response to these problems was an attempt to understand cultural differences and to provide training as necessary. Technology sharing was seen to be a good means of overcoming marketing problems associated with distance and cultural differences.

Implications of International Technology Transfer

The experts' view of the long-term implications of international technology transfer was one of risks and opportunities. On the positive side, international technology transfer was seen as a way to "avoid reinventing the wheel" or, in other words, reducing development costs. Technology transfer was seen as enabling the firm to remain competitive, increase market share and provide growth.

Caution was expressed about the negative commercial implications of international technology transfer. Proper management of technology transfer was seen as important in preventing a loss of domestic manufacturing capacity along with jobs and competitiveness such as was seen in the decline of the U.S. color television industry. One executive stated that international technology transfer had almost always created competition, both for his firm and the industry. National security issues associated with technology transfer were also a concern.

Effect of U. S. Government Restrictions on Technology Transfers

The cost and time delays associated with obtaining an export license were cited as a negative influence on export sales. A minimum of 90 days was required for a validated export license and some took as long as 6 to 9 months. These tight restrictions were seen as unrealistic in light of the fact that oftentimes similar technology is available in other countries. This situation causes enormous setbacks in certain high technology firms as foreign buyers seek overseas suppliers in order to avoid overly restrictive U.S. government export controls. The response of these firms was to support export control reform. Those firms exporting under the general destination export license category did not find U.S. government restrictions excessive.

The Extent of U. S. Government Control on Transfers

The respondents unanimously supported the idea of controlling technology transfers to protect the national security of the United States. However, the respondents disagreed with current government policy regarding the description of strategic defense items. The respondents felt that the list was too long and included items easily obtainable in other countries, particularly Japan. Restricting export of these products was seen as damaging only U.S. firms and contributing nothing to national defense.

One CEO of an electronics firm expressed his opinion as follows:

> The government certainly has an interest in looking after the high technology transfers. They should, however, limit themselves to levels of technology which are not obtainable from other countries. We tend to embargo a number of technology items far too long, thereby taking away from the competitive position that our companies could enjoy. Our foreign competitors, therefore, take market share from us and those research and development dollars and enjoy a heavier percentage of market penetration. Government should work closer with industry rather than having an adversarial relationship. Government does not trust industry, particularly Department of Defense, and I do not see this changing in the future.

A few respondents expressed concern regarding the fact that U.S. companies are forbidden to transfer technology that is freely available to students from all lands in our university system. It was felt that in the case of true leading edge technology, where breakthroughs are strategically important, the technology should be protected or controlled in the early stages, including the university level as well as the industrial level.

Corporate Goals of International Technology Transfer

Increasing market share was the most common company goal sought through the use of international technology transfer. Also important were:

1. increasing competitiveness;
2. increasing profits by reducing development costs;
3. enhancing the technological position of the firm within its industry;
4. reducing prices while maintaining quality; and
5. earning royalties from remote markets.

Trends

Emerging trends in international technology transfer which were identified by the respondents are:

1. A major trend in technology transfer currently taking place, reportedly, is in direct reflection of the different government attitudes toward protectionism (companies are beginning to take strategic steps that would protect themselves in case of controls in import/export activities; by having license agreements or manufacturing facilities or joint ventures in other countries, they are somewhat insulated from this trend);

2. joint ventures with the Peoples Republic of China;
3. a shift in major activity from Europe to the Pacific Rim. China (PRC) will join Japan by 2050 as a developed industrial economy;
4. more awareness of what technology is available from other countries;
5. more and more sophisticated technology being transferred; and
6. Increased regulatory control of imports by host governments will require increased transfer of technology to maintain/increase market penetration.

SUMMARY AND RECOMMENDATIONS

The purpose of the study was to examine international technology transfer issues as perceived by international executives of selected firms. The major problems associated with international technology transfer as identified by the study are:

1. government export licensing policies on high tech products/technology were seen as overly restrictive, hurting the competitive position of U.S. producers;
2. cultural problems, with language being the number one problem;
3. lack of trained technicians and servicing problems in the recipient countries, including industrialized countries;
4. fluctuating foreign exchange rates; and
5. lack of an international technology transfer policy on the part of most firms.

The opportunities presented to firms by international technology transfers were seen as a way for firms to reduce development costs, remain competitive, increase market share and provide growth.

In conclusion, international technology transfer issues are a concern to firms responding to the survey. Only a few of the firms surveyed have policies in place to deal with the problems and opportunities presented by international technology transfers. The majority of the firms are reacting to the problems after the technology has crossed national borders.

The following recommendations are in order.

1. International technology transfer issues should be integrated into the strategic planning process of the firm.
2. U.S. firms should investigate the recipients and suppliers of technology before transfers occur.
3. Overly restrictive U. S. government controls on transferred technology which is easily available elsewhere in the world are a serious concern

to the responding firms. Export control reform is called for to ensure that sensitive defense-related technology will remain controlled while allowing industry the ability to export commercial products quickly. The ability to respond quickly to commercial export orders would seem to be in the best interests of the U. S. economy by enabling domestic manufacturers to remain competitive worldwide while reducing the U. S. trade deficit.

APPENDIX:
QUESTIONNAIRE

International Technology Transfer Issues
International Business Institute
Mankato State University

1. A. What are the method(s) your firm is using to transfer its technology? (Please rank in order of importance, with "1" being the most important. If a method is not applicable, please indicate with a "NA").

    _____Wholly owned   _____sale of technological products
       subsidiary
    _____joint ventures   _____sale of technological services
    _____licensing   _____emulation (your technology
                                 being copied by a foreign firm
                                 aka reverse engineering)

    B. What country(ies) is your firm transferring technology to?
2. What country(ies) is your firm transfering technology from?
    By what methods?
3. What products/services/technology do you transfers?
4. Does your firm hvae a policy in regard to technology transfer?
    If so, what is that policy?
5. Does your company have different technology transfer policies for different regions of the world? Please explain.
6. When transferring technology to less developed countries:
    A. What problems have been experienced by your firm?
    B. How does your firm respond to these problems?
7. When transferring technology to developing countries:
    A. What problems have been experienced by your firms?
    B. How does your firm respond to these problems?
8. When transferring technology to industrialized countries:
    A. What prolems have been experienced by your firm?
    B. How does your firm respond to these problems?

9. On a scale of 1-10, with 10 being the highest level of technology, what level of technology is your firm transferring? If different levels of technology are being transferred, please indicate each level.

1	3	5	7	10
low		medium		high

10. In your opinion, what implications does international technology transfer have on the long run competitiveness of your firm? Of your industry?
11. What U.S. Government restrictions does your firm encounter in transferring technology to foreign countries? How does your firm respond?
12. Under what, if any, circumstances should the U.S. Government regulate/control technology transfers?
13. What is your definition of international technology transfer?
14. What corporate goals and objectives are you trying to achieve by transferring technology?
15. What do you perceive as emerging trends in international technology transfers?

NAME: _____

POSITION: _____

COMPANY: _____

TELEPHONE NUMBER: _____ (_____) _____

REFERENCES

Brooks, H., & Guile, B.R. (1987). *Technology and global industry.* Washington, DC: National Academy Press.

Castro, J. (1987). Tussle over high technology. *Time, 129*(4), 48.

Frame, J.D. (1983). *International business and global technology.* Lexington, MA: Lexington Books.

Gall, N. (1986). Does anyone really believe in free trade? *Forbes, 138*(13), 115-120.

Gray, H.J. (1985). The new technologies: An industrial revolution. *Journal of Business Strategy, 5,* 83-85.

High tech—trade deficit in '86. (1987, May-June). *Research Management,* pp. 2-3.

Lassere, P. (1984). Selecting a foreign partner for technology transfer. *Long Range Planning, 17,* 43-49.

News Action, International Trade and Technology. (1987, Fall). Northwestern University.

Price tag put on damage from U.S. technology transfer. (1985). *Research and Development, 27*(5), 75.

Stobaugh, R., & Wells, L.T. (1984). *Technology crossing borders.* Boston: Harvard Business School Press.

PART III

STRATEGY-TECHNOLOGY INTEGRATION

MANAGING STRATEGIES AND TECHNOLOGIES

Charles C. Snow and Edward J. Ottensmeyer

High technology firms face unique management challenges as increasingly they compete in industries that are at the forefront of new approaches to strategic management. Competitive success for these firms will largely depend on their ability to manage both business strategies and various technologies. What do we know about managing the critical link between these two powerful forces in the high technology firm? The basic premises of this chapter are straightforward: (a) there are a limited number of successful competitive strategies, (b) new strategies are likely to be combinations or extensions of currently known strategies, and (c) the organization structure required to implement new competitive strategies is presently available but it is difficult to manage. A conceptual framework is presented that can help managers of high technology firms to determine the appropriate fit among strategy, technology, and organization structure.

BACKGROUND

One of the hottest consumer electronics products in history is the videocassette recorder (VCR). Its genesis can be traced to the introduction of television after World War II. Four decades later, it represents a multibillion-dollar global business. The market leader in VCRs, Japan's Matsushita Electric Company, generates over $3 billion in revenues from this product alone.

The path leading to this product's resounding success, however, is strewn with missed strategic opportunities and technological failures (Rosenbloom & Cusumano, 1987). For example, Ampex, the U.S. company that pioneered the original product technology, was not able to produce a consumer version of its successful industrial machine. Taking a different tack, RCA invested heavily in a competing product technology. In 1981, it offered consumers a product called the Selectavision VideoDisc. Three years later, RCA announced that it would discontinue production of the VideoDisc after sustaining losses estimated at nearly $600 million. Today it markets VCRs manufactured in Japan. Finally, Sony developed a successful VCR called the Betamax, but after initial market success, sales declined to a miniscule share of the U.S. market.

Every day, we see around us dramatic reminders of the powerful, sometimes mysterious link between technology and business success (and failure). The growing numbers of advanced technology products in the marketplace—personal computers, medical diagnostic equipment, industrial robots, and others—provide evidence not only of the power of technology to change our lives but also to transform the very structure of industries. New information technologies allow firms to cross traditional industrial boundaries. Critical, but less visible, are new process technologies that have moved mature, "low tech" industries into the "high tech" age. Computer-aided design and manufacturing, as well as a host of other process developments, have breathed new life into moribund firms and industries.

Investment by firms in these new product, process and information technologies is also of interest to public policymakers, since national productivity growth and global competitiveness are at stake. Robert M. White, President of the National Academy of Engineering, stated that managing technology is "... one of the most critical issues that confront the country ..." (American Association of Engineering Societies, 1987, p. 14). Former Deputy Secretary of Commerce Clarence Brown has gone further, claiming that "Nothing could be more important to our future [than the management of technology]" (p. 14).

TECHNOLOGY: ITS MEANING AND IMPACT

In its broadest meaning, technology is the commercialization of science (see Figure 1). As such, technology refers to the systematic application of scientific knowledge in a new product, process or service (Bahrami & Evans, 1987). For most firms, making important technology decisions is like gambling. As one CEO of a high technology firm puts it: "Managing a high technology company means figuring out what to bet on and when to bet." Not surprisingly, the exciting activities and challenges of such firms

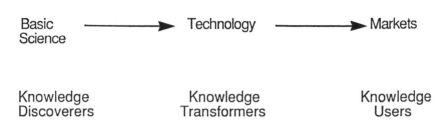

Figure 1. What is Technology?

have generated much interest on the part of management theorists. These observers have catalogued a dizzying array of management concepts and approaches—intrapreneuring, skunkworks, coventuring, and so on—that have been innovated by high technology firms.

Technology affects firms of all types and sizes, in every industry, and at every point on a firm's value chain (Porter, 1985). Similarly, strategic technology issues emerge throughout the three major stages of a firm's adaptive cycle—entrepreneurial, engineering, and administrative (Miles & Snow, 1978). In the entrepreneurial stage, product technology is dominant as firms experiment with alternative technologies and attempt to find the right mix of products and product designs to attract buyers in the early stages of a product life cycle. Process technology becomes the prime focus in the engineering stage as product designs stabilize, markets mature and greater efficiencies are sought in manufacturing. Solving administrative problems means that managers need to draw upon both information technologies and management systems to improve the chances for success of both product and process technologies.

These adaptive stages can be observed in operation in large, established firms as well as in small, start-up firms. Large firms, like Matsushita, Sony and RCA in VCRs, face a set of critical technology questions based largely on administrative complexity. For example, which new product technologies have sufficient market potential to pursue profitably given their higher cost structures? Which new product technologies are synergistic with existing product lines? How can more effective technology transfer occur in order to get ideas out of expensive corporate research labs and into product divisions? Which new manufacturing technologies will yield the highest efficiency? How can effective cooperative agreements or alliances be worked out with customers, independent R&D labs, or even competitors?

Small start-up firms struggle with quite different technology problems. These include convincing skeptical customers to try new products based on new technologies, transforming a product idea into a commercial success,

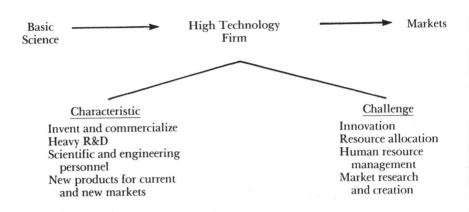

Figure 2.   What Is a High Technology Firm?

fighting off attacks from larger, better-financed competitors for favorable market position, and moving from entrepreneurial to professional top management teams.

Whether large or small, high technology firms can be distinguished from other firms in several important ways (see Figure 2). High technology firms commercialize inventions described in patents; spend a major portion of their budgets on research and development activities; are staffed by scientific and engineering personnel; and sell novel products, often to new market segments (Heidegger, 1977; Sherman, 1981). Because of these characteristics, high technology firms face unique management challenges, including how to (a) ensure continuous innovation; (b) allocate resources under conditions of high uncertainty; (c) manage professionals, and (d) create new markets.

STRATEGIC MANAGEMENT OF TECHNOLOGY

In high technology firms, technology and strategy issues require constant top-management attention: How and why do technological successes and failures occur? How can the technology component of competitive strategy be managed more successfully? Definitive answers to these basic questions often prove to be elusive or temporary. For example, success does not appear to result solely from foresight, persistence or serendipity. Neither does failure appear to be due simply to ignorance or recklessness. Success or failure in managing technology appears to be probabilistic—sometimes firms win, sometimes they do not. Can a company somehow improve its batting average so that, over time, technological success is more likely to occur than failure? That is, are there better ways to manage technology? And, if so, what are the key questions and issues on which top managers should focus their attention?

In our view, effective management of technology requires an understanding of how the development of technology, and the products and services it spawns, relates to the shifting realities of the marketplace. A conceptual approach that aids in this understanding could be called the *strategic management of technology*. Such an approach would help firms link their overall competitive strategy with appropriate product, process, and information technologies. While the conceptual integration of the literatures of strategic and technology management is presently at an early stage of development, there are points of convergence that can be identified. In the following sections, we attempt to move toward this important conceptual integration.

GENERIC COMPETITIVE STRATEGIES

Competitive strategies identify both a firm's intended position as well as the means by which those intentions are pursued. Firms, through their aspirations, plans, and actions, (a) develop modes of competing within particular industries (i.e., business strategies); and (b) select those industries in which they wish to participate (i.e., corporate or multi-business strategies). Generic strategies, those commonly found across a variety of industries, reflect fundamental choices about diversification, product offerings, competitive strengths and, of course, the role of technology.

A high technology firm's choices must be made within the existing structure of competition in an industry. Technology may have the power to transform an industry, so the way key technologies are managed shapes such factors as long-term and short-term profitability, market share, and downstream strategic options. Thus, it is crucial for a firm to manage technology in a way that is congruent with its overall competitive orientation.

Multi-Business Strategies and Technology

At the multi-business or corporate strategy level, firms grapple with the fundamental strategic issue of diversity and its management. How broadly should we diversify? How important is financial or operating synergy to our business? Should we attempt to achieve technological synergy across business units or leave them free to pursue their own separate opportunities? Which organization structures and management systems are best suited for our level of diversity? In answering these basic questions, a firm must select from a familiar array of corporate strategies (Pitts & Snow, 1986; Rumelt,

Prospector (First Mover)

Analyzer (Fast Follower)

Defender (Late Follower)

Specialist (Segmenter)

Generalist

Figure 3.   Generic Competitive Strategies

1974). Essentially, firms must first decide whether to concentrate on a few businesses or diversify into many businesses. If the choice is to diversify, then come decisions about whether the firm should seek financial or operating (including technological) synergies across its units. Technology considerations intersect portfolio choices most obviously in the case of firms that choose to consistently diversify around one or more product or process technologies. Corning Glass provides a ready example of such a technology-based diversification strategy. Conglomerate strategies, on the other hand, mainly seek financial synergy, making technological considerations of strategic importance primarily within operating units.

Business Strategies and Technology

At the business level, technology and strategy decisions must address specific questions about how to compete successfully within a given business. These questions revolve around product or service offerings, competitor strengths and weaknesses, production processes, marketing and distribution approaches, and so forth. As with corporate strategy, there are several generic strategies for competing in a particular business (Ansoff & Stewart, 1967; Miles & Snow, 1978; Porter, 1980) (see Figure 3).

With respect to product and information technologies, *Prospectors* are "early movers" or "pioneers." They value being first to market with a new product, service or application. There are some clear competitive advantages associated with the early-mover strategy—a head start on moving down the experience curve, obtaining market share without fighting competitors head to head, and so forth—and this strategy is best implemented by employing flexible organization structures that are highly responsive to market change.

Examples of Prospectors include Hewlett-Packard in precision measuring instruments, 3M in materials bonding, and Citibank in consumer banking.

A second business strategy is called the *Analyzer*. Often described as "fast followers" in the technological arena, Analyzers are adept at monitoring industry developments and then quickly selecting and improving upon the product technologies developed by more pioneering competitors. One of the features that permits rapid imitation and enhancement is the state-of-the-art process technology maintained by the aggressive Analyzer. This overall strategic orientation allows the Analyzer to avoid major technological and product failures. Classic examples of the Analyzer strategy are Matsushita in consumer electronics and Compaq Computer in its early years.

A third business strategy is the *Defender*. Technologically, Defenders are "late movers"—if they respond at all. They are slow to imitate product, market or technological developments, choosing instead to focus on a limited product or service line, often from a position of considerable market strength gained earlier in product life cycles. Defenders typically get to positions of industry strength by rationalizing process technologies in these earlier periods. Defenders emphasize efficiency, and those that operate in industry segments where products largely have become commodities can achieve the status of "low-cost producer." Examples here include Lincoln Electric in arc-welding supplies and equipment, White Consolidated in major home appliances, and McDonald's. Defenders tend to invest most heavily in improvements to their current process technologies.

Variations of these generic strategies have also been identified (Carroll, 1984; Hannan & Freeman, 1977; Pitts & Snow, 1986; Porter, 1980). One variation has been referred to as a "specialist," "segmentation," or "focus" strategy. The defining characteristic of this approach is a small market. Segmenters or specialists operate in industry niches, usually are left undisturbed by their larger rivals, and may employ either an early-mover or late-mover strategy. For example, Dansk Designs develops housewares for the "top of the table" and is well-known for its innovative product designs. Similarly, Cray Research is a designer and producer of supercomputers for a worldwide, but nevertheless, small market. Conversely, many specialist newspapers, book publishers, recording companies and "boutique" breweries serve loyal customers but are not noted for their innovative products. Thus, specialists serve only small, focused markets, but they emphasize either product or process technologies depending on their strategic orientation.

The opposite of the specialist strategy is the "generalist" strategy. Here the defining characteristic is a broad market coupled with a combination of Prospector, Analyzer, and/or Defender approaches. In a generalist firm, it is sometimes difficult to identify a dominant competitive strategy since a generalist firm overwhelms its industry with innovative as well as traditional products, uses new and old manufacturing processes, and so forth. Usually the generalist is a resource-rich firm that can afford the simultaneous pursuit of several competitive strategies, and thus it may employ multiple product and/or process technologies. Firms using this strategy include Prentice-Hall in college textbook publishing and IBM in electronic data processing.

In recent years, some industries—for example, electronics, computers, communications, and factory and office automation equipment—have undergone changes that require rethinking how these generic competitive strategies are used (Astley & Brahm, 1989). In these increasingly global industries dominated by powerful competitors, there is little room for error in the choice of strategy. Moreover, because these are healthy, growing industries, potential entrants and innovative smaller competitors (e.g., clone producers) are constantly pressing for change and improvement. In these and similar industries, technology life cycles are shorter and more interdependent. This causes, among other things, industry boundaries to become blurred. Under shifting competitive circumstances, it is difficult to achieve lasting industry standards, and firms find themselves not only competing but also collaborating in a variety of arenas in order to protect and promote the overall business.

Thus, some high technology industries require competitors to be adept at pursuing *all* of the above generic strategies, and to form alliances with other firms if resources or expertise are limited. Firms must be able to innovate, respond quickly to the actions of competitors, lower costs without diluting quality, and tailor products or services to a variety of market segments in order to survive. According to Peters (1987), the new management principles are "world-class quality and service, enhanced responsiveness through greatly increased flexibility and continuous, short-cycle innovation and improvement" to create markets. This skill is becoming known as "fast-cycle capability" (Bower & Hout, 1988).

STRATEGY, TECHNOLOGY AND ORGANIZATION DESIGN

Recent years have witnessed a number of important developments in the ways organizations can be designed to support competitive strategies (see Figure 4). Each new design solves the problems associated with its predecessor and facilitates the pursuit of new strategies. Combined with technical developments in manufacturing and information processing, these new organizational arrangements hold promise for high technology firms that are attempting to compete in the complex, changing industries that increasingly comprise the global marketplace.

Hierarchically Based				Market Based
Functional	Matrix	Multidivisional	Internal Co-Venture	Network
			Examples:	Examples:
			Intrapreneuring	Joint ventures
			Corporate venture capital funds	Licensing
			Autonomous workgroups	Franchising
				Leasing

Figure 4. Generic Organization Designs

New strategies require new organization structures for their successful implementation. This phenomenon has occurred throughout American business history (Chandler, 1962). Thus, the functional organization structure, developed in the middle to late 1800s, was best suited to stable, efficiency-oriented strategies such as those pursued by Defenders. Firms that attempted to diversify, especially those prospecting for new product technologies, found that they needed more flexible structures such as divisions or project teams. These structures flourished in the post-World War II period. In the 1960s, many firms wanted to pursue competitive strategies that required them to be simultaneously efficient and flexible, and they turned to the matrix form of organization.

In the 1970s and 1980s an interesting new way of organizing has appeared and spread. It is called the network organization (Miles & Snow, 1986). In its ultimate form, the network organization is a series of independent firms (or business units) linked together in a system that designs, produces, and markets a product or service (see Figure 5). For the individual firm (or component), the primary benefit of participation in the network is the opportunity to pursue its particular distinctive competence. Each network component complements rather than competes with the other components, and a properly constructed network can display the technical specialization of the functional structure, the market responsiveness of the divisional structure and the balanced orientation characteristic of the matrix. Because each component may be an independent legal entity, business groups are assembled by or located through brokers. In some cases, a single broker plays a lead role and subcontracts for needed services. In other cases, linkages among equal partners are created by various brokers specializing in a

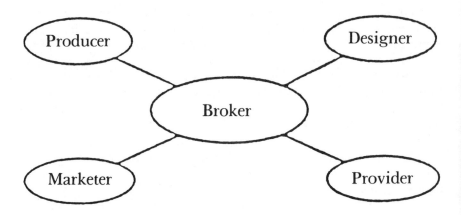

Figure 5.   Dynamic Network Structure

particular service. In still other cases, one of the network components may assume the broker's role while also making its contribution to the overall business.

Examples of network organizations abound. Nike, the sports-shoe giant, has used the network structure since its inception in 1964. Nike is essentially a research, development and marketing corporation, and from the beginning it has used offshore contract manufacturers to produce its products and independent retailers to sell them. IBM used a network structure for only a limited time as a way of entering the personal computer market. Invented by Apple Computer in 1976, the personal computer was well into the growth stage by the time IBM decided to enter the market in 1981. Instead of designing and manufacturing the machine in-house, IBM set up its Entry Systems Division, which relied heavily on off-the-shelf components and contract manufacturers to get its PC to market quickly and keep costs down. These efforts were supported by a vast network of independent software designers who competed against each other to create programs for the new machine. Later, after IBM had established itself in the market, the company reintegrated portions of the network into its primary operating system.

Perhaps the ultimate network organization is Lewis Galoob Toys. In 1988, Galoob sold over $120 million of its Micro Machines and other trendy toys—20 times its 1981 total—and today it is one of the country's most successful toy companies. A mere 115 employees run Galoob's entire operation. Independent inventors and entertainment companies dream up most of Galoob's products, while outside specialists do most of the design and engineering. Galoob farms out manufacturing and packaging to a dozen or so contractors in Hong Kong, and they, in turn, pass on the most labor-intensive work to factories in China. When the toys land in the United States, they are distributed by commissioned manufacturers' representatives. Galoob does not even collect its accounts. It sells its receivables to Commercial Credit Corporation, a factoring company that also sets Galoob's credit policy. In short, Galoob essentially performs a set of complex brokering relations among a far-flung group of designers, producers, suppliers and marketers.

The network organization emerged as a response to competitive pressures. This form of organization, and the principles underlying its design, have helped to accelerate two phenomena that are central to the success of many high technology firms: (a) the so-called "externalization" of work (Pfeffer & Baron, 1988); and (b) the use of "intrapreneuring" and other internal approaches designed to accelerate the process of innovation (e.g., Dean, 1987; Galbraith, 1982; Pinchot, 1985; Quinn, 1979). In many high technology firms, human resources are temporary or leased. At Apple Computer, for example, 17 percent of the workforce is temporary (Kirkpatrick, 1988). And in an increasing number of companies, the types of human resources provided by external vendors include not only clerical help but professional, scientific and executive as well (How to temp, 1988). Coupled with this externalization of work are a variety of intrapreneurial approaches intended to make firms more responsive and nimble. In effect, these approaches encourage permanent employees to act as internal subcontractors providing updated ideas and services to the corporation.

With respect to technology, the network structure creates a dilemma for strategists in high technology firms. On the one hand, technology development can be spun off to outside vendors, freeing the firm to participate in a variety of technological partnerships as opportunities arise. Such flexibility allows a firm to focus on its distinctive competence (research and development, marketing, production, brokering, and so forth). On the other hand, the act of "taking technology outside" may expose the firm to substantial risk. Nevertheless, the network structure offers an important new strategic option for firms in select industry contexts.

CONCLUSION

The strategic management of technology requires that high technology firms develop a management process that fosters the consistent commercialization of new scientific developments. Certain management approaches may facilitate commercialization, such as having senior executives guide technology development in a particular area, creating stable project teams that focus on a specific technology but have the flexibility to change directions if necessary, and so forth. However, it is an inescapable fact that achieving technological success over time requires a clear link between competitive strategy and technology policy. This relationship can only be forged effectively through the active participation of senior management, and these executives have a limited number of generic strategies and structures from which to choose. Therefore, in closing, we would like to offer some general guidance to CEOs and other corporate strategists about technology and its connection to business strategies. This guidance, based upon different types of technological certainty and uncertainty faced by top managers, is captured in four pithy phrases:

What we know we know—This refers to the current core technologies of the firm. Normally these are the most profitable technologies, but they are also the most vulnerable to competition. These technologies should be constantly evaluated to determine if they will continue to support business strategies.

What we know we don't know—This refers to (a) extensions of current technologies and (b) peripheral technologies that are being monitored rather than actively developed. The basic strategic issue here is which of the peripheral technologies should be added to the corporate portfolio and when.

What we don't know we know—This refers to (a) undeveloped technological synergies within the company and (b) unexplored applications of current technologies. From a strategic perspective, these represent latent business opportunities over which the firm has almost monopolistic control. The trick, of course, is how to surface these opportunities and capitalize on them. Intrapreneurs, product champions, and "skunks" are the likely sources of useful information, but management may have to offer specific rewards for locating new business opportunities within the firm.

What we don't know we don't know—This refers to those unknown technologies that revolutionize a business or even an entire industry. History shows that most technological revolutions start outside the business they ultimately affect, so firms are naturally reluctant to invest substantial resources in developing ways to protect against unknown threats. At a minimum, however, high technology firms should assign evaluation teams to explore tangential technologies, hire consultants to forecast future technological breakthroughs, and so forth, in order to protect the integrity of their current business strategies.

REFERENCES

American Association of Engineering Societies. (1987). *Management of technology: The key to America's Competitive Future.* Report of the 1987 AAES Public Affairs Workshop. Washington, DC: National Academy of Sciences.

Ansoff, H.I., & Stewart, J.M. (1967). Strategies for a technology-based business. *Harvard Business Review, 45,* 71-83.

Astley, W.G., & Brahm, R.A. (1989). Organizational designs for post-industrial strategies: The role of interorganizational collaboration. In C.C. Snow (Ed.), *Strategy, Organization Design, and Human Resource Management* (pp. 233-270). Greenwich, CT: JAI Press.

Bahrami, H., & Evans, S. (1987). Stratocracy in high technology firms. *California Management Review, 30,* 51-66.

Bower, J.L., & Hout, T.M. (1988). Fast-cycle capability for competitive power. *Harvard Business Review, 66,* 110-118.

Carroll, G.R. (1984). The specialist strategy. *California Management Review, 26,* 126-137.

Chandler, A.D. Jr. (1962). *Strategy and structure.* Garden City, NY: Doubleday.

Dean, J.W. Jr. (1987). *Deciding to innovate: How firms justify advanced technology.* Cambridge, MA: Ballinger.

Galbraith, J.R. (1982, Winter). Designing the innovating organization. *Organizational Dynamics,* 5-25.

Hannan, M.T., & Freeman, J.H. (1977). The population ecology of organizations. *American Journal of Sociology, 82,* 929-964.

Heidegger, M. (1977). *The question concerning technology* (W. Lovitt, Trans.). New York: Harper & Row.

"How to 'temp' as a top executive." (1988, September 12). *Business Week,* p. 125.

Kirkpatrick, D. (1988, December 15). Smart new ways to use temps. *Fortune,* pp. 110-113.

Miles, R.E., & Snow, C.C. (1978). *Organizational strategy, structure, and process.* New York: McGraw-Hill.

———— (1986). Network organizations: New concepts for new forms. *The McKinsey Quarterly,* pp. 53-66.

Peters, T. (1987). *Thriving on chaos: Handbook for a management revolution.* New York: Knopf.

Pfeffer, J., & Baron, J.N. 1988. Taking the workers back out: Recent trends in the structuring of employment. In B.M. Staw & L.L. Cummings (Eds.), *Research in organizational behavior,* Volume 10: Greenwich, CT: JAI Press.

Pinchot, G., III. (1985). *Intrapreneuring.* New York: Harper & Row.

Pitts, R.A., & Snow, C.C. (1986). *Strategies for competitive success.* New York: Wiley.

Porter, M.E. (1980). *Competitive strategy.* New York: Free Press.

———— (1985). *Competitive advantage.* New York: Free Press.

Quinn, J.B. (1979). Technological innovation, entrepreneurship, and strategy. *Sloan Management Review, 20,* 19-30.

Rosenbloom, R.S., & Cusumano, M.A. (1987). Technological pioneering: The birth of the VCR industry. *California Management Review, 29,* 51-76.

Rumelt, R.P. (1974). *Strategy, structure, and economic performance.* Cambridge, MA: Harvard University Press.

Sherman, P.M. (1981). *Strategic planning for technology industries.* Reading, MA: Addison-Wesley.

VAPORWARE CONTAINMENT:
SOFTWARE START-UPS' METHODS
FOR MANAGING CHANGE

Judith B. Kamm

Computer software has been called "vaporware" for two reasons. Venture capitalists have learned that many software companies and their products disappear soon after starting up (Ingrassia, 1986). In addition, users have learned that the wait for promised new software products may be as long as two years (Fitz Simon, 1988; Wheelwright, 1987) and in some instances, they never materialize (Kneale, 1985; Pollack, 1986). This paper attempts to better understand the vaporware phenomenon by viewing it as an example of managing change in high technology firms.

Because environmental factors can determine whether start-ups survive (Aldrich, 1979; Aldrich & Mueller, 1982; Hannan & Freeman, 1978), it is reasonable to assume that they are the main sources of change with which software entrepreneurs and managers must cope in order to prevent their firms and products from evaporating. Conversations with software entrepreneurs as well as articles in the business press lead to the proposition that rapid computer hardware innovation, fluctuating availability of venture capital, unpredictability in copyright protection and increasing user demands for protection from inadequate products are important external factors challenging new entrants to the software industry of the 1980s.

This chapter not only explores these forces for change, but also describes how three software start-up firms manage it and the impact of their coping methods on the firms' interpersonal relationships and ultimately on their performance. These firms were studied as part of an ongoing research project on organizational behavior in small, young companies.

THE RESEARCH PROJECT

Assuming that human problems in very small, young businesses are significant because such firms lack the extra time, money and energy needed to cope with their symptoms, such as absenteeism, low productivity and turnover, the objective of this study is to better understand the relationship of interpersonal and group relationships to organizational performance, including the ability to successfully cope with externally imposed change. Because micro-organizational behavior in start-up firms appears to be a relatively uncharted field of inquiry, familiarity with the phenomenon itself is needed in order to generate hypotheses for testing and theory construction (Roethlisberger, 1977).

The descriptive case methodology is widely recognized as the most appropriate and effective for early knowledge building (Roethlisberger, 1977; Selltiz, Wrightsman & Cook, 1976; Van Maanen, 1979a). In fact, more systematic case research has been recommended to improve knowledge about the field of entrepreneurship and small business in general (Churchill & Lewis, 1986). Thus, our research design calls for a series of cases about companies during the first two years of their existence. In order to ensure an abundant supply of such firms, we chose the software industry in the Boston area.

In 1984 we used a listing of all new incorporations produced by the Massachusetts Secretary of State's Office, Department of Corporations, to select nine nonretail firms with the word software in their names that had been incorporated before June 1, 1983. Of the three firms that responded favorably, two were actually studied. The sampling process was replicated in July 1985, producing another site, and in March 1988 producing two more sites. Table 1 presents a summary description of the first three firms about which cases were written.

Data about the companies are gathered during bimonthly site visits and interim telephone conversations. Interviews with the owner(s) and all other key personnel, whether or not they work full time for the company, are the primary data collection method. Adapting the "triangulation" approach (Jick, 1979; Light, 1979), however, direct observation and examination of internal correspondence, policy and planning documents, public statements, press articles and promotional materials are also used. After data have been collected for a calendar year, the case is written. The structure of each case is standardized in order to permit patterns to be recognized across

Table 1. Sample Software Start-up Firms

	Company Name		
Features	Software Action Team	Applied Programs Co., Inc.	International Software Centre
Business	Marketing service for minicomputer software authors	Development and marketing of technical word processing for IBM PCs	Foreign language translation service for minicomputer software
Incorporated	1983	1983	1984
No. of Entrepreneurs	2 at incorp.; 1 at study's end	2 at incorp.; 3 at study's end	3 at incorp., 2 at study's end
Education	B.S. degrees: 1 engineering, 1 nonengineering	2 PhDs: OR and EE; 1 B.S. in Psychology	3 Bachelors degrees
Previous S/W Industry Experience	yes for both	3 no	2 no; 1 yes
Previous Middle Mgt. Experience	yes for both	2 no; 1 yes	3 yes
Source of Capital	self-financed	self-financed	self-financed
Number of Employees at Study's End	4	7	25
Sales Performance	1 copy of its 1 client's $50,000 S/W package—Not at break even.	150 packages of its 1 product ($53,000)—At break even.	$500,000. At break even.

cases. Information about the software industry is collected continuously from published sources in order to track the environmental changes that are occurring.

SOURCES OF CHANGE IN THE U.S. SOFTWARE INDUSTRY

Rapid Advancement in Computer Hardware Technology

A key strategic decision for software industry entrants is with which computer hardware system to align themselves. Although much work is being done to create links (Carroll, 1987b, 1988a, 1988b; Schlender, 1988c; Verity & Lewis, 1987), machine incompatibilities continue to necessitate substantial rewriting of programs for different computers. Most start-up firms lack the human or financial resources to introduce programs for more than one type of hardware at a time. The growth and market share of the chosen hardware system initially create demand for the software, although software availability and quality in turn can spur demand for hardware (Carroll, 1988b).

Furthermore, as a particular hardware system's technology improves, its software programs also must be upgraded to take advantage of its increased capabilities. For example, a new microcomputer semiconductor has been introduced by Intel, which has been adopted by IBM, the dominant force in that segment of the hardware industry. Over 95% of IBM personal computers use an operating system produced by Microsoft, which has recently announced shipment of an upgraded version (OS/2) to take advantage of Intel's innovation (Schlender, 1988d). Originally, it was expected that smaller software firms could begin writing applications programs based upon this operating system as soon as it was released (Carroll, 1987a). Although 4,000 OS/2 developer kits costing $3,000 each have been purchased, however, many small firms have been too overwhelmed by the huge volume of data the kits contained to begin writing new products (Schlender, 1988d).

It appears, then, that such hardware changes have a number of implications for start-up firms. They provide seemingly infinite potential for incumbents' growth by new product development. On the other hand, they can once again lower barriers to entry to the industry, thereby increasing the likelihood of even more competitors for recently established firms (Standard & Poor's, 1987). In addition, rapid hardware advancement strains young software firms' already precarious resources. Simultaneously developing new versions of programs while trying to sell enough existing ones to become and maintain a presence in the still highly fragmented industry of an estimated 5,000 companies (Davis & Miller, 1986) requires large amounts of human and financial investment. Writing software is notoriously more time-consuming and problem-ridden than is ever anticipated (Kneale, 1985). Expenses for even the most basic advertising for new products can run between $10,000 and $17,000 per month (Ingrassia, 1986).

One of the firms in our study, Applied Programs Co., was particularly affected by this source of change, not only because of technological advancement in the IBM PCs for which its program was written, but because of improvements in and proliferation of printers, which required program modifications. As one of the firm's entrepreneurs noted, "We have to run very, very fast just to stay in place." These changes were managed by recognizing that the company's primary resource was its star programmer, Peter, who was also one of its owner/founders.

This resource was "conserved" by devising ways to relieve Peter of as many nonessential tasks as possible so that he could dedicate his genius solely to product development. For example, Scott, the marketing expert who recently had been brought into the firm, showed Peter how to use a dictaphone and persuaded him to dictate memos that were the start of the users' manual for the second version of the product. He also had Peter write a program enabling Scott to create printer-drivers so that the new product could be used on 30 different printers. Scott wanted to be able to transfer much of what he had taken upon himself to either his office manager or to a "computer hacker" as well as to find even more mechanisms for reducing Peter's workload.

Such specialization is unusual and difficult to achieve in very small, young firms (Cohn & Lindberg, 1974; Drucker, 1969; Hoy & Hellreigel, 1982; Welsh & White, 1981). At APCI, before the marketing expert was brought into the firm, Peter believed that the stress of the programming demands had caused him to gain weight and become short-tempered. He had become increasingly concerned about burning out. These feelings were straining his relationships, not only with his family, but also with APCI's other owner. Nonetheless, because at the time of the study Peter was not drawing a salary from APCI, but rather was relying on his income from a full-time associate professorship at an out-of-state university, the out-of-pocket costs to the firm of such specialization were minimal.

Fluctuating Availability of External Capital

The major sources of external capital to finance software start-ups have been venture capital companies, which have themselves proliferated greatly since the mid-1970s ("A special report," 1986, p. 38D), and the over-the-counter stock market. In addition, some states recently have begun to provide seed money to high technology start-ups, including software firms, as part of their economic development programs (Gupta, 1987). Apart from the inherent drawbacks of external financing, such as reduced equity and operating control, that make some entrepreneurs reluctant to use it, however, its availability to software start-ups has fluctuated markedly during the 1980s.

It has been said that the term "vaporware" was first coined by venture capitalists, some of whom had been burned by their investments in the software industry between 1984 and 1986. At the end of 1984 it was observed, "Gone are the glory days of 1979 to 1983 when computer-related companies were being formed at record rates. Some call it 'the golden age of software' because of the large number of personal computer software companies. At that time new venture money, notably from pension funds which could start to invest in high-risk companies, started to flood the market" (Rosenberg, 1984, p. A99). In 1984 it was estimated that only 15 percent of software and related service firms were funded by venture capital, ranking second after computer hardware and systems start-ups, of which 23 percent were funded by this source ("A special report," 1986).

Between 1984 and 1986 the microcomputer segment of the software industry followed the slump in hardware sales, but starting in the spring of 1987 the situation began to change for the better. By early October it was reported, "appetite is hot for software stocks ... sales are really booming" ("Hot PC sales," 1987a, p. 45). Even the stock market crash of October 19th did not seem to greatly affect software companies' stock prices. For example, Lotus Development Corp.'s and Cullinet's stock prices actually rose in the following week ("How area stocks fared," 1987b, p. 51). For small, young companies whose owners want to take them public, however, there was a freeze on initial public offerings that sent them back to venture capitalists for second and third rounds of financing (Gupta, 1987).

Nonetheless, in December 1987, Inc.'s list of the 500 fastest growing small firms included more than 40 firms that develop, publish or distribute software, eliciting the following observation: "You saw it in the stock market. You've seen it in the merger-and-acquisition activity ... Software is hot." This strength is expected to continue due to a wave of new products and the belief that "as the hardware becomes more and more like a commodity business ... the software ... becomes the high-stakes arena" ("The 500," 1987, p. 75).

As Table 1 indicates, the sample companies' primary way of coping with this external source of change was to insulate themselves from it by self-financing. Software Action Team's founder, John Sottile, used some of the termination settlement he negotiated with his former employer to capitalize his new firm with $117,000 in cash, foregone salary, and nonreimbursed expenses. Relying upon personal savings, his partner invested a total of $13,300 in the same way. APCI was initially capitalized with $50,000 loaned to it by Bill Jameson, one of the entrepreneurs, and his wife. They made another loan during the second year. Peter's countless unpaid hours of programming were another form of investment. International Software Centre was capitalized entirely by its founder, who invested approximately $100,000, most of which resulted from the terms of his departure from his former employer.

Self-financing as a method of coping with changing availability of external capital appears to have had some negative effects on relationships within the firms studied. At Software Action Team, when only one copy of the product had been sold after eight months of effort, Paul, the primary salesman, noted that corporate bill-paying raised most of the anxiety and caused team members to become short-tempered with each other. "The bank balance dictates what it's O.K. to do. If we met our sales quotas, people wouldn't get excited about $20 worth of letterhead." John, the majority shareholder, spoke more of *his* company and *his* money and became more directive. He began to pressure the minority shareholder, Ted, and Paul to be more aggressive in selling, thereby causing friction among the three principals in the firm. Ted left the company a few months later, followed shortly thereafter by Paul.

At APCI, the last loan was made by the Jamesons in August of 1984. One area of difference among the directors arose on the topic of repaying the firm's debt to them. Peter wanted a commitment from them and a schedule of what would happen financially to be prepared. Rachel Jameson was reluctant to do this before checking with professional accountants about what to do next. Bill Jameson hoped that a recent limited mailing of literature notifying current customers that the product had been made compatible with a popular type of circuit board would generate enough sales to fund a more general mailing announcing the product extension.

Peter felt that nothing was being done to sell the product, however, and that the company needed more capital, but that the Jamesons should not be expected to loan any more to it. He became quite depressed and did little productive work for the company during the autumn and winter months until Scott was brought in to take over the marketing function.

When International Software Centre had difficulty in getting new contracts in May of 1986, overhead was cut by relocating its offices back with the owner's other business, an executive search firm. ISC's chief operating officer perceived that the owner, who controlled ISC's books, was reducing his commitment to his software company. In the COO's view, ISC was a "poor cousin" of the owner's other business, which was "given an allowance and told how to spend it." The result was that if the marketing director wanted to attend a trade show on the West Coast in order to pursue sales leads, the COO felt he had to "make a big deal" of it in order to get the travel funding. He felt isolated from the owner and unable to interest him in the start-up and its problems. Shortly after the study ended, the company was liquidated.

Among the reasons the owner gave for the evaporation of ISC was the fact that the firm's major source of new business, minicomputer manufacturers, was trying to reduce costs in the slumping industry by no longer translating software in advance of taking it overseas. Instead, manufacturers were hiring translators in the target country. Most microcomputer software firms that ISC approached were also start-ups and lacked sufficient funds to translate their products. In addition, some small software companies' entrepreneurs were wary of entering foreign markets in which copyright protection was not provided.

Unpredictable Copyright Protection

Because computer software is considered to be intellectual property, software authors may copyright it to prevent it from being copied. There are two sources of infringement threat: competitors and users. Illegal copying by competitors means lower prices and profit margins (Davis & Miller, 1986). On the other hand, software start-ups having the mission of competing on the basis of lower prices for comparable programs are liable to be sued for copyright infringement. Illegal duplication by users means lost potential sales. It is particularly threatening to vulnerable start-up firms that are often extremely dependent upon sales to generate cash to continue operations. Legal costs can be substantial, thereby lowering their chances for survival.

In 1985 Mitchell Kapor, founder and then CEO of Lotus Development Corp., whose microcomputer integrated spreadsheet program "1-2-3" was already on its way to becoming the best-selling software in the industry's history, identified "the extent of copycat behavior, sort of a failure of entrepreneurial nerve" as *the* significant industry issue (Denison, 1985, p. 2). Lotus has been a major target of imitators, which it claims sell programs with the "look and feel" of its products, but at prices much lower than the $495 per copy charged for "1-2-3" (Standard & Poor's, 1987; Tell, 1987).

Microsoft, the largest U.S. software company, has been engaged in a dispute with the Brazilian government over its reluctance to prevent its software firms from copying Microsoft's products, and its likely imposition of a duty on software imports of as high as 200 percent (Barham, 1987, 1988).

In September 1987, arbitrators resolved the legal battle between IBM and Fujitsu over Fujitsu's copying of IBM's proprietary mainframe computer software. The binding decision gave the Japanese company access to IBM's source codes for a fee. IBM had also brought suit against Hitachi for similar infringement (Miller, 1987). Thus infringement by competitors is a threat regardless of the market segment (mainframe, mini- or micro-computers) in which the software is sold.

Illegal duplication of programs by users appears to be more of a threat, however, in the microcomputer software segment of the industry. Users with computers having dual disk drives need only insert a program in one drive and a blank disk in the other, give a copy command, and obtain a free copy of what was originally a several hundred dollar product. For every software program sold, it has been estimated that up to ten copies of it are made illegally. The "piracy ratio" is particularly high in foreign markets, estimated to be 250 copies for each program (Standard & Poor's, 1987).

Enforcement of ambiguous laws governing software copyrights has been inconsistent (Verity, 1987), leading one industry observer to note "neither U.S. Copyright Office nor the courts have given clear guidance" (Tell, 1987, p. 31). One response has been to form industry groups, such as Adapso, that lobby state governments for stronger anti-duplication laws (Kneale, 1985). Additionally, large software firms appear to be turning to the courts more often (Standard & Poor's, 1987), which may in time clarify interpretation of the existing laws. Nonetheless, software entrepreneurs continue to face a great deal of uncertainty as they decide upon how much investment of time and money to make in legal protection against copyright infringement or against being sued for infringement.

Of the companies in the study reported here, only APCI was directly affected by this source of change because it was the only company that developed its own software. The original name of its technical typists' software was similar to the name and some of the capabilities of a program already established by Tandy Corp. Although Rachel Jameson, a lawyer, had performed a copyright search to minimize the firm's liability before the product was shipped, when the marketing expert, Scott, was brought into the firm, he was concerned about the similarity. He changed the product's name after it had been on the market for several months. At the end of the study it was not clear whether this change had a negative effect on sales.

Rachel Jameson, one of the firm's investors, was on APCI's board of directors and was the company's treasurer and clerk. She did not charge for her legal services, which also included preparing site license letters for foreign users. Although Scott's decision to change the product's name could have caused tension in his relationship with Rachel, she had disengaged herself from any of the firm's activities once he joined it. There was no evidence that she resented his second-guessing her original judgment that the product name and function were safe from suits by competitors.

APCI, then, initially relied upon legal protection to cope with the uncertainty surrounding copyright infringement. It could afford to do so because one of its directors was a lawyer who was willing to work *gratis*. This is a relatively inaccessible method for many start-up software companies, however, some of whom have tried to rely upon devices built into their software products for protection against piracy. Nonetheless, such devices, which take the form of codes written into the software, have problems of their own. Not only can they be disarmed by skilled programmers, but also they make the product more difficult to use (Standard & Poor's, 1987).

Increasing Demands by Users

Until the slump in growth in the mid-1980s, which probably reflected and certainly increased users' bargaining power with software producers, the software industry was notorious for its relative disregard for many user needs (Pollack, 1986). Historically, this revolutionary new industry has grown by proving to consumers that they need never-before-imagined products. At first the market consisted of only technically sophisticated consumers, primarily programmers themselves, for whom ease of use was less important than power to perform. As the market grew, shortages of skilled programmers and other specialists necessitated programs that could be operated by less sophisticated users.

Furthermore, the introduction of the microcomputer in the late 1970s broadened the market even more to include people not only lacking in experience and skill with programming, but also totally unfamiliar and uncomfortable with computers. Users increasingly demanded ease of use, or "friendliness" from software, in addition to better support in the form of comprehensible manuals and "hotlines" to call for answers to questions (Kneale, 1985; Pollack, 1986). Apple Computer, IBM, and other large firms, as well as start-ups like Mitchell Kapor's ON Technology, are devising ways to make software easier to use (Carroll, 1987c).

Users have also become more demanding about product quality. The software industry has been described as acting in "ways that would be suicidal in selling cars or videocassette recorders. Companies admit they knowingly ship programs with small flaws, fixing them in later versions and charging early buyers for the revisions" (Kneale, 1985, p. 33). Many firms explicitly stated that their products were not guaranteed in "as-is warranties." A number of individuals and users' groups, however, have taken political action that threatens to create state regulations to protect consumers from faulty products (Kneale, 1985). To avoid regulation, software executives belonging to Adapso ultimately created a more consumer-oriented warranty that has been adopted by many industry firms (Pollack, 1986).

Another growing user demand has been for software that operates on more than one kind of computer system, thereby overcoming the problem of incompatibility. Large corporate users, in particular, have complained about their inability to connect their machines of different sizes and makes, thus limiting the uses of software they have. Software firms have responded in at least two ways. They are creating more links between different sizes of systems, such as minicomputers and microcomputers and between different brands of machines, such as Apple and IBM (Carroll, 1988a, 1988b; Schlender, 1988b, 1988c; Verity & Lewis, 1987).

Users have also begun to demand more use of industry standards. As one journalist observed: "Software companies have found that they have confused customers to the point that they will sit on the sidelines until they are convinced that the software technology they buy will be the one that survives ... software companies are increasingly trying to settle the technological questions among themselves and present ... a single solution" (Carroll, 1988a, p. 30). For example, AT&T's Unix operating system software has been endorsed as a standard by both IBM and Apple Computer (Waldman, 1988).

These increasing user demands have several implications for software start-up companies. Ease of program use requires entrepreneurs to understand users' problems that call for new software and difficulties with current software that call for improvements. Successful start-ups in the industry appear to have "a product designed for a highly focused market; a willingness to make a heavy investment in product improvements; and close and continual communication with customers" (Hartman, 1987, p. 136; Ingrassia, 1988).

Performing market research, writing good instruction manuals to accompany software, and providing customer service representatives to answer questions and solve problems are concrete ways to meet these requirements. If they are to meet them, however, entrepreneurs must spend more time engaged in these activities or in searching for and training employees to carry them out. As a result, product development time typically increases, as do costs, thereby reducing margins and lengthening the period of time before profitability is achieved.

Warranties promising free replacement of faulty programs, programming effort allocated to correcting minor problems in existing products, and time and effort spent in testing new software products also add to start-ups' costs of doing business. Furthermore, new products may be delayed in being introduced to the market. The adjective "long-awaited" accompanies almost every announcement of a major new software product in the business press.

Joint ventures between software companies appear to be an increasingly popular method for responding to users' demands for product compatibility and standardization. Indeed, some start-ups have linked up with more established members of the industry in order to pool the resources necessary to achieve these difficult goals (Brandt, 1988). While compatibility and standards can widen markets for both hardware and software, however, thereby fostering growth potential, there are some negative implications for imitative start-ups. They must wait until the leading software is available, and the delays can be substantial. Furthermore, once the standard is available, other low-cost imitators and applications authors can enter the market more quickly, reducing the time period during which early firms can enjoy much-needed high margins to finance survival and growth by new product development (Tell, 1987).

Software Action Team and International Software Centre were not affected by changing user demands because they did not have direct contact with users. Their business was to provide services to software authors, thus their customers were these authors. Applied Programs Co.'s business, however, required direct contact with users, which its entrepreneurial pair had established early in the firm's development. They wanted to provide users with a "first class" manual, but realized their limited experience, skill and time. They discovered the existence of an emerging portion of the software industry: documentation service. Thus they contracted with another small, young company to prepare the manual for their new product.

The technical typist software was still evolving during the documentation period and the contractor had to critique some of the program's commands, requiring the authors' explanations. While this process resulted in refining the product, it turned out to be costly and painful. The documentation cost two and a half times the original estimate, it was late, and portions of it were unusable. Both entrepreneurs felt "burned" by this experience.

Bill Jameson also attempted to stay in contact with users by sending out a newsletter to update information about the product and to get ideas from them about new uses and improvements for it. The newsletter was to be printed in the same format as the users' manual so that it could be added to it. In the first issue he requested users to send their articles on diskettes so that he could edit, combine, and print them out in subsequent issues. In the interim the firm's only employee left and Bill used an answering service to field inquiries. He and Peter had taken notes from some of the calls they had time to return, and had kept a list of users, but felt that they really did not know how to stay in touch with them.

One of the reasons they brought the marketing expert, Scott, into the firm was that he was anxious to talk to these people as well as to other prospective users who had called. In fact, he recommended telemarketing to them as a strategy. Their method of coping with user demands after product introduction, therefore, consisted of a newsletter and differentiating the company's functions by adding a marketing specialist. Because they could not afford to pay Scott in cash, they eventually formed a separate company to market their one product, and promised him a third of its ownership if he achieved the sales goals he set for himself.

These methods of coping with user demands did have an impact upon relationships within the firm. Bill's original role in the start-up was chief strategist and marketer, while Peter's was product development. Bill's contact with users via telephone and newsletter put him in the position of making suggestions to Peter about ways to improve the product, many of which Peter believed were too difficult to do. Once Scott came into the firm, however, and made similar suggestions, Peter became more willing to try to accommodate some of them. Scott actually began to work closely with Peter on developing the second version of the product, thereby distracting him from marketing the existing version and delaying the achievement of the sales goals he had set for himself with the approval of Bill and Peter.

Nonetheless, Bill and Peter felt so dependent upon Scott that they did not withhold shares from him because he missed his deadlines. Bill and Rachel turned over to Scott all of the operating responsibilities for the technical typist product. They removed themselves almost completely from the new company that Bill, Peter and Scott had formed. Scott's employee performed the necessary daily functions of APCI. Scott became the CEO of the new company and saw himself as the filter between Peter and Bill. Thus the original relationship between Bill and Peter became more distant psychologically as well as in terms of geographical location. Nonetheless, at the end of the study APCI was continuing to make sales and Scott was deciding how to finance the introduction of the new version of the product.

MANAGING CHANGE IN SOFTWARE FIRMS: SOME OBSERVATIONS

Four external forces for change in the software industry—rapid hardware innovation, fluctuating availability of capital, unpredictable copyright protection and increasing user demands—appear to at least partially contribute to the vaporware phenomenon. Increasing computer power and proliferation of peripherals mean that software authors have to write programs that can keep up, or make that power and versatility accessible to users. The nature of the programming task takes time. By the time a product is ready, even more changes in it are needed. At some point the process must be stopped and the product launched, even though its developers know that it could be better, that is, that it could have fewer "bugs" and that it could do more. Consequently much software is late, or it is never released, due to unsolvable problems or indications that the hardware it is written for will not gain sufficient market share to make the necessary marketing investment worthwhile.

One method of coping with rapid hardware changes is to find and pay experienced, gifted programmers to specialize in product development. This method, however, requires that the firm be sufficiently capitalized to afford such talent. Changes in the availability of external capital, as well as the perceived loss of entrepreneurial control that often accompanies external funding, is dealt with by self-financing. This method of managing change, which could be called insulation, can lead to late software market introductions as well as to start-up failure to survive. Self-financing can mean that resources are more limited so costs have to be kept as low as possible. If the entrepreneur is inexperienced in the industry, he or she may misallocate resources, spending too little on marketing and personnel or too much on physical facilities or other overhead, perhaps in an effort to establish credibility in an industry that historically relied upon such credibility instead of warranties.

Self-financing may also mean that the start-up relies very heavily upon sales revenues for cash flow, and if sales are made more slowly than expected, marketing and further development may be delayed at a time when speed is crucial because of hardware innovations and proliferation of competitors. Tight budgets can strain interpersonal relationships, in turn impeding productivity, whether it takes the form of aggressively pursuing sales leads, as in the Software Action Team and International Software Centre cases, or of developing the product, as in APCI's case.

The threat of copyright infringement can lead to vaporware because it presents a risk to authors and publishers that prevents them from expanding or from finding new business, as in the case of ISC. It could not diversify into the microcomputer software translation service business because many potential customers were reluctant to take their products into foreign markets where copyright laws either did not exist or were not enforced. Illegal copies reduce sales revenues that are especially needed for self-financed firms.

The difficulty of proving infringement encourages the proliferation of "me-too" start-ups that compete by offering comparable products at substantially lower prices because their new products do not require huge investments in R&D and marketing, and they do not suffer from long time delays in product introductions. Consequently, software prices may be driven down, thereby reducing profit margins while marketing and personnel costs rise. If copyright infringement enforcement is tightened, many imitator start-ups could evaporate as well.

The most common method for managing this external source of change is to obtain legal protection. Lawyers' fees for copyright search and other services can be very high and such protection may not stand up in court. Joining a trade association to influence the passage of protective laws generally takes more time than entrepreneurs can spare and the legislative process can take more time than most start-ups can expect to survive (three years). Building protective codes into the software itself, another method of coping with changing copyright protection enforcement, dissuades some users from purchasing the product because it can be less easy to use.

Table 2. Methods For Managing Externally Imposed Change

Acquiescence	Isolation	Influence
• speed product development	• self-finance	• join trade associations
• write for a variety of hardware types	• write in copy deterrents	• set industry standards
• improve existing products	• hire legal services	
• test new products		
• provide better support		
• follow industry standards		

Increased user demands for products that are easy to use have not only prevented software start-ups from using the least expensive way of protecting themselves from piracy, but they have also contributed to vaporware by subscribing to the notion of standards among various types of programs. While standards reduce user confusion, they force software authors to line up behind leaders who set the standards. If the leaders are late, so are the followers. From a start-up's perspective, meeting customers' increasing demands for good support in the form of better documentation and packaging are also time-consuming and expensive and are just one more way for cash-starved start-ups to spend money that they do not have. Thus they are pushed ever closer to the evaporation point (and rightly so, consumer advocates would add).

It is not surprising, then, that the software industry has been experiencing greater consolidation as start-ups fail, merge with each other, or are bought out by larger firms (Standard & Poor's, 1987). The forces driving change interact with each other, as do the coping methods, reflecting a very complex set of relationships in this industry. Start-ups' methods of coping with their turbulent industry environment may be as likely to send them up in vapor as to contain them.

The methods observed thus far in this study of the software industry can be grouped into three broad approaches to managing change: acquiescing to it and trying to keep up, insulating against it and influencing its source, as summarized in Table 2.

The acquiescence approach includes ways of keeping up with the speed and direction of externally-imposed changes. It was taken by APCI, which tried to keep up with the pace of technological advancement by trying to speed product development. It was also taken by APCI when it tried to satisfy users' needs for good product support and continuing improvements.

The isolation approach consists of ways to reduce the impact of changes upon the firm. It was taken by all three firms that tried to buffer themselves from the vagaries of external capital availability by self-financing. It was also taken by APCI in its reliance upon formal legal measures against copyright liability suits. Moving outside of the firm and working to modify the source of change in some way is the influence approach. It was not in evidence in the firms studied, although it is used by those software entrepreneurs who join trade associations and attempt to get legislation passed that clarifies and strengthens copyright protection laws. It is also taken by companies that join partnerships with other firms to set industry standards.

While the categorization of individual methods is still tentative, the groupings themselves provide a way of thinking about start-ups' strategies as they enter rapidly changing environments such as the computer software industry. More research is needed to better understand under which conditions these change management methods are most effective in the software industry, as well as their usefulness in other high technology industries.

REFERENCES

Aldrich, H.E. (1979). *Organizations and environments.* Englewood Cliffs, NJ: Prentice-Hall.
Aldrich, H.E., & Mueller, S. (1982). The evolution of organizational forms: Technology, coordination, and control. In B.M. Staw & L.L. Cummings (Eds.), *Research in organizational behavior* (Vol. 4). Greenwich, CT: JAI Press.
Barham, J. (1987, November 19). Measure to protect computer software advances in Brazil. *Wall Street Journal,* p. 5.
―――. (1988, January 21). Brazilian panel is conciliatory on software. *Wall Street Journal,* p. 8.
Brandt, R. (1988, February 8). It's grab-your-partner time for software makers. *Business Week,* pp. 86-87.
Carroll, P.R. (1987a, November 4). IBM to ship new software in December. *Wall Street Journal,* p. 4.
―――. (1987b, November 23). Mainframe slowdown and stiff competition put pressure on IBM. *Wall Street Journal,* pp. 1, 16.
―――. (1987c, December 14). Computer firms step up efforts to make machines easier to use. *Wall Street Journal,* p. 27.
―――. (1988a, January 14). Ashton-Tate/Microsoft accord shows unusual teamwork in competitive field. *Wall Street Journal,* p. 30.
―――. (1988b, January 22). Patching up software occupies programmers and disables systems. *Wall Street Journal,* pp. 1, 13.
Churchill, N.C., & Lewis, V.L. (1986). Entrepreneurship research: Directions and methods. In D. Sexton & R. Smilor (Eds.), *Art and science of entrepreneurship* (pp. 333-365). Cambridge, MA: Ballinger.
Cohn, T., & Lindberg, R.A. (1974). *Survival and growth management strategies for the small firm.* New York: Amacom.
Davis, B., & Miller, M.W. (1986, March 27). Software sales soar. *Wall Street Journal,* p. 1.
Denison, D.C. (1985, January 27). Mitchell D. Kapor. *Boston Sunday Globe Magazine,* pp. 2, 32.
Drucker, P. (1969). *The practice of management.* London: Heinemann.

Fitz Simon, J. (1988, October 8). Lotus product delayed again. *Boston Globe,* p. 21.

The 500. (1987). *Inc. 9*(13), 75-130.

Gupta, U. (1987, November 9). States play expanding role in funding technology firms. *Wall Street Journal,* p. 29.

Hannan, M.T., & Freeman, J.H. (1978). The population ecology of organizations. In M.W. Meyer & Associates (Eds.), *Environments and organizations: Theoretical and empirical perspectives.* San Francisco, CA: Jossey-Bass.

Hartman, C. (1987). The *Inc.* 500 honor roll. *Inc., 9*(13), 136-139.

Hot PC sales boost software stocks. (1987a, October 6). *Boston Globe,* p. 45.

How area stocks fared. (1987b, October 22). *Boston Globe,* p. 51.

Hoy, F., & Hellreigel, D. (1982). The Kilmann and Herden model of organizational effectiveness criteria for small business managers. *Academy of Management Journal, 25*(2), 308-322.

Ingrassia, L. (1986, May 19). A shout in the dark. *Wall Street Journal,* p. 21D.

_____. (1988, October 11). Small software companies profit by exploiting niches. *Wall Street Journal,* p. B1.

Jick, T.D. (1979). Mixing qualitative and quantitative methods: Triangulation in action. *Administrative Science Quarterly, 24*(4), 602-611.

Kneale, D. (1985, October 2). Buyer beware: Software plagued by poor quality and poor service. *Wall Street Journal,* p. 30.

Light Jr., D. (1979). Surface data and deep structure: Observing the organization of professional training. *Administrative Science Quarterly, 24*(4), 551-559.

Miller, M.W. (1987, October 7). U.S. software firms complain Fujitsu gained edge in IBM copyright decision. *Wall Street Journal,* p. 4.

Pollack, A. (1986, September 28). Softening up software publishers. *New York Times,* p. 12.

Roethlisberger, F.J. (1977). *The elusive phenomena* (G.F.F. Lombard, ed.). Boston: Division of Research, Graduate School of Business Administration, Harvard University.

Rosenberg, R. (1984, December 9). Tough times ahead for venture capitalists. *Boston Sunday Globe,* pp. A93, A99.

Schlender, B.R. (1988a, January 25). Microsoft predicts industry wide sales of personal computers will surge 26%. *Wall Street Journal,* p. 3.

_____. (1988b, January 14). Apple to unveil family of laser printers, software to access IBM PCs, compatibles. *Wall Street Journal,* p. 3.

_____. (1988c, January 18). Apple, Digital Equipment outline pact to devise ways to link their computers. *Wall Street Journal,* p. 6.

_____. (1988d, October 31). IBM, Microsoft enter pc-display battle. *Wall Street Journal,* p. B1.

Selltiz, C., Wrightsman, L.S., & Cook, S.W. (1976). *Research methods in social relations (3rd Ed.).* New York: Holt, Rinehart and Winston.

A special report: Small business. (1986, May 19). *Wall Street Journal,* pp. 10-440.

Standard & Poor's. (1987, October). *Industry Surveys,* pp. C93-C103.

Tell, L.J. (1987, August 31). Software copyrights: Keep out the pirates—but let innovators in. *Business Week,* p. 31.

Van Maanen, J. (1979a). Reclaiming qualitative methods for organizational research: A preface. *Administrative Science Quarterly, 24*(4), 520-526, 539-550.

_____. (1979b). The fact of fiction in organizational ethnography. *Administrative Science Quarterly, 24*(4), 539-550.

Verity, J. (1987, October 5). The market for mainframes will never be the same. *Business Week,* p. 62.

Verity, J.W., & Lewis, G. (1987, November 30). Computers: The new look. *Business Week,* pp. 112-123.

Waldman, P. (1988, February 10). Apple and IBM issue endorsements of Unix computer-operating system. *Wall Street Journal*, p. 24.

Welsh, J.A., & White, J.F. (1981, July-August). A small business is not a little big business. *Harvard Business Review*, pp. 18-32.

Wheelwright, G. (1987, May 19). The industry suffers a case of the vapours. *The Times*, p. 29.

THE LIFE CYCLE OF
TECHNOLOGY-BASED FIRMS:
BUILDING NECESSARY FLEXIBILITY

Robert P. McGowan

The innovation process within U.S.-based businesses has frequently been called the critical edge in competing in an increasingly turbulent global economy and marketplace. In fact, a recent study of innovation management practices of nearly four hundred publicly-held companies found that innovation today is of industry-wide importance and will remain so in the foreseeable future (Arthur Young, 1985). The study also reports that, while many companies seem interested in giving high priority to innovation, they often lack effective systems for evaluation and management.

While the concept of innovation can have application across a number of industrial sectors, the relationship between technology and innovation has particular bearing in the field of corporate strategy and competitive success (Bitondo & Frohman, 1981; Frohman, 1982; Maidique & Hayes, 1984; Pappas, 1984; Quinn, 1979). A number of recent works and research has also focused on the need for technology-based firms to understand the significance of change in making strategic decisions regarding markets to enter, future financial investments, R&D efforts, exit decisions and the like. While the concept of organizational change has a rich and varied background in the field of management, its application to the field of technology and innovation management is unique since it must incorporate several product/market life cycles, and organizational life cycles. This paper will delineate the key theoretical issues involved in these life cycles. By examining several technology-based firms at the various stages of growth, a model is developed that addresses organizational barriers to change and innovation. In addition, a framework for future research on the subject is suggested.

The Concept of Organizational Change

The notion of organizational change has interested a variety of disciplines, ranging from management and industrial psychology to sociology and anthropology. Frequently, the subject of organizational change has been closely associated with the promotion of organizational development: that is, organizations that are undergoing change need to view it as a long-term effort that pervades the entire organization.

Greiner, as part of a larger study on organizational change, looked at the process as one involving successive phases (Greiner, 1967). According to Greiner, successful change involves two core elements: a redistribution of power with greater emphasis on shared power and a developmental process of change. Greiner concludes that the critical ingredients to successful change involves a "master blueprint" and greater participation in the change process at all levels.

Other writers, such as Lawrence (1969) and Kotter and Schlesinger (1979) argue that a critical element in organizational change is understanding the forces that resist change. According to Lawrence, it isn't understanding the technical nature of the change that is the key. Rather, managers need to develop a keener awareness of the human factors (i.e., ignoring the know-how of those involved in the change, not using understandable terms, and so on).

Kotter and Schlesinger take a similar approach in advocating a diagnostic approach. In addition, they develop a continuum of approaches that range from education and communication to explicit and implicit coercion.

In recent years, a new body of writing and research has taken a different avenue and has focused more on the relationship between change and the innovation process. This group is represented by authors such as Rosabeth Moss Kanter (1983, p. 279):

> Change involves the crystallization of new action possibilities (new policies, new behaviors, new patterns, new methodologies, new products or new market ideas) based on reconceptualized patterns in the organization. The architecture of change involves the design and construction of new patterns, or the reconceptualization of old ones, to make new, and hopefully more productive, actions possible.

Kanter, in a related work on the role of the middle manager, found innovation flourished in companies where territories overlap and people have contact across functions: information flows freely; numbers of people have excesses in their budgets; many managers are in open-ended positions; and reward systems look to the future, not the past (Kanter, 1982, p. 95). Of additional note, Kanter found, in a study across several industrial sectors, that the most entrepreneurial firms were high tech firms that used a decentralized-matrix or mixed-matrix form of organization. In addition, emphasis in these firms was on horizontal communication; and the concept of corporate culture was clear.

TECHNOLOGY AND CHANGE

In focusing in on the relationship between change and innovation within high tech firms, it is important to consider aspects of such firms that make them particularly unique. First, high tech firms must constantly innovate and build innovative structures to be competitive. This differs markedly from other firms in which new entrants to that industry must have the innovative product or service at their early stage of development to grow and mature. Once these other firms have grown and developed an initial degree of success, they tend to build in functionalized structures and control systems. High tech firms, regardless of size of stage of development, must look to ways to be constantly innovative. For example, 3M derives 25% of its annual revenue from *new* products introduced.

Second, a characteristic of most high tech firms is a significant portion of their budgets that are allocated to R&D—usually on the order of 12-15%. Given this sizable amount, there is a compelling need to develop mechanisms for monitoring technical trends—ranging from formal university-industry linkages to technology transfer programs.

Third, turnover and mobility of personnel is quite high within technology-oriented organizations as the focus of scientists and engineers is oriented more toward the rewards associated with working on break-through projects as opposed to traditional organizational rewards and benefits. High tech firms are continually experimenting with ways of motivating such personnel, including the use of paid sabbaticals to work on specific projects or nondirected, basic research.

Finally, the rate of technological change is usually quite rapid; and in many cases, what once took three years to evolve from the field of basic research now takes eighteen months. The rapidity of this change is determined by several factors—not the least of which is increasing competition for the purpose of maintaining as well as sustaining a technological edge.

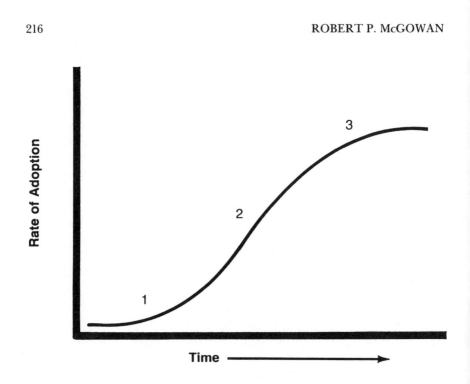

Figure 1.   Innovation Stages

THE INNOVATION PROCESS

The technology innovation process is often thought to proceed in a
nonlinear manner as illustrated in Figure 1. In this classic S-curved
approach, the rate of technological innovation is initially slow at Stage One.
Often accompanying radical or breakthrough inventions or applications,
there may exist some initial hesitancy to make further investments in R&D
or delay may be linked to competing technologies and their associated sunk
cost of investments. A current example which vividly illustrates this is the
introduction of *high definition television* (HDTV) technology. While the
consumer may be quite ready and willing to purchase this particular
commodity, adoption by the industry calls for a significant change in the
generation of broadcast signals and transmission rates. In addition, current
television sets would not be able to accept the proposed standards. The
industry therefore is poised on the threshold. Some proponents of the new
technology argue that a radical change-over needs to take place immediately
to prevent foreign competition from dominating the market. Opponents
argue for a "go-slow" approach to accommodate those firms that have
investments in current technology. The final resolution appears to be a

compromise to both groups; in which new HDTV sets have to accommodate both technologies—not unlike the manner in which color television sets were introduced into the market. An interesting side note to this Stage One process is that this compromise solution was also an explicit action to buy some time relative to foreign competition.

In other instances, the time lag from basic invention to commercial applications may result, in part, from regulatory hurdles that are imposed. This is clearly evident in the field of biotechnology, which can range from animal and human pharmaceutical to environmental applications. The significant initial investments that must be made in the areas of basic and applied research are weighed against a lengthy testing and licensing procedure that may prevent successful commercial introduction for several years.

At Stage Two, rapid growth is experienced. Here the innovation process is driven by increasing acceptance and application of the technology. In addition, market pull conditions are such that enhancements to the technology fuel further growth. Investment criteria at Stage Two is focused on rapid deployment of the technology into the market as well as exploitation of additional market segments. Innovations today in the field of VLSI (Very Large Scale Integration) chip technology would be characteristic of this stage of development. It should also be noted that the marketing function also involves a high degree of market intelligence for gaining competitive advantage as well as determining whether the firm should take a position as leader or follower (Porter, 1983).

Finally, Stage Three involves slowing the rate of growth and development. The technological innovation process slows as the application reaches physical limits of growth. This stage is also characterized by incremental improvements to the application, and often a technologically superior successor begins to emerge. A critical strategic decision at this stage involves "crossing over" to the successor:

> The changeover points may occur when the performance of the new innovation is *significantly* better than the old one. This is because of the economic, social and political factors that tend to resist technological change. An industry may have so much fiscal and human capital invested in a given technology that it is unwilling to change to the new one, even when the latter is markedly superior. Indeed, often such a change is imposed by a company outside the industry. (Martin, 1984, p. 77)

While the technology S-curve can be utilized to trace the progress of a specific application, they typically function as a series of S-curves which operate in successive stages within what is termed the "envelope curve." Figure 2 illustrates this phenomenon in which X1, X2, and X3 are the changeover points.

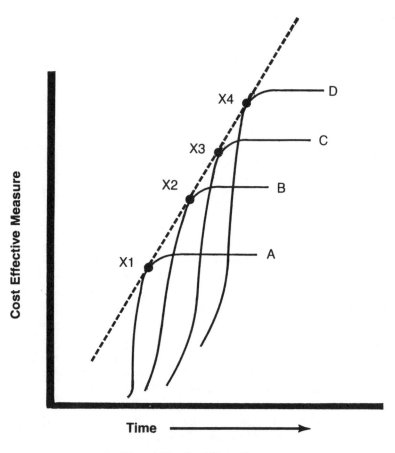

Figure 2. Envelope Curve

The critical set of factors in this relationship between stage of evolution and the innovation process is that corporate management can successfully exploit technology as a competitive weapon, yet this is rarely the case. In order to do so, technology management must be successfully integrated with corporate strategy making (Jelinek & Burstein, 1982; Lawless, 1986; Maidique & Patch, 1980).

TECHNOLOGY AND STRATEGY

The role of technology in helping to shape corporate strategy has been firmly established in the literature. As noted by Porter (1983), technology and technological change can often be the great "equalizer" by nullifying the advantage of incumbents as well as helping others to overcome entry barriers. In addition, firms can shift from product to process changes as a means of maintaining their advantage.

In examining specific technology-based corporate strategies, a number of factors must also be incorporated. This would include, among others: the specific stage of the innovation (previously discussed); the amount and level of investment that the firm is capable of, and willing to, commit to R&D; the rate of change within the industry; competing technologies; the competency and skill base of the organization; and organizational policies and procedures. These can be offset by approximately six variants of technology-based strategy.

The first form is often labeled "offensive" or technology leader. Firms often adopt an offensive position if they have access to, or proprietary rights in, a technological advance. Semiconductor chips that allow for dual processing of tasks have triggered a new round of efforts by computer manufacturers and software designers to speed products to market. Firms that have adopted an offensive or leadership position frequently have a significant investment in applied directed research as well as experimental development and design that necessitates gaining and maintaining market share. Since one of the critical variables to a successful offensive strategy is the ability to get to the market as quickly as possible, efficient structural mechanisms must be in place. These would include such forms as venture teams in which the researcher or scientist is working closely with personnel from operations, marketing, and the like. Depending on the specific technology, these firms will also adopt an aggressive patent and licensing posture in order to create entry barriers for others.

The second predominant technological strategy is a defensive or "follower" position. As opposed to the offensive position, this strategy involves less risk as the firm prefers to observe how the market first reacts to the innovation. While the commitment to research and development is usually not as focused on applied directed research, there is usually a significant commitment to advanced development and design enhancements that can be used to exploit a new innovation once it has proven to be successful. A defensive strategy firm, to be successful, must also counter for late market entry by placing a premium on superior product or process development, marketing intelligence and responsiveness. The choice between a leadership/offensive position and follower/defensive position is influenced by several factors, among which are: the technological opportunity to influence cost or differentiation, the uniqueness of the firm's technological skills, first mover advantages, and continuity of technological change (Porter, 1983). It should also be noted that large, diversified firms may adopt a combination approach in which it adopts an offensive approach in certain domains and a defensive approach in others. This strategy allows the firm the ability to offset risks as well as the potential to profit from new innovations.

An imitative strategy is one in which the firm is development- and design-intensive as opposed to research-intensive. Firms that adopt an imitative strategy do not have the extensive research and development investments of either an offensive or defensive approach, yet they must frequently purchase access to the specific technology through licenses and agreements. The imitative firm also tends to compete on the basis of lower costs, which necessitates efficient manufacturing and production processes. Perhaps a classic example of successful execution of an imitative approach is within the personal computer industry. The emergence of numerous clones, combined with aggressive pricing, has forced such dominant firms as IBM to change strategy.

The fourth technology-based strategy involves an interstitial or "niche" approach. Common across a number of industrial sectors, the emphasis here is toward applications engineering—in other words, making refinements or enhancements to the innovation that are suited for a specific market segment. The break-up of the Bell system, while driven by technological and economic, as well as political forces, created an entire substrata of niche firms that were able to address specific telecommunications needs—for example, customized office PBX (private branch exchange) systems. Successful niche firms place strong emphasis on market analysis and intelligence in order to identify segments and provide "after-sales" service. Certain firms have also emerged as offensive or defensive players after having gained a toehold within the market. Another critical ingredient for the adoption of this strategy is the ability of the company to exit certain segments as market conditions change.

A fifth strategy involves a "branch plant" approach. Usually characteristic of multinational corporations (MNCs), this strategy involves an effort to export the technology in offshore markets. Recent attention to the potential of the China market illustrates the viability of such a strategy—particularly for those firms that can gain a decisive edge in early market entry.

Finally, an absorbent strategy involves the use of either joint ventures or direct acquisition as a means of gaining access to a new product or service line. For high tech firms, absorbent strategies are particularly effective for acquiring a technology knowledge base. For example, Japanese firms have recently developed a joint venture with Boeing for the purpose of eventually entering into aerospace development and manufacturing. One of the concerns, particularly with the joint venture approach, is the determination of whether the partnership is "value-added" on both parts.

As a means of examining the relationship between forms of technology-based strategies and the stage of innovation, Figure 3 lists the various combinations.

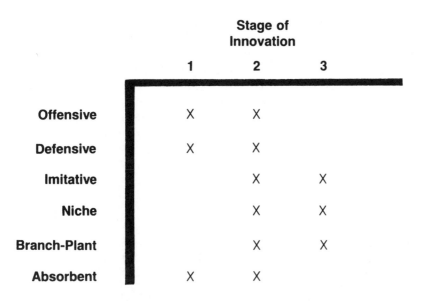

Figure 3. Stages of Innovation and Technology Strategies

At the initial stage of the innovation process (Stage One), the relative choice of strategies is largely constrained to offensive, defensive or absorbent. As Porter (1983) notes, the selection of the strategy to adopt is determined by several factors, not the least of which are first mover advantages.

For the second stage of innovation, characterized by rapid acceleration of the technology, the array of possible technology-based strategies widens as firms position themselves around market segments. The final stage of innovation, in which the rate of technological change begins to decline, shows a high degree of market exit.

In sum, the choice of strategy is largely determined, not only by market conditions or the degree of buyer/supplier control, but by the life cycle of the technology itself.

INTEGRATING STRATEGY, STRUCTURE AND PEOPLE

Up to this point, we have considered the various aspects of managing in a high tech environment—beginning with the concept of change and leading to consideration of the rate of innovation as well as technology-based strategies. Yet, as noted earlier, the concept of change needs to be considered in an integrated manner. Maidique and Hayes (1984), in looking at critical success factors for high tech firms, note that the central dilemma in the management of these firms was the ability to manage two conflicting trends: continuity and rapid change. They go on to argue that, due to the evolutionary nature of both the firm and technology itself, such firms need to alternate accordingly:

> (A) way which we believe is more powerful and pervasive is to manage differently at different times in the evolutionary cycle of the firm. The successful high technology firm alternates periods of consolidation and continuity with sharp reorientations that can lead to dramatic changes in the firm's strategies, structures, controls, and distribution of power—followed by a period of consolidation. (p. 28)

Figure 4 portrays the phenomenon to which Maidique and Hayes as well as others have alluded. Briefly, T-1 and T-2 show portions of the technology S-curve and the technology envelope that have previously been discussed. F-1 is the life cycle of the firm itself, and P-1 is the product or service life cycle. Figure 4 overlays the three curves using the two dimensions of time and rate of change/growth. Consistent with Maidique and Hayes, a period of consolidation would take place in time frame B, as firms begin to implement control systems to harness the rapid growth that is taking place. One distinguishing factor here is the use of matrix and mixed-matrix structures, as opposed to functional units/divisions.

As the life cycles proceed into time frame C, sharp reorientations take place as the firm must quickly adapt from T-1 to T-2. This is often achieved through the use of strategic business unit approaches tailored to particular technologies and markets as well as through various absorbent strategies previously discussed. General Electric has been quite successful in this approach as it has changed its product/service mix from core appliances to new technologies (e.g., medical equipment) and services (e.g., credit and financial services)—largely within the last five years. As the firm migrates from T-1 to T-2, it will often employ a divest strategy with the obsolete product or service—either outright liquidation and transfer of assets or "spinning off" the unit to an interested party (whether external or internal to the organization). GTE successfully employed the latter strategy when it chose to spin off the PBX division to a group of employees. They arranged temporary bridge financing for the unit and are now one of the division's major customers. The decision to spin off was triggered by a decision to enter new sectors within the extremely competitive technology of telecommunications.

In migrating to T-2, one of the critical strategy questions is one of how to best enter the new technology sector. It is important to note that, for high technology firms, this decision varies by the type of technology being

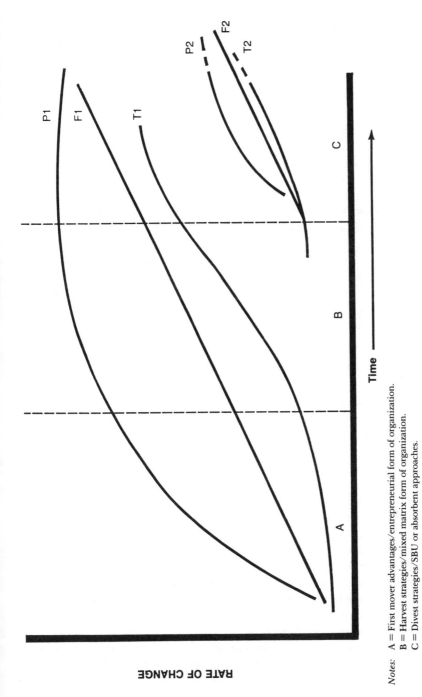

RATE OF CHANGE

Time

Figure 4. The Life-Cycle of the Firm

Notes: A = First mover advantages/entrepreneurial form of organization.
B = Harvest strategies/mixed matrix form of organization.
C = Divest strategies/SBU or absorbent approaches.

223

considered. A common misunderstanding is that the rate of change is equal across all high technology industries. For the field of microelectronics, the rate of technological change has decreased in recent years from approximately *three years to eighteen months*. In the area of biotechnology, the technology life cycle ranges from five to seven years. This suggests the need to develop a typology of technologies and associated strategies for this transition phase. With a longer technology life cycle, a firm may wish to consider an internal growth strategy as a means of amortizing the significant entry barriers. (For biotechnology, this translates to extremely expensive lab and basic research expenses.) Another variant, which is gaining increased attention, is the use of joint-venture strategies at this stage. Joint ventures allow both parties to mitigate risks to some degree.

With a shorter technology life cycle, an absorbent strategy is strongly suggested. This allows the firm to quickly gain a toe-hold position in the new field. There are, of course, risks associated with an absorbent strategy. Perhaps the foremost risk is less financial than organizational. A determination needs to be made early on whether to quickly merge both cultures or to allow for some degree of autonomy. Since, in the high tech arena, the work force tends to be well-educated and motivated by several factors, an absorbent strategy can quickly backfire as key talent may leave.

SUMMARY AND IMPLICATIONS

This paper has examined the issues of change within technology-based firms, and the extent to which strategic decisions are shaped, not only by concerns of traditional organizational evolution, but also by the rate of technological change. As such, a critical ingredient is for managers to understand key integration issues of technology, product, and organizational life cycles. As the firm evolves from early growth stages to maturity, a number of the traditional management concepts of building in control systems and experimenting with matrix and mixed-matrix forms would hold. However, at the critical stage of maturity and sustained growth, the ability to make an effective transition to new technological advances becomes critical. One of the central concerns is a strategic choice between internal- versus external-driven growth. An issue for further research in this area is the extent to which internal growth has proven to be more successful than joint-venture or acquisition activities. This can be measured against several criteria—including ROI or internal rate of return. In addition, these need to be assessed over several years as opposed to one point in time. A related question involves how well fully-integrated firms have performed relative to those firms that have been granted some autonomy.

Both sets of issues raise some interesting questions as technology-driven companies seek to be competitive in an increasingly global economy. While some may argue that the concept of change is nothing unique relative to organizational strategy, it is the increasing *rate of change* that poses a set of interesting decisions.

REFERENCES

Bitondo, D., & Frohman, A. (1981). Linking technological and business planning. *Research Management, 24,* 19-23.

Frohman, A. (1982). Technology as a competitive weapon. *Harvard Business Review, 63,* 97-104.

Greiner, L. (1964). Patterns of organization change. *Harvard Business Review, 45*(3), 119-128.

Jelinek, M., & Burstein, M. (1982). The production administrative structure: A paradigm for strategic fit. *Academy of Management Review, 7,* 242-252.

Kanter, R. (1982). The middle manager as innovator. *Harvard Business Review, 60*(4), 95-105.

———. (1983). *The change masters.* New York: Simon & Schuster.

Kotter, J., & Schlesinger, L. (1979). How to deal with resistance to change. *Harvard Business Review, 57*(2), 106-114.

Lawless, M. (1986a). *The structure of strategy: A taxonomic study of competitive strategy and technology substrategy* (Working paper No. 86-114). Boulder, CO: University of Colorado Graduate School of Business.

———. (1986b). *Competitive and structural issues in strategy classification: A synthesis* (Working paper No. 86-5). Boulder, CO: University of Colorado Graduate School of Business.

Lawrence, P. (1969). How to deal with resistance to change. *Harvard Business Review, 47*(1), 4-13.

Maidique, M., & Hayes, R. (1984). The art of high technology management. *Sloan Management Review, 25,* 17-31.

Maidique, M., & Patch, P. (1980). *Corporate strategy and technological policy* (Note No. 9-679-033). Cambridge, MA: Harvard Business School.

Martin, M. (1984). *Managing technological innovation and entrepreneurship.* Reston, VA: Reston.

Pappas, C. (1984). Strategic management of technology. *Journal of Product Innovation Management, 1,* 30-35.

Porter, M. (1983). *Research on technological innovation, management and policy: Vol. 1.* Greenwich, CT.: JAI Press.

Quinn, J. (1979.) Technological innovation, entrepreneurship, and strategy. *Sloan Management Review, 20,* 19-30.

Arthur Young & The Institute for Innovation. (1985). *Innovation: The agenda for American business.* New York: Author.

MANAGING THE DESIGN/ MANUFACTURING INTERFACE IN SELECTED HIGH TECHNOLOGY FIRMS

Michael Hottenstein

Thirty-four manufacturing sites were visited throughout the United States where advanced manufacturing technology has been or is being installed. Twenty-seven of these companies are considered to be high technology firms. The purpose of each visit was to explore with managers and engineers at these sites a number of issues involved in the installation and management of advanced, computer-based manufacturing technology. Each visit typically consisted of one-on-one interviews with managers and engineers, group discussions and tours of manufacturing facilities, manufacturing research and development laboratories, and electronic engineering work stations. In advance of each visit, each company host was mailed a list of research issues to be explored. While discussions generally followed the research issues, each visit had very unique characteristics. This was often a function of the entry point into each organization which varied from corporate staff units to autonomous line operations. The companies included in the study ran the gamut from manufacturers of penny-a-piece candy to manufacturers of 100 million dollar satellites. However, one thing that most companies had in common was their reaction to a new, more competitive environment by making rather radical changes in how they do manufacturing and in how they manage.

CHANGES IN COMPETITIVE ENVIRONMENT

The first major issue discussed with each company was the nature of the forces that were stimulating changes in their manufacturing. While these forces frequently included a more competitive environment, the forces behind change often were more diverse. In no particular order of importance or frequency, these forces included:

1. rapidly developing technologies;
2. accelerated product-life cycles;
3. global, world-class competition;
4. ability of competitors to clone products;
5. more complex products;
6. more sophisticated and discriminating consumers (both organizational and individual);
7. less government regulation;
8. over-valued dollar;
9. more highly fragmented markets; and
10. supply uncertainties and sourcing difficulties.

In order to compete in this changing environment, many of the companies felt that they had to develop two critical organizational capabilities. First, they had to compress the R&D cycle to speed up the introduction of new products. One manager with an electronics firm put it this way: "Things are changing so fast in this industry that you can't deal with traditional lead times from conception of a new product idea to its eventual availability on the market." Depending on the industry, the desired compression might be from five years to three, from 36 months to 18, from one year to six months, and so on. Second, for new and existing products they had to be able to compete on the basis of cost, quality and service. In more traditional times, cost, quality and service were considered to be "trade-offs," with the need to focus on one or two but seldom on all three (Miller, 1983). An executive in the aircraft industry said: "Up to recently, the most important motivator for manufacturing was the schedule. That is, it was most important to get aircraft produced on time to meet the agreed upon due dates with customers. However, with worldwide competition, cost was becoming as equally important as the schedule. Of course, it was always important to have high quality products because of how the product was used and the tremendous cost of liability in case of failure." Rather than cost, quality and service being viewed as "trade-offs," in more and more companies, they are being viewed as "multipliers." The challenge, of course, is to improve quality and service while, at the same time, reducing costs.

A key to developing these two critical organizational capabilities is a concept called "design for manufacturability" or "design for producibility." Whatever the name, the idea is to speed up the design process and, at the same time, have designs that manufacturers can turn into competitive products in terms of cost, quality and service (Buffa & Sarin, 1987). This is no easy task, even in the best managed organizations. What is required, at a minimum, is better interfaces between design and manufacturing, two often separate and sometimes antagonistic organizational entities.

OBSTACLES TO DEVELOPING CAPABILITIES

The research revealed a number of organizational and systems obstacles to the effective interfacing of design and manufacturing. These included:

1. A paper-based system for engineering design drawings;
2. Lack of compatibility of hardware and software among designers and between design and manufacturing;
3. Lack of standardized databases between design and manufacturing.
4. No uniform parts numbering system across the company;
5. Sequential, compartmentalized design cycle;
6. Inappropriate incentive and reward systems for designers;
7. Different cultures between design and manufacturing;
8. Often physical distance between design function and manufacturing;
9. Late involvement of manufacturing in the design cycle;
10. Poor communication from manufacturing to design concerning process capabilities and manufacturing constraints.

Surprisingly, up until recently, a large number of the companies in the study were still using drafting boards for their design functions. A paper-based system is slow, contains no built-in test capabilities and is difficult to revise. Blueprints must be carried or mailed to move them sequentially through the design cycle. Engineering changes often are cumbersome, leading to high probabilities that errors will be experienced. A paper-based design system not only slows down the design process but it creates many obstacles for interaction and cooperation between design and manufacturing (Boyer, 1977).

Even where companies used electronic engineering work stations, frequently there would be a lack of compatibility among the wide variety of hardware and software systems used leading to difficulties in designers communicating electronically with one another, let alone communicating with manufacturers. This problem might arise where hardware and software acquisition decisions are made on a highly decentralized basis. Or it could arise because of organizational relationships such as the following situation from one of the aerospace companies in the study:

> One of the difficulties with installing a universal CIM system is the relationship between manufacturing and the product groups. While each product group has a number of products, these products do not have any interaction to one another. Consequently, there is no need for product organizations within product groups to talk to one another or to have any communication links with one another. However, all of these product organizations have to be able to talk and communicate with the manufacturing group. Since each product organization has its own autonomy and uniqueness, it is difficult to come up with any standard, in terms of equipment or software, to form the basis for a CIM type of system. Currently, the company is trying to install local area networks and devices for communicating to other networks. However, not all equipment that is currently owned is compatible with one another.

While many of the companies in the study had electronic databases, there was often a separate database for engineering, for manufacturing, for purchasing, for finance, and so forth. In only a few instances was there a common database accessible by all functions needing access to such data. Often the same data was stored in several databases; however, because of lack of linkages among these databases, a high likelihood existed for poor data integrity (Goldhar, 1985).

If a company or autonomous operating division did not have a uniform parts numbering system, duplication and proliferation of parts likely would result. Furthermore, engineers often would design parts that already existed because they had no easy way of retrieving parts information.

Up until recently, many of the companies in the study followed a sequential, compartmentalized design process. This process is typified by the experience of one of the systems companies in the study where it was reported that:

> In their traditional way of doing business, it was taking about 30 months to design and get built plastic molded parts for their products. This was shortened somewhat by getting their own plastic injection molding machines. In their traditional way of doing business, which they called reaction, a number of events took place sequentially. For example, product development did their thing and then released information for tool development which did its thing and typically, followed by engineering changes, tools would be built. This probably would lead to further engineering changes until finally the product, the process, and the tools would be fully developed. They call this an over-the-wall design with lots of engineering changes.

In the past, in many of the companies studied, there was little incentive for designers to closely examine the consequences of their designs for manufacturing. Incentives and rewards are often based on criteria other than manufacturability. Approvals, both formal and informal, came from marketing and design engineering and placed a premium on function, appearance, size, weight and elegance. Peer acceptance was a powerful motivator.

Perhaps one of the most significant barriers to effective interfacing between design and manufacturing was the difference in cultures between these two groups. Many of these differences can be traced back to engineering school where design was pushed as "where the action is" and where the "pure engineering is practiced." On the other hand, manufacturing was often portrayed as "being dirty, hot, messy, with little opportunity to practice other than grunt engineering." As a result, often the "best and brightest" went into design and only the "uninitiated" into manufacturing. These stereotypes often continue on the job and are frequently reinforced by the working environments of both groups. Design people usually are housed in modern office structures located in urban areas. The design engineer often is viewed as king in that organization given the importance of new product development. Visiting the factories is like going out to the provinces and is barely tolerated. The manufacturing engineer, on the other hand, has an office on or near the factory floor in a factory located in a remote, rural, small town. Traditionally, this engineer spent a great deal of time "fixing things" to help get out the production. It is no wonder that these two cultures seldom interface very effectively in many firms (Gunn, 1987).

The so-called "over-the-wall" relationship between design and manufacturing is only a slight exaggeration in many of the companies in the study, at least in the recent past. Often, manufacturing was not a party to the design process until late in the cycle and then too late to make a difference without costly redesign. The design was thrown over the wall with a "take it or leave it" attitude (Wheelwright, 1987).

The problem is not always or exclusively the fault of design engineering. Manufacturing often does a poor job communicating with design concerning process capabilities and manufacturing constraints. Over-generalizations and vagueness about what constitutes a good design from a production point of view are often cited as reasons why design engineers are not more responsive to manufacturing.

Effective management of the design/manufacturing interface requires a coherent set of strategies for removing these obstacles. Many of the firms in the study are beginning to do this successfully. We will now turn to these strategies.

STRATEGIES FOR INTERFACING DESIGN AND MANUFACTURING

Most of the companies in the study were well into developing strategies for more effectively managing the design/manufacturing interface. For convenience, these strategies have been divided into four basic categories:

1. Interfacing via technology;
2. Interfacing via parts simplification program;
3. Interfacing via organizational relationships;
4. Interfacing via supraorganizational efforts.

It should be pointed out that some overlap exists among these interfacing strategies and usually they are mutually supportive rather than being mutually exclusive.

Interfacing Via Technology

This strategy attempts to more effectively manage the interface by developing paperless, electronic hardware, software and database systems to link design and manufacturing. The basic components of the strategy are:

1. promoting the use of computer-aided design (CAD);
2. developing the capability for the direct transfer of electronic design database to manufacturing via computer-aided manufacturing (CAM);
3. providing designers with database of preferred materials/components and menus of process capabilities;
4. providing designers with manufacturing derived principles for designing for producibility or for automation;
5. using Artificial Intelligence (AI) to find best ways of manufacturing given certain design constraints; and
6. setting standards of compatibility for hardware, software, and databases so interfacing and networking are feasible.

Creating a "paperless" design environment with electronic links to manufacturing can dramatically reduce the design cycle. As an executive in one aircraft company put it: "With a paper oriented sequential design-built process, months could be taken up with the simple design of a part, perhaps one of thousands that go into an aircraft. Making this process more electronic through CAD/CAM systems, the time sequence could be compressed to a matter of weeks, if not days." Most of the companies were not mandating CAD/CAM systems but, rather, were trying to promote them. One company developed a videotape that highlighted the efficacy of CAD/CAM systems as a means of selling design engineers on this technology. Another company set up a "hit squad" of CAD experts who, if contacted, would bring to the engineer an electronic engineering work station and teach the engineer to use the system.

One systems company was working to create databases to link up design with manufacturing. They were using what they called a DB2 file to store three kinds of information: the drawings themselves, reference documents such as bills of material and process routings and various technical publications that were needed to support the design and manufacturing of the product. The problem was linking this stage and the CAD database file to manufacturing. The goal of the company was to create a paperless manufacturing environment from design to production. They feel that they are 40 percent there. One major effect linking design with manufacturing is an EC folder, which is an electronic worksheet for the part, change numbers, bills of materials, process information, and so forth. The EC folder can electronically provide manufacturing with all the information required to manufacture a part for its eventual assembly into some new product.

Another company was using an electronic database called Colossus, a database on preferred materials and electronic components. Another company had an integrated database that contained a master engineering parts list. The impact of both databases was to limit the freedom of choice of designers, whenever possible, by having them stick to materials and components with which the company had experience in order to avoid surprises later. In yet another high tech company, manufacturing was developing electronic menus of the available manufacturing processes and their capabilities. Thus, when the engineer designed a part or product, it was possible to do so interactively with the database of manufacturing process capabilities.

Several companies have begun to formulate sets of guidelines or principles for producibility and are articulating them to design. In one company, manufacturing developed a book entitled *Designing for the Automatic Factory*, which is input information to product design people. In another company, a number of principles for designing for automation were developed and have served as a basis for design engineers for designing and redesigning for automation. They said that "you definitely have to design the product for automation. It's virtually impossible to take an existing product and try to design a system for automatically producing it." Another company has gone a step further by using Artificial Intelligence (AI) to look at the CAD data system and to try to find the best way to manufacture a product.

The success of this strategy of interfacing via technology requires a high degree of compatibility of hardware, software and electronic databases. Many companies have begun to set standards for compatibility for new purchases and are developing ways of networking components that were acquired at different times from different vendors and, consequently, did not talk easily to one another.

Interfacing Via Parts Simplification Program

This strategy brings design and manufacturing people together by having them focus on the common goal of parts and product simplification. The basic components of this strategy are:

1. developing a universal parts numbering system;
2. reducing the number of parts per product;
3. reducing part numbers per product;
4. using more standard or preferred parts;
5. eliminating fasteners or reducing variety of fasteners; and
6. using modular designs or common parts or common assemblies.

Design engineers need to know what parts currently exist in the company. It is virtually impossible to know this in the absence of a universal parts numbering system. A good numbering system would provide clues to the part's material, geometry, size, function, and so forth. An inventory file of parts by number would provide an opportunity for the designer to search for already existing parts to meet a requirement and, if one is found, eliminate the need to develop a new part. Implementing a parts numbering system would frequently uncover duplicates, lead to the simplification of parts, reduce parts proliferation, and make the design or redesign of parts somewhat more simple.

In one company, the parts simplification program led to the reduction of part numbers within one product from 3,200 to 52 and in another product from over 200 to 16. Other, less dramatic examples were found in many other companies. One company was able to save tens of thousands of dollars simply by getting designers to cut back on bolt and nut sizes they specified for assemblies. In putting the product together, the assembler or robot would need to make fewer tool changes. Another company has been trying to eliminate fasteners altogether by redesigning product parts that snap together.

One common strategy, especially in the electronics industry, is to use modular concepts in the design of products. The idea is to develop a full product family by using different configurations of common product modules. Such a strategy will result in fewer part numbers in total since products in a family share many common parts and common assemblies.

Interfacing Via Organizational Relationships

This strategy attempts to improve the design/manufacturing interface by reducing some of the cultural differences between design and manufacturing. Some of the components of this strategy are:

1. rotating design engineers to manufacturing;
2. early involvement of manufacturing in the design cycle;
3. manufacturing sign-off on engineering changes;
4. creating multi-functional product teams for the design responsibility;
5. developing incentives and rewards for designing right the first time; and
6. reducing the physical distance between design and manufacturing.

The following are some examples from the study of activities going on in the firms that cut across many of the components of this strategy.

Equipment Manufacturer

There have been a number of steps made to bring design and manufacturing closer together. As a first step, methods, standards, and I.E. types were combined to focus on a product type. This way they can take more pride and identify more with a product. A second step was to combine product engineering with process engineering for each product. The third step was to assign assembly engineering to design right from the outset. One of the remaining problems is communication between people in that product engineering is about a half mile away from the assembly plant. This problem is being addressed by rotating design engineers between design and manufacturing.

Systems Company

Part of the problem of linking up design with manufacturing is to break down some of the barriers that typically have existed between engineering and manufacturing. For example, teams are formed now which are cross-functional and start with the outset of new product development through the manufacturing of that particular product. There is also a sign off process on design changes by manufacturing. This forces design engineers to think through design changes before submitting them to manufacturing. Many site managers want to radically change the organization in order to bring together all functions concerned with the same product.

Automobile Company

To address the problems that most companies have between their design engineers and their manufacturing engineers, we have been trying to have engineers spend more time on the line before moving into engineering. In Japan, engineers out of school first go to the line for two or three years before they go into R&D or into manufacturing engineering. While this probably would not work in the United States, we have our engineers spend about 18 weeks on a line before moving them into engineering.

Systems Company

Traditionally, products were not designed from a manufacturing point of view. Now there is a lot more focus on designing for cost. It forces the designer to take a manufacturing view when designing a product. It also forces manufacturing to tell laboratories what processes are available and what those process capabilities are. There seems to be a great deal of overlap of manufacturing people with design people at various stages in the design cycle. Manufacturing is brought in a lot earlier in the design cycle than in the past in order that products coming out of the design function are capable of being manufactured at competitive costs. This also has significantly reduced the cycle time from idea to production from about five years to less than two years.

Interfacing Via Supraorganizational Efforts

This strategy attempts to improve the effectiveness of the management of the design/manufacturing interface through the creation of new organizational structures and by changes in corporate culture and climate. Included in this strategy are the following components:

1. improving the status of manufacturing;
2. creating corporate-level advanced manufacturing R&D units; and
3. changing corporate culture and climate.

In most of the firms in the study, manufacturing has been improving in stature. Many companies are beginning to realize the potential for competitive advantage through manufacturing and are paying a lot more attention to it. This is being translated into cleaner, more modern, technologically sophisticated plants and with manufacturing capabilities playing a more central role in corporate strategy. As a result, some of the "best and brightest" engineers and managers are being attracted into manufacturing from other parts of the organization. A manufacturing assignment is not being viewed as a punishment to the extent that it often was viewed in the past.

A number of companies in this study have created corporate or division level organization units dedicated to manufacturing research and development. These units might undertake basic research on process technologies or on management technologies and then look for application opportunities within the company. Another approach is to respond to needs expressed by operating units and, if a significant change can be made, to try to leverage that improvement in similar units throughout the company. Such units often develop expertise in technologies like computer-aided design (CAD), computer-aided-manufacturing (CAM), computer-integrated-manufacturing (CIM), robotics, automatic testing, simulation, artificial intelligence (AI), and management information systems (MIS). Often these units have laboratories where they can test and debug systems and processes before moving them to the manufacturing floor.

Many of the companies in the study are seriously committed to changing their philosophy of management and their company culture from ones based on adversarial relations with employees to ones based on trust and mutual respect. Many companies are beginning to use teams, natural work groups or other group concepts that accomplish shared goals in a cooperative rather than confrontational atmosphere. Other cultural change strategies are oriented toward encouraging people or teams to develop a sense of ownership and commitment toward products and processes and to take responsibility for quality.

In some companies, a different sort of cultural change was underway, motivated in part by the need to become more competitive through manufacturing. One systems company said they were in a major tug-of-war about their strategic direction. While their culture has been very much oriented toward creativity and autonomy, some of the new directions needed to be more efficient are putting these values in conflict with values needed for consolidation and standardization.

In many of the companies, strong signals are being sent from top management to the effect that traditional ways of doing business are no longer appropriate. What is needed is a new way of doing business that, among other things, calls into question the typical compartmentalization of business functions.

SUMMARY

This paper was based on an investigation of 34 U.S. companies where advanced manufacturing technology has been or is being installed. Twenty-seven of these companies can be classified as "high technology." In order to compete in changing, more competitive environments, many of these companies felt that they had to develop two critical organizational capabilities. First, they had to compress the R&D cycle to speed up the introduction of new products. Second, for new and existing products, they had to have the manufacturing capability to compete on the basis of cost and quality and service. A key to developing these capabilities is a concept called "design for manufacturability." To implement this concept, it is necessary to develop better interfaces between design and manufacturing. This is not always easy to do because of the many barriers that often separate these two organizational functions.

Most of the companies in this study were well into developing strategies for more effectively managing the design/manufacturing interface. This paper explored interfacing strategies, which were divided for convenience into four categories depending on whether interfacing was based predominantly on: (1) technology; (2) a parts simplification; (3) organizational relationships; or (4) supraorganizational efforts. Most companies were using a combination of strategies from several of these categories.

REFERENCES

Boyer, C.H. (1977). Lockheed links design and manufacturing. *Industrial Engineering, 22*(1), 14-21.

Buffa, E.S., & Sarin, R.K. (1987). *Modern production/operations management* (8th ed.). New York: Wiley.

Goldhar, J.D. (1985, March-April). The transparent factory. *CIM*, pp. 2-5.

Gunn, T.G. (1987). *Manufacturing for competitive advantage*. Cambridge, MA: Ballinger.

Miller, S.S. (1983). Make your plant manager's job manageable. *Harvard Business Review, 61*(1), 68-74.

Wheelwright, S.C. (1987). Restoring the competitive edge in U.S. manufacturing. In D.J. Teece (Ed.), *The competitive challenge* (pp. 83-100). Cambridge, MA: Ballinger.

BIOGRAPHICAL SKETCHES

Srinivasan Balakrishnan is Assistant Professor at the Carlson School of Management, University of Minnesota. Professor Balakrishnan received his Ph.D. in strategic management from the University of Michigan and specializes in acquisitions, sell-offs, joint-ventures, leasing and other arrangements for restructuring corporate assets. His research focuses on the strategic, financial and international aspects of such arrangements. He has published several papers on the subject of intercorporate relationships. Professor Balakrishnan also has extensive international consulting experience in organizing joint ventures and technical collaboration with corporations in developing countries.

Jay B. Barney received his Ph.D. in Sociology and Administrative Sciences from Yale University. He then accepted an appointment at the Anderson Graduate School of Management at UCLA. In 1986, Professor Barney moved from UCLA to the Department of Management at Texas A&M University.

Professor Barney's research and teaching interests have been in the areas of Organizational Economics and Strategic Management. He has written a book with William G. Ouchi entitled *Organizational Economics,* along with several articles that examine the role of idiosyncratic firm attributes in creating sustained competitive advantage. These articles have been published in the *Academy of Management Review, Management Science, Strategic Management Journal,* and elsewhere.

Barry Baysinger is an Associate Professor of Management at Texas A&M University. Professor Baysinger received his doctorate in Economics in 1978 from the Virginia Polytechnic Institute and State University. His current research interests include organizational economics, organization theory, the management of innovation, and risk taking in the context of multiproduct firms.

Professor Baysinger's research has appeared in such publications as the *Academy of Management Review, Strategic Management Journal, Academy of Management Journal, Journal of Law and Economics, Business Horizons* and the *Sloan Management Review.*

Allen L. Brown has a B.A. in Engineering from Dartmouth University and an M.A. in Planning from the University of Oregon; he is currently a Ph.D. candidate in the Resources Planning Program at Stanford University.

Gregory A. Daneke received his Ph.D. from the University of California in 1976. He has taught at several institutions, including the University of Michigan and Stanford University, and has been a fellow with the U.S. General Accounting Office. He is currently on the faculty of the School of Public Affairs at Arizona State University.

John D. Daniels received his Ph.D. from the University of Michigan and is Professor of International Business at Indiana University. He is a Fellow and 1988-89 President of the Academy of International Business. He will be President of the International Division of the Academy of Management for 1991. Most of his research has been on the strategy for companies' international operations; and this research has appeared in leading business journals. Among his books are *Foreign Direct Investment in the United States* and the coauthored text, *International Business: Environments and Operations,* which is in its fifth edition. He has served on the editorial boards of the *Academy of Management Journal, Essays in International Business, Journal of Business Research,* and the *Journal of International Business Studies.*

George S. Day is a Professor of Marketing at the University of Toronto and Executive Director of the Strategic Planning Institute in Cambridge, Massachusetts. He previously taught at the University of Western Ontario and Stanford University. He is a member of the Research Advisory Council for the Strategic Planning Institute and a member of the Research Committee for the National Center for Management Research and Development. Dr. Day holds degrees from UBC, University of Western Ontario, and Columbia University. He is editor of the West Publishing series on "Strategic Market Management." He has authored more than 80 articles, and published nine books in the areas of marketing and strategic business planning. His next book, *Competing for Markets,* will be published in 1990.

Andre Delbecq is Professor of Management of the Leavey School of Business at Santa Clara University. His research has focused on creative problem solving techniques, incuding the nominal group process, and on organizational structures that underline innovation. In recognition of his scholarship, he was named "Fellow" of the Academy of Management in 1975.

Jonathan Freeman is a doctoral candidate at the University of Toronto. A past Managing Director with ten years experience in a British company, he has degrees from the University of Manchester and York University. His research interests include the evolution of markets, the identification of factors contributing to the success or failure of businesses, product innovation and discussion, and competitive and cooperative business strategies.

Luis R. Gomez-Mejia, Ph.D. in Industrial Relations, University of Minnesota, is a full Professor of Management at Arizona State University. Previously, he was a co-director of the High Technology Management Research Center at the University of Colorado. He has had over four years of full time field experience at Control Data Corporation and has also been a consultant on human resource problems to numerous high technology firms. Dr. Gomez-Mejia has over 50 publications appearing in such journals as *Administrative Science Quarterly, Academy of Management Journal, Strategic Management Journal, Industrial Relations* and *Personnel Psychology.*

Farid Harianto has assumed a teaching position at the Institute for Management Education, Jakarta, Indonesia, after completing his Ph.D. from the Wharton School of Business, University of Pennsylvania. His research interests include the role of innovation in strategy, corporate governance structure and corporate restructuring. He has published his works, and is now involved in ongoing research and projects concerning innovation, strategic capabilities and corporate restructuring.

Ray M. Haynes is a native Californian who grew up in the bilingual border town of Nogales, Arizona. He holds a B.S. in aerospace engineering and an M.B.A. in management from the University of Arizona. He is currently completing the requirements for the Ph.D. degree in Business Logistics at Arizona State University. He has accepted a position of Associate Professor of Operations Management at California Polytechnic State University (SLO) as of January 1989.

He has worked for eighteen years at various high tech companies including AiResearch, RCA, TRW, Fujitsu and Citicorp. He has extensive domestic and international consulting experience with companies such as IBM, Sears, VISA, Texaco and EDS/GM.

He has published in the areas of electronic banking, service operations, productivity and quality and technology implementation.

Thomas E. Hendrick has been Professor of Production/Operations Management at Arizona State University since 1965. Previously, he was Professor of P/OM and Management Science at the University of Colorado at Boulder. Dr. Hendrick received his doctorate from the University of Oregon and his B.S. and M.B.A. degrees from the University of Washington. He was president of the Western Academy of Management in 1981 and is a member of the American Production and Inventory Control Society, the Decision Sciences Institute, and the Operations Management Association.

Dr. Hendrick has worked as a staff engineer at Martin-Marietta Aerospace and has been a Special Advisor to the Republic of China. His numerous consulting assignments include Motorola, Hewlett-Packard, Contel, Samsonite and RAND Corporation.

Dr. Hendrick has published numerous books and articles in the areas of production/operations, JIT and business performance measurement. His current book (co-authored with F.G. Moore), *Production/Operations Management: Fundamental Concepts and Methods,* is in its third edition.

Michael P. Hottenstein is Assistant Dean and Faculty Director of Graduate Programs, College of Business Administration, Pennsylvania State University. He is Professor of Management in the Management Science Department. He was formerly Head, Department of Management Science and Organizational Behaivor and was Director of the MBA Program.

His research has been concerned with the computer simulation of production and service systems and most recently studied U.S. manufacturing companies at various stages of implementing advanced computer-based manufacturing technologies.

Dr. Hottenstein's publications include two books, *Models and Analysis for Production Management* and *PROSIM: A Production Management Simulation.* Major research papers have been published in the *Journal of Production and Inventory Management, AIIE Transactions, The Naval Research Logistics Quarterly* and the *International Journal of Production Research.* He is a member of the Academy of Management, the Decision Science Institute and the Society of Manufacturing Engineers.

Basil J. Janavaras is the Director of the International Business Institute and Professor of International Business at Mankato State University, Mankato, Minnesota. He has been active in both public and private sector efforts to address the need for international business education and training in the state and nation.

Dr. Janavaras holds a doctorate from Northern Illinois University and has been a faculty member at Mankato State since 1969. He has published and presented many papers on issues relating to international business and trade. Dr. Janavaras is professionally active in a number of academic/trade groups including the Academy of International Business, the Minnesota District Export Council, the Minnesota World Trade Association, the Southern Minnesota International Trade Group and the Active Corps of Executives at SCORE.

Dr. Judith Brown Kamm is currently the principal investigator of a research project at Bentley College on the role of entrepreneurial teams in the new venture creation process. A Doctor of Business Administration from Harvard Business School, she has written numerous cases and given presentations on the topic of organizational behavior in small, young companies in the software and other industries, including *An Integrative Approach to Managing Innovation, How to Manage the New Product Development Process,* and articles appearing in *Human Relations* and the *Journal of Business Strategy.*

Dr. Mitchell P. Koza is Assistant Professor of Business Policy at the European Institute of Business Administration (INSEAD) in Fontainebleau, France. His research interests focus on problems of collective choice. He is currently examining the management of interorganizational arrangements (joint ventures, licensing, long term contracting, and the like) and the ways in which the organization of top management teams influences the formulation of policy. He has presented and published many papers on joint ventures, regulation and public policy. Professor Koza received his doctorate from the University of Chicago and his master's degree from Harvard University.

Michael Lawless, Ph.D. in Strategic Analysis, Anderson Graduate School of Management, UCLA, is Associate Professor at the Graduate School of Business, University of Colorado at Boulder and Director of the High Technology Management Research Center. His experience includes staff and consulting positions at the RAND Corporation and System Development Corporation. Professor Lawless' research on competitive strategy, innovation and strategic management of technology has been published in *Strategic Management Journal, Management Science, Human Relations, Journal of Management, Omega,* and other journals. Dr. Lawless is Associate Editor of the *Journal of High Technology Management Research* and an editorial board member at the *Journal of Management.*

Robert P. McGowan is an Associate Professor of Management at the College of Business, University of Denver. Dr. McGowan researches in the area of technology management and corporate strategy as well as economic development policy for emerging industries. In addition, Dr. McGowan has served as consultant to the Colorado Advanced Technology Institute and was recently a participant in the Faculty in Residence Program at US West, Inc., in corporate strategic planning.

Edward J. Ottensmeyer is Assistant Professor of Management in the Graduate School of Management at Clark University. His research examines the management systems used by top executives to identify and act upon strategic issues. This research has been published recently in the *Academy of Management Review*. His related work on strategic processes in not-for-profit organizations has appeared in *Policy Studies Review, Growth and Change* and *Economic Development Commentary*. These research projects have attracted funding from the Spencer Foundation, the Mellon Foundation, the U.S. Department of Commerce and the Tenneco Fund. He conducts numerous executive development programs, for both private and public sector executives, on such topics as strategic management, technology management and business-government relations. He also serves as a consultant to both industrial and public sector enterprises, and is an active member of both the Academy of Management and the Strategic Management Society.

Johannes M. Pennings is Associate Professor of Management at the Wharton School at the University of Pennsylvania. Previously, he was at Carnegie Mellon University and Columbia University. He earned his Ph.D. at the University of Michigan in 1973. His research has dealt with organization-environment relationships, new ventures, corporate governance and innovation. Recent publications include *Organizational Strategy and Change* (Jossey Bass, 1985) and *New Technology as Organizational Innovation* (Ballinger, 1987).

Charles C. Snow is Professor of Business Administration and Chair of the Management and Organization Department at The Pennyslvania State University. His research interests are in the areas of competitive strategy and organization design, and he is editor and co-author of *Strategy, Organization Design, and Human Resource Management* (JAI Press, 1989). Currently, he is conducting a study of industry synergy—the notion that competitors in an industry must perform certain roles in order for the industry to maintain its long-term health. He has appeared on National Technological University's TV Satellite Network.

Gerardo Rivera Ungson earned his Ph.D. degree at Pennsylvania State University. He is presently an Associate Professor of Management and Department Head, Management Department at the University of Oregon. His current research interests include global strategies. He has recently completed a book, *Competitive Strategies in High Technology: Responding* *to Organizational, Strategic, and Institutional Challenges* (Lexington Press).

Joseph Weiss received his M.A. from Boston College and his Ph.D. from the University of Wisconsin-Madison. He is the author of *Management of Change and Regional Cultures, Managerial Behavior and Entrepreneurship: An International Perspective.* He is currently on the faculty of Bentley College in Waltham, Massachusetts.

INDEX